Mastering Apache Spark 2.x

Second Edition

D0775304

Scalable analytics faster than ever

Romeo Kienzler

BIRMINGHAM - MUMBAI

Mastering Apache Spark 2.x

Second Edition

First published: September 2015

Second Edition: July 2017

Production reference: 1190717

Published by Packt Publishing Ltd.
Livery Place
35 Livery Street
Birmingham
B3 2PB, UK.
ISBN 978-1-78646-274-9

www.packtpub.com

Credits

Author
Romeo Kienzler

Reviewer
Md. Rezaul Karim

Commissioning Editor
Amey Varangaonkar

Acquisition Editor
Malaika Monteiro

Content Development Editor
Tejas Limkar

Technical Editor
Dinesh Chaudhary

Copy Editor
Tasneem Fatehi

Project Coordinator
Manthan Patel

Proofreader
Safis Editing

Indexer
Tejal Daruwale Soni

Graphics
Tania Dutta

Production Coordinator
Deepika Naik

About the Author

Romeo Kienzler works as the chief data scientist in the IBM Watson IoT worldwide team, helping clients to apply advanced machine learning at scale on their IoT sensor data. He holds a Master's degree in computer science from the Swiss Federal Institute of Technology, Zurich, with a specialization in information systems, bioinformatics, and applied statistics. His current research focus is on scalable machine learning on Apache Spark. He is a contributor to various open source projects and works as an associate professor for artificial intelligence at Swiss University of Applied Sciences, Berne. He is a member of the IBM Technical Expert Council and the IBM Academy of Technology, IBM's leading brains trust.

Writing a book is quite time-consuming. I want to thank my family for their understanding and my employer, IBM, for giving me the time and flexibility to finish this work. Finally, I want to thank the entire team at Packt Publishing, and especially, Tejas Limkar, my editor, for all their support, patience, and constructive feedback.

About the Reviewer

Md. Rezaul Karim is a research scientist at Fraunhofer Institute for Applied Information Technology FIT, Germany. He is also a PhD candidate at the RWTH Aachen University, Aachen, Germany. He holds a BSc and an MSc degree in computer science. Before joining the Fraunhofer-FIT, he worked as a researcher at Insight Centre for Data Analytics, Ireland. Prior to that, he worked as a lead engineer with Samsung Electronics' distributed R&D Institutes in Korea, India, Vietnam, Turkey, and Bangladesh. Previously, he worked as a research assistant in the Database Lab at Kyung Hee University, Korea. He also worked as an R&D engineer with BMTech21 Worldwide, Korea. Prior to that, he worked as a software engineer with i2SoftTechnology, Dhaka, Bangladesh.

He has more than 8 years' experience in the area of Research and Development with a solid knowledge of algorithms and data structures in C/C++, Java, Scala, R, and Python focusing on big data technologies (such as Spark, Kafka, DC/OS, Docker, Mesos, Zeppelin, Hadoop, and MapReduce) and Deep Learning technologies such as TensorFlow, DeepLearning4j, and H2O-Sparking Water. His research interests include machine learning, deep learning, semantic web/linked data, big data, and bioinformatics. He is the author of the following books with Packt Publishing:

- **Large-Scale Machine Learning with Spark**
- **Deep Learning with TensorFlow**
- **Scala and Spark for Big Data Analytics**

I am very grateful to my parents, who have always encouraged me to pursue knowledge. I also want to thank my wife, Saroar, son, Shadman, elder brother, Mamtaz, elder sister, Josna, and friends, who have always been encouraging and have listened to me.

www.PacktPub.com

For support files and downloads related to your book, please visit www.PacktPub.com.

Did you know that Packt offers eBook versions of every book published, with PDF and ePub files available? You can upgrade to the eBook version at; www.PacktPub.com and as a print book customer, you are entitled to a discount on the eBook copy. Get in touch with us at service@packtpub.com for more details.

At www.PacktPub.com, you can also read a collection of free technical articles, sign up for a range of free newsletters and receive exclusive discounts and offers on Packt books and eBooks.

https://www.packtpub.com/mapt

Get the most in-demand software skills with Mapt. Mapt gives you full access to all Packt books and video courses, as well as industry-leading tools to help you plan your personal development and advance your career.

Why subscribe?

- Fully searchable across every book published by Packt
- Copy and paste, print, and bookmark content
- On demand and accessible via a web browser

Customer Feedback

Thanks for purchasing this Packt book. At Packt, quality is at the heart of our editorial process. To help us improve, please leave us an honest review on this book's Amazon page at `https://www.amazon.com/dp/1786462745`.

If you'd like to join our team of regular reviewers, you can e-mail us at `customerreviews@packtpub.com`. We award our regular reviewers with free eBooks and videos in exchange for their valuable feedback. Help us be relentless in improving our products!

Table of Contents

Preface

Apache Spark is an in-memory, cluster-based, parallel processing system that provides a wide range of functionality such as graph processing, machine learning, stream processing, and SQL. This book aims to take your limited knowledge of Spark to the next level by teaching you how to expand your Spark functionality.

The book opens with an overview of the Spark ecosystem. The book will introduce you to Project Catalyst and Tungsten. You will understand how Memory Management and Binary Processing, Cache-aware Computation, and Code Generation are used to speed things up dramatically. The book goes on to show how to incorporate H20 and Deeplearning4j for machine learning and Juypter Notebooks, Zeppelin, Docker and Kubernetes for cloud-based Spark. During the course of the book, you will also learn about the latest enhancements in Apache Spark 2.2, such as using the DataFrame and Dataset APIs exclusively, building advanced, fully automated Machine Learning pipelines with SparkML and perform graph analysis using the new GraphFrames API.

What this book covers

Chapter 1, *A First Taste and What's New in Apache Spark V2*, provides an overview of Apache Spark, the functionality that is available within its modules, and how it can be extended. It covers the tools available in the Apache Spark ecosystem outside the standard Apache Spark modules for processing and storage. It also provides tips on performance tuning.

Chapter 2, *Apache Spark SQL*, creates a schema in Spark SQL, shows how data can be queried efficiently using the relational API on DataFrames and Datasets, and explores SQL.

Chapter 3, *The Catalyst Optimizer*, explains what a cost-based optimizer in database systems is and why it is necessary. You will master the features and limitations of the Catalyst Optimizer in Apache Spark.

Chapter 4, *Project Tungsten*, explains why Project Tungsten is essential for Apache Spark and also goes on to explain how Memory Management, Cache-aware Computation, and Code Generation are used to speed things up dramatically.

Chapter 5, *Apache Spark Streaming*, talks about continuous applications using Apache Spark streaming. You will learn how to incrementally process data and create actionable insights.

Chapter 6, *Structured Streaming*, talks about Structured Streaming – a new way of defining continuous applications using the DataFrame and Dataset APIs.

Chapter 7, *Classical MLlib*, introduces you to MLlib, the de facto standard for machine learning when using Apache Spark.

Chapter 8, *Apache SparkML*, introduces you to the DataFrame-based machine learning library of Apache Spark: the new first-class citizen when it comes to high performance and massively parallel machine learning.

Chapter 9, *Apache SystemML*, introduces you to Apache SystemML, another machine learning library capable of running on top of Apache Spark and incorporating advanced features such as a cost-based optimizer, hybrid execution plans, and low-level operator re-writes.

Chapter 10, *Deep Learning on Apache Spark using H20 and DeepLearning4j*, explains that deep learning is currently outperforming one traditional machine learning discipline after the other. We have three open source first-class deep learning libraries running on top of Apache Spark, which are H2O, DeepLearning4j, and Apache SystemML. Let's understand what Deep Learning is and how to use it on top of Apache Spark using these libraries.

Chapter 11, *Apache Spark GraphX*, talks about Graph processing with Scala using GraphX. You will learn some basic and also advanced graph algorithms and how to use GraphX to execute them.

Chapter 12, *Apache Spark GraphFrames*, discusses graph processing with Scala using GraphFrames. You will learn some basic and also advanced graph algorithms and also how GraphFrames differ from GraphX in execution.

Chapter 13, *Apache Spark with Jupyter Notebooks on IBM DataScience Experience*, introduces a Platform as a Service offering from IBM, which is completely based on an Open Source stack and on open standards. The main advantage is that you have no vendor lock-in. Everything you learn here can be installed and used in other clouds, in a local datacenter, or on your local laptop or PC.

Chapter 14, *Apache Spark on Kubernetes*, explains that Platform as a Service cloud providers completely manage the operations part of an Apache Spark cluster for you. This is an advantage but sometimes you have to access individual cluster nodes for debugging and tweaking and you don't want to deal with the complexity that maintaining a real cluster on bare-metal or virtual systems entails. Here, Kubernetes might be the best solution. Therefore, in this chapter, we explain what Kubernetes is and how it can be used to set up an Apache Spark cluster.

What you need for this book

You will need the following to work with the examples in this book:

- A laptop or PC with at least 6 GB main memory running Windows, macOS, or Linux
- VirtualBox 5.1.22 or above
- Hortonworks HDP Sandbox V2.6 or above
- Eclipse Neon or above
- Maven
- Eclipse Maven Plugin
- Eclipse Scala Plugin
- Eclipse Git Plugin

Who this book is for

This book is an extensive guide to Apache Spark from the programmer's and data scientist's perspective. It covers Apache Spark in depth, but also supplies practical working examples for different domains. Operational aspects are explained in sections on performance tuning and cloud deployments. All the chapters have working examples, which can be replicated easily.

Conventions

In this book, you will find a number of text styles that distinguish between different kinds of information. Here are some examples of these styles and an explanation of their meaning.

Code words in text, database table names, folder names, filenames, file extensions, pathnames, dummy URLs, user input, and Twitter handles are shown as follows: "The next lines of code read the link and assign it to the to the `BeautifulSoup` function."

A block of code is set as follows:

```
import org.apache.spark.SparkContext
import org.apache.spark.SparkContext._
import org.apache.spark.SparkConf
```

Any command-line input or output is written as follows:

```
[hadoop@hc2nn ~]# sudo su -
[root@hc2nn ~]# cd /tmp
```

New terms and **important words** are shown in bold. Words that you see on the screen, for example, in menus or dialog boxes, appear in the text like this: "In order to download new modules, we will go to **Files** | **Settings** | **Project Name** | **Project Interpreter**."

Warnings or important notes appear in a box like this.

Tips and tricks appear like this.

Reader feedback

Feedback from our readers is always welcome. Let us know what you think about this book-what you liked or disliked. Reader feedback is important for us as it helps us develop titles that you will really get the most out of.

To send us general feedback, simply e-mail feedback@packtpub.com, and mention the book's title in the subject of your message.

If there is a topic that you have expertise in and you are interested in either writing or contributing to a book, see our author guide at www.packtpub.com/authors.

Customer support

Now that you are the proud owner of a Packt book, we have a number of things to help you to get the most from your purchase.

Downloading the example code

You can download the example code files for this book from your account at http://www.packtpub.com. If you purchased this book elsewhere, you can visit http://www.packtpub.com/support and register to have the files e-mailed directly to you.

You can download the code files by following these steps:

1. Log in or register to our website using your e-mail address and password.
2. Hover the mouse pointer on the **SUPPORT** tab at the top.

3. Click on **Code Downloads & Errata**.
4. Enter the name of the book in the **Search** box.
5. Select the book for which you're looking to download the code files.
6. Choose from the drop-down menu where you purchased this book from.
7. Click on **Code Download**.

Once the file is downloaded, please make sure that you unzip or extract the folder using the latest version of:

- WinRAR / 7-Zip for Windows
- Zipeg / iZip / UnRarX for Mac
- 7-Zip / PeaZip for Linux

The code bundle for the book is also hosted on GitHub at `https://github.com/PacktPubl ishing/Mastering-Apache-Spark-2x`. We also have other code bundles from our rich catalog of books and videos available at `https://github.com/PacktPublishing/`. Check them out!

Downloading the color images of this book

We also provide you with a PDF file that has color images of the screenshots/diagrams used in this book. The color images will help you better understand the changes in the output. You can download this file from `https://www.packtpub.com/sites/default/files/down loads/MasteringApacheSpark2x_ColorImages.pdf`.

Errata

Although we have taken every care to ensure the accuracy of our content, mistakes do happen. If you find a mistake in one of our books-maybe a mistake in the text or the code-we would be grateful if you could report this to us. By doing so, you can save other readers from frustration and help us improve subsequent versions of this book. If you find any errata, please report them by visiting `http://www.packtpub.com/submit-errata`, selecting your book, clicking on the **Errata Submission Form** link, and entering the details of your errata. Once your errata are verified, your submission will be accepted and the errata will be uploaded to our website or added to any list of existing errata under the Errata section of that title.

To view the previously submitted errata, go to https://www.packtpub.com/books/content/support and enter the name of the book in the search field. The required information will appear under the **Errata** section.

Piracy

Piracy of copyrighted material on the Internet is an ongoing problem across all media. At Packt, we take the protection of our copyright and licenses very seriously. If you come across any illegal copies of our works in any form on the Internet, please provide us with the location address or website name immediately so that we can pursue a remedy.

Please contact us at copyright@packtpub.com with a link to the suspected pirated material.

We appreciate your help in protecting our authors and our ability to bring you valuable content.

Questions

If you have a problem with any aspect of this book, you can contact us at questions@packtpub.com, and we will do our best to address the problem.

1
A First Taste and What's New in Apache Spark V2

Apache Spark is a distributed and highly scalable in-memory data analytics system, providing you with the ability to develop applications in Java, Scala, and Python, as well as languages such as R. It has one of the highest contribution/involvement rates among the Apache top-level projects at this time. Apache systems, such as Mahout, now use it as a processing engine instead of MapReduce. It is also possible to use a Hive context to have the Spark applications process data directly to and from Apache Hive.

Initially, Apache Spark provided four main submodules--SQL, MLlib, GraphX, and Streaming. They will all be explained in their own chapters, but a simple overview would be useful here. The modules are interoperable, so data can be passed between them. For instance, streamed data can be passed to SQL and a temporary table can be created. Since version 1.6.0, MLlib has a sibling called SparkML with a different API, which we will cover in later chapters.

The following figure explains how this book will address Apache Spark and its modules:

Kafka	Flume	MQTT							
Streaming			MLLib	ML	SQL	GraphX	DeepLearning4J	H2O	SystemML
ApacheSpark Core									

The top two rows show Apache Spark and its submodules. Wherever possible, we will try to illustrate by giving an example of how the functionality may be extended using extra tools.

We infer that Spark is an **in-memory** processing system. When used at scale (it cannot exist alone), the data must reside somewhere. It will probably be used along with the Hadoop tool set and the associated ecosystem.

Luckily, Hadoop stack providers, such as IBM and Hortonworks, provide you with an open data platform, a Hadoop stack, and cluster manager, which integrates with Apache Spark, Hadoop, and most of the current stable toolset fully based on open source. During this book, we will use **Hortonworks Data Platform (HDP®) Sandbox 2.6**. You can use an alternative configuration, but we find that the open data platform provides most of the tools that we need and automates the configuration, leaving us more time for development.

In the following sections, we will cover each of the components mentioned earlier in more detail before we dive into the material starting in the next chapter:

- Spark Machine Learning
- Spark Streaming
- Spark SQL
- Spark Graph Processing
- Extended Ecosystem
- Updates in Apache Spark
- Cluster design
- Cloud-based deployments
- Performance parameters

Spark machine learning

Machine learning is the real reason for Apache Spark because, at the end of the day, you don't want to just ship and transform data from A to B (a process called **ETL (Extract Transform Load)**). You want to run advanced data analysis algorithms on top of your data, and you want to run these algorithms at scale. This is where Apache Spark kicks in.

Apache Spark, in its core, provides the runtime for massive parallel data processing, and different parallel machine learning libraries are running on top of it. This is because there is an abundance on machine learning algorithms for popular programming languages like R and Python but they are not scalable. As soon as you load more data to the available main memory of the system, they crash.

Apache Spark in contrast can make use of multiple computer nodes to form a cluster and even on a single node can spill data transparently to disk therefore avoiding the main memory bottleneck. Two interesting machine learning libraries are shipped with Apache Spark, but in this work we'll also cover third-party machine learning libraries.

The Spark MLlib module, Classical MLlib, offers a growing but incomplete list of machine learning algorithms. Since the introduction of the **DataFrame**-based machine learning API called **SparkML**, the destiny of MLlib is clear. It is only kept for backward compatibility reasons.

This is indeed a very wise decision, as we will discover in the next two chapters that structured data processing and the related optimization frameworks are currently disrupting the whole Apache Spark ecosystem. In SparkML, we have a machine learning library in place that can take advantage of these improvements out of the box, using it as an underlying layer.

SparkML will eventually replace MLlib. Apache SystemML introduces the first library running on top of Apache Spark that is not shipped with the Apache Spark distribution. SystemML provides you with an execution environment of R-style syntax with a built-in cost-based optimizer. Massive parallel machine learning is an area of constant change at a high frequency. It is hard to say where that the journey goes, but it is the first time where advanced machine learning at scale is available to everyone using open source and cloud computing.

Deep learning on Apache Spark uses **H20**, **Deeplearning4j** and **Apache SystemML**, which are other examples of very interesting third-party machine learning libraries that are not shipped with the Apache Spark distribution.

While H20 is somehow complementary to MLlib, Deeplearning4j only focuses on deep learning algorithms. Both use Apache Spark as a means for parallelization of data processing. You might wonder why we want to tackle different machine learning libraries.

The reality is that every library has advantages and disadvantages with the implementation of different algorithms. Therefore, it often depends on your data and Dataset size which implementation you choose for best performance.

However, it is nice that there is so much choice and you are not locked in a single library when using Apache Spark. Open source means openness, and this is just one example of how we are all benefiting from this approach in contrast to a single vendor, single product lock-in. Although recently Apache Spark integrated GraphX, another Apache Spark library into its distribution, we don't expect this will happen too soon. Therefore, it is most likely that Apache Spark as a central data processing platform and additional third-party libraries will co-exist, like Apache Spark being the big data operating system and the third-party libraries are the software you install and run on top of it.

Spark Streaming

Stream processing is another big and popular topic for Apache Spark. It involves the processing of data in Spark as streams and covers topics such as input and output operations, transformations, persistence, and checkpointing, among others.

Apache Spark Streaming will cover the area of processing, and we will also see practical examples of different types of stream processing. This discusses batch and window stream configuration and provides a practical example of checkpointing. It also covers different examples of stream processing, including Kafka and Flume.

There are many ways in which stream data can be used. Other Spark module functionality (for example, SQL, MLlib, and GraphX) can be used to process the stream. You can use Spark Streaming with systems such as **MQTT** or **ZeroMQ.** You can even create custom receivers for your own user-defined data sources.

Spark SQL

From Spark version 1.3, data frames have been introduced in Apache Spark so that Spark data can be processed in a tabular form and tabular functions (such as `select`, `filter`, and `groupBy`) can be used to process data. The Spark SQL module integrates with Parquet and JSON formats to allow data to be stored in formats that better represent the data. This also offers more options to integrate with external systems.

The idea of integrating Apache Spark into the Hadoop Hive big data database can also be introduced. Hive context-based Spark applications can be used to manipulate Hive-based table data. This brings Spark's fast in-memory distributed processing to Hive's big data storage capabilities. It effectively lets Hive use Spark as a processing engine.

Additionally, there is an abundance of additional connectors to access NoSQL databases outside the Hadoop ecosystem directly from Apache Spark. In Chapter 2, *Apache Spark SQL*, we will see how the Cloudant connector can be used to access a remote ApacheCouchDB NoSQL database and issue SQL statements against JSON-based NoSQL document collections.

Spark graph processing

Graph processing is another very important topic when it comes to data analysis. In fact, a majority of problems can be expressed as a graph.

A **graph** is basically a network of items and their relationships to each other. Items are called **nodes** and relationships are called **edges**. Relationships can be directed or undirected. Relationships, as well as items, can have properties. So a map, for example, can be represented as a graph as well. Each city is a node and the streets between the cities are edges. The distance between the cities can be assigned as properties on the edge.

The **Apache Spark GraphX** module allows Apache Spark to offer fast big data in-memory graph processing. This allows you to run graph algorithms at scale.

One of the most famous algorithms, for example, is the traveling salesman problem. Consider the graph representation of the map mentioned earlier. A salesman has to visit all cities of a region but wants to minimize the distance that he has to travel. As the distances between all the nodes are stored on the edges, a graph algorithm can actually tell you the optimal route. GraphX is able to create, manipulate, and analyze graphs using a variety of built-in algorithms.

It introduces two new data types to support graph processing in Spark--VertexRDD and EdgeRDD--to represent graph nodes and edges. It also introduces graph processing algorithms, such as PageRank and triangle processing. Many of these functions will be examined in Chapter 11, *Apache Spark GraphX* and Chapter 12, *Apache Spark GraphFrames*.

Extended ecosystem

When examining big data processing systems, we think it is important to look at not just the system itself, but also how it can be extended and how it integrates with external systems so that greater levels of functionality can be offered. In a book of this size, we cannot cover every option, but by introducing a topic, we can hopefully stimulate the reader's interest so that they can investigate further.

We have used the H2O machine learning library, SystemML and Deeplearning4j, to extend Apache Spark's MLlib machine learning module. We have shown that Deeplearning and highly performant cost-based optimized machine learning can be introduced to Apache Spark. However, we have just scratched the surface of all the frameworks' functionality.

What's new in Apache Spark V2?

Since Apache Spark V2, many things have changed. This doesn't mean that the API has been broken. In contrast, most of the V1.6 Apache Spark applications will run on Apache Spark V2 with or without very little changes, but under the hood, there have been a lot of changes.

The first and most interesting thing to mention is the newest functionalities of the Catalyst Optimizer, which we will cover in detail in Chapter 3, *The Catalyst Optimizer*. Catalyst creates a **Logical Execution Plan** (**LEP**) from a SQL query and optimizes this LEP to create multiple **Physical Execution Plans** (**PEPs**). Based on statistics, Catalyst chooses the best PEP to execute. This is very similar to cost-based optimizers in **Relational Data Base Management Systems** (**RDBMs**). Catalyst makes heavy use of Project Tungsten, a component that we will cover in Chapter 4, *Apache Spark Streaming.*

Although the **Java Virtual Machine** (**JVM**) is a masterpiece on its own, it is a general-purpose byte code execution engine. Therefore, there is a lot of JVM object management and **garbage collection** (**GC**) overhead. So, for example, to store a 4-byte string, 48 bytes on the JVM are needed. The GC optimizes on object lifetime estimation, but Apache Spark often knows this better than JVM. Therefore, Tungsten disables the JVM GC for a subset of privately managed data structures to make them L1/L2/L3 Cache-friendly.

In addition, code generation removed the boxing of primitive types polymorphic function dispatching. Finally, a new first-class citizen called Dataset unified the RDD and DataFrame APIs. Datasets are statically typed and avoid runtime type errors. Therefore, Datasets can be used only with Java and Scala. This means that Python and R users still have to stick to DataFrames, which are kept in Apache Spark V2 for backward compatibility reasons.

Cluster design

As we have already mentioned, Apache Spark is a distributed, in-memory, parallel processing system, which needs an associated storage system. So, when you build a big data cluster, you will probably use a distributed storage system such as Hadoop, as well as tools to move data such as Sqoop, Flume, and Kafka.

We wanted to introduce the idea of edge nodes in a big data cluster. These nodes in the cluster will be client-facing, on which reside the client-facing components such as Hadoop NameNode or perhaps the Spark master. Majority of the big data cluster might be behind a firewall. The edge nodes would then reduce the complexity caused by the firewall as they would be the only points of contact accessible from outside. The following figure shows a simplified big data cluster:

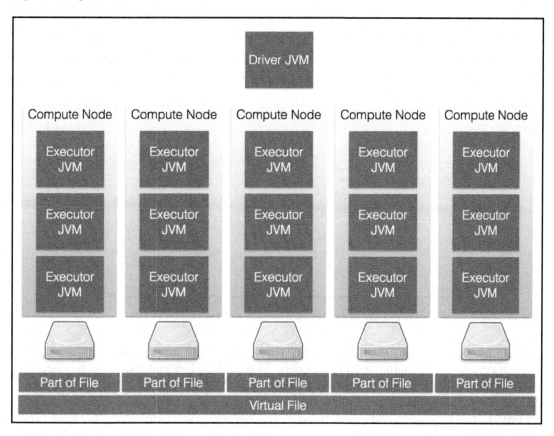

It shows five simplified cluster nodes with executor JVMs, one per CPU core, and the Spark Driver JVM sitting outside the cluster. In addition, you see the disk directly attached to the nodes. This is called the **JBOD (just a bunch of disks)** approach. Very large files are partitioned over the disks and a virtual filesystem such as HDFS makes these chunks available as one large virtual file. This is, of course, stylized and simplified, but you get the idea.

The following simplified component model shows the driver JVM sitting outside the cluster. It talks to the Cluster Manager in order to obtain permission to schedule tasks on the worker nodes because the Cluster Manager keeps track of resource allocation of all processes running on the cluster.

As we will see later, there is a variety of different cluster managers, some of them also capable of managing other Hadoop workloads or even non-Hadoop applications in parallel to the Spark Executors. Note that the Executor and Driver have bidirectional communication all the time, so network-wise, they should also be sitting close together:

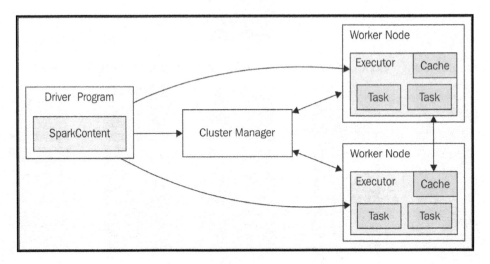

Figure source: https://spark.apache.org/docs/2.0.2/cluster-overview.html

Generally, firewalls, while adding security to the cluster, also increase the complexity. Ports between system components need to be opened up so that they can talk to each other. For instance, Zookeeper is used by many components for configuration. Apache Kafka, the publish/subscribe messaging system, uses Zookeeper to configure its topics, groups, consumers, and producers. So, client ports to Zookeeper, potentially across the firewall, need to be open.

Finally, the allocation of systems to cluster nodes needs to be considered. For instance, if Apache Spark uses Flume or Kafka, then in-memory channels will be used. The size of these channels, and the memory used, caused by the data flow, need to be considered. Apache Spark should not be competing with other Apache components for memory usage. Depending upon your data flows and memory usage, it might be necessary to have Spark, Hadoop, Zookeeper, Flume, and other tools on distinct cluster nodes. Alternatively, resource managers such as YARN, Mesos, or Docker can be used to tackle this problem. In standard Hadoop environments, YARN is most likely.

Generally, the edge nodes that act as cluster NameNode servers or Spark master servers will need greater resources than the cluster processing nodes within the firewall. When many Hadoop ecosystem components are deployed on the cluster, all of them will need extra memory on the master server. You should monitor edge nodes for resource usage and adjust in terms of resources and/or application location as necessary. YARN, for instance, is taking care of this.

This section has briefly set the scene for the big data cluster in terms of Apache Spark, Hadoop, and other tools. However, how might the Apache Spark cluster itself, within the big data cluster, be configured? For instance, it is possible to have many types of the Spark cluster manager. The next section will examine this and describe each type of the Apache Spark cluster manager.

Cluster management

The Spark context, as you will see in many of the examples in this book, can be defined via a Spark configuration object and Spark URL. The Spark context connects to the Spark cluster manager, which then allocates resources across the worker nodes for the application. The cluster manager allocates executors across the cluster worker nodes. It copies the application JAR file to the workers and finally allocates tasks.

The following subsections describe the possible Apache Spark cluster manager options available at this time.

Local

By specifying a Spark configuration local URL, it is possible to have the application run locally. By specifying `local[n]`, it is possible to have Spark use *n* threads to run the application locally. This is a useful development and test option because you can also test some sort of parallelization scenarios but keep all log files on a single machine.

Standalone

Standalone mode uses a basic cluster manager that is supplied with Apache Spark. The spark master URL will be as follows:

```
Spark://<hostname>:7077
```

Here, `<hostname>` is the name of the host on which the Spark master is running. We have specified `7077` as the port, which is the default value, but this is configurable. This simple cluster manager currently supports only **FIFO (first-in first-out)** scheduling. You can contrive to allow concurrent application scheduling by setting the resource configuration options for each application; for instance, using `spark.core.max` to share cores between applications.

Apache YARN

At a larger scale, when integrating with Hadoop YARN, the Apache Spark cluster manager can be YARN and the application can run in one of two modes. If the Spark master value is set as `yarn-cluster`, then the application can be submitted to the cluster and then terminated. The cluster will take care of allocating resources and running tasks. However, if the application master is submitted as `yarn-client`, then the application stays alive during the life cycle of processing, and requests resources from YARN.

Apache Mesos

Apache Mesos is an open source system for resource sharing across a cluster. It allows multiple frameworks to share a cluster by managing and scheduling resources. It is a cluster manager that provides isolation using Linux containers and allowing multiple systems such as Hadoop, Spark, Kafka, Storm, and more to share a cluster safely. It is highly scalable to thousands of nodes. It is a master/slave-based system and is fault tolerant, using Zookeeper for configuration management.

For a single master node Mesos cluster, the Spark master URL will be in this form:

`mesos://<hostname>:5050.`

Here, `<hostname>` is the hostname of the Mesos master server; the port is defined as `5050`, which is the default Mesos master port (this is configurable). If there are multiple Mesos master servers in a large-scale high availability Mesos cluster, then the Spark master URL would look as follows:

`mesos://zk://<hostname>:2181.`

So, the election of the Mesos master server will be controlled by Zookeeper. The `<hostname>` will be the name of a host in the Zookeeper quorum. Also, the port number, `2181`, is the default master port for Zookeeper.

Cloud-based deployments

There are three different abstraction levels of cloud systems--**Infrastructure as a Service (IaaS)**, **Platform as a Service (PaaS)**, and **Software as a Service (SaaS)**. We will see how to use and install Apache Spark on all of these.

The new way to do IaaS is Docker and Kubernetes as opposed to virtual machines, basically providing a way to automatically set up an Apache Spark cluster within minutes. This will be covered in `Chapter 14`, *Apache Spark on Kubernetes*. The advantage of Kubernetes is that it can be used among multiple different cloud providers as it is an open standard and also based on open source.

You even can use Kubernetes in a local data center and transparently and dynamically move workloads between local, dedicated, and public cloud data centers. PaaS, in contrast, takes away from you the burden of installing and operating an Apache Spark cluster because this is provided as a service.

There is an ongoing discussion whether Docker is IaaS or PaaS but, in our opinion, this is just a form of a lightweight preinstalled virtual machine. We will cover more on PaaS in `Chapter 13`, *Apache Spark with Jupyter Notebooks on IBM DataScience Experience*. This is particularly interesting because the offering is completely based on open source technologies, which enables you to replicate the system on any other data center.

One of the open source components we'll introduce is Jupyter notebooks, a modern way to do data science in a cloud based collaborative environment. But in addition to Jupyter, there is also Apache Zeppelin, which we'll cover briefly in `Chapter 14`, *Apache Spark on Kubernetes*.

Performance

Before moving on to the rest of the chapters covering functional areas of Apache Spark and extensions, we will examine the area of performance. What issues and areas need to be considered? What might impact the Spark application performance starting at the cluster level and finishing with actual Scala code? We don't want to just repeat what the Spark website says, so take a look at this URL:
`http://spark.apache.org/docs/<version>/tuning.html`.

Here, `<version>` relates to the version of Spark that you are using; that is, either the latest or something like `1.6.1` for a specific version. So, having looked at this page, we will briefly mention some of the topic areas. We will list some general points in this section without implying an order of importance.

The cluster structure

The size and structure of your big data cluster is going to affect performance. If you have a cloud-based cluster, your IO and latency will suffer in comparison to an unshared hardware cluster. You will be sharing the underlying hardware with multiple customers and the cluster hardware may be remote. There are some exceptions to this. The IBM cloud, for instance, offers dedicated bare metal high performance cluster nodes with an InfiniBand network connection, which can be rented on an hourly basis.

Additionally, the positioning of cluster components on servers may cause resource contention. For instance, think carefully about locating Hadoop NameNodes, Spark servers, Zookeeper, Flume, and Kafka servers in large clusters. With high workloads, you might consider segregating servers to individual systems. You might also consider using an Apache system such as Mesos that provides better distributions and assignment of resources to the individual processes.

Consider potential parallelism as well. The greater the number of workers in your Spark cluster for large Datasets, the greater the opportunity for parallelism. One rule of thumb is one worker per hyper-thread or virtual core respectively.

Hadoop Distributed File System

You might consider using an alternative to HDFS, depending upon your cluster requirements. For instance, IBM has the **GPFS (General Purpose File System)** for improved performance.

The reason why GPFS might be a better choice is that, coming from the high performance computing background, this filesystem has a full read write capability, whereas HDFS is designed as a write once, read many filesystem. It offers an improvement in performance over HDFS because it runs at the kernel level as opposed to HDFS, which runs in a **Java Virtual Machine (JVM)** that in turn runs as an operating system process. It also integrates with Hadoop and the Spark cluster tools. IBM runs setups with several hundred petabytes using GPFS.

Another commercial alternative is the **MapR file system** that, besides performance improvements, supports mirroring, snapshots, and high availability.

Ceph is an open source alternative to a distributed, fault-tolerant, and self-healing filesystem for commodity hard drives like HDFS. It runs in the Linux kernel as well and addresses many of the performance issues that HDFS has. Other promising candidates in this space are **Alluxio** (formerly **Tachyon**), **Quantcast**, **GlusterFS**, and **Lustre**.

Finally, **Cassandra** is not a filesystem but a NoSQL key value store and is tightly integrated with Apache Spark and is therefore traded as a valid and powerful alternative to HDFS--or even to any other distributed filesystem--especially as it supports predicate push-down using `ApacheSparkSQL` and the Catalyst optimizer, which we will cover in the following chapters.

Data locality

The key for good data processing performance is avoidance of network transfers. This was very true a couple of years ago but is less relevant for tasks with high demands on CPU and low I/O, but for low demand on CPU and high I/O demand data processing algorithms, this still holds.

 We can conclude from this that HDFS is one of the best ways to achieve data locality as chunks of files are distributed on the cluster nodes, in most of the cases, using hard drives directly attached to the server systems. This means that those chunks can be processed in parallel using the CPUs on the machines where individual data chunks are located in order to avoid network transfer.

Another way to achieve data locality is using `ApacheSparkSQL`. Depending on the connector implementation, SparkSQL can make use of data processing capabilities of the source engine. So for example when using MongoDB in conjunction with SparkSQL parts of the SQL statement are preprocessed by MongoDB before data is sent upstream to Apache Spark.

Memory

In order to avoid **OOM (Out of Memory)** messages for the tasks on your Apache Spark cluster, please consider a number of questions for the tuning:

- Consider the level of physical memory available on your Spark worker nodes. Can it be increased? Check on the memory consumption of operating system processes during high workloads in order to get an idea of free memory. Make sure that the workers have enough memory.
- Consider data partitioning. Can you increase the number of partitions? As a rule of thumb, you should have at least as many partitions as you have available CPU cores on the cluster. Use the `repartition` function on the RDD API.

- Can you modify the storage fraction and the memory used by the JVM for storage and caching of RDDs? Workers are competing for memory against data storage. Use the **Storage** page on the Apache Spark user interface to see if this fraction is set to an optimal value. Then update the following properties:
- `spark.memory.fraction`
- `spark.memory.storageFraction`
- `spark.memory.offHeap.enabled=true`
- `spark.memory.offHeap.size`

In addition, the following two things can be done in order to improve performance:

- Consider using Parquet as a storage format, which is much more storage effective than CSV or JSON
- Consider using the DataFrame/Dataset API instead of the RDD API as it might resolve in more effective executions (more about this in the next three chapters)

Coding

Try to tune your code to improve the Spark application performance. For instance, filter your application-based data early in your ETL cycle. One example is when using raw HTML files, detag them and crop away unneeded parts at an early stage. Tune your degree of parallelism, try to find the resource-expensive parts of your code, and find alternatives.

ETL is one of the first things you are doing in an analytics project. So you are grabbing data from third-party systems, either by directly accessing relational or NoSQL databases or by reading exports in various file formats such as, CSV, TSV, JSON or even more exotic ones from local or remote filesystems or from a staging area in HDFS: after some inspections and sanity checks on the files an ETL process in Apache Spark basically reads in the files and creates RDDs or DataFrames/Datasets out of them.

They are transformed so they fit to the downstream analytics application running on top of Apache Spark or other applications and then stored back into filesystems as either JSON, CSV or PARQUET files, or even back to relational or NoSQL databases.

Finally, I can recommend the following resource for any performance-related problems with Apache Spark: `https://spark.apache.org/docs /latest/tuning.html`.

Cloud

Although parts of this book will concentrate on examples of Apache Spark installed on physically server-based clusters, we want to make a point that there are multiple cloud-based options out there that imply many benefits. There are cloud-based systems that use Apache Spark as an integrated component and cloud-based systems that offer Spark as a service. Even though this book cannot cover all of them in depth, it would be useful to mention some of them:

- Chapter 13, *Apache Spark with Jupyter Notebooks on IBM DataScience Experience*, is an example of a completely open source based offering from IBM
- Chapter 14, *Apache Spark on Kubernetes*, covers the Kubernetes Cloud Orchestrator, which is available as offering of on many cloud services (including IBM) and also rapidly becoming state-of-the-art in enterprise data centers

Summary

In closing this chapter, we invite you to work your way through each of the Scala code-based examples in the following chapters. The rate at which Apache Spark has evolved is impressive, and important to note is the frequency of the releases. So even though, at the time of writing, Spark has reached 2.2, we are sure that you will be using a later version.

If you encounter problems, report them at `www.stackoverflow.com` and tag them accordingly; you'll receive feedback within minutes--the user community is very active. Another way of getting information and help is subscribing to the Apache Spark mailing list: `user@apachespark.org`.

By the end of this chapter, you should have a good idea what's waiting for you in this book. We've dedicated our effort to showing you practical examples that are, on the one hand, practical recipes to solve day-to-day problems, but on the other hand, also support you in understanding the details of things taking place behind the scenes. This is very important for writing good data products and a key differentiation from others.

The next chapter focuses on `ApacheSparkSQL`. We believe that this is one of the hottest topics that has been introduced to Apache Spark for two reasons.

First, SQL is a very old and established language for data processing. It was invented by IBM in the 1970s and soon will be nearly half a century old. However, what makes SQL different from other programming languages is that, in SQL, you don't declare how something is done but what should be achieved. This gives a lot of room for downstream optimizations.

This leads us to the second reason. As structured data processing continuously becomes the standard way of data analysis in Apache Spark, optimizers such as Tungsten and Catalyst play an important role; so important that we've dedicated two entire chapters to the topic. So stay tuned and enjoy!

2
Apache Spark SQL

In this chapter, we will examine ApacheSparkSQL, SQL, DataFrames, and Datasets on top of **Resilient Distributed Datasets (RDDs)**. DataFrames were introduced in Spark 1.3, basically replacing SchemaRDDs, and are columnar data storage structures roughly equivalent to relational database tables, whereas Datasets were introduced as experimental in Spark 1.6 and have become an additional component in Spark 2.0.

We have tried to reduce the dependency between individual chapters as much as possible in order to give you the opportunity to work through them as you like. However, we do recommend that you read this chapter because the other chapters are dependent on the knowledge of DataFrames and Datasets.

This chapter will cover the following topics:

- SparkSession
- Importing and saving data
- Processing the text files
- Processing the JSON files
- Processing the Parquet files
- DataSource API
- DataFrames
- Datasets
- Using SQL
- User-defined functions
- RDDs versus DataFrames versus Datasets

Before moving on to SQL, DataFrames, and Datasets, we will cover an overview of the SparkSession.

The SparkSession--your gateway to structured data processing

The **SparkSession** is the starting point for working with columnar data in Apache Spark. It replaces SQLContext used in previous versions of Apache Spark. It was created from the Spark context and provides the means to load and save data files of different types using DataFrames and Datasets and manipulate columnar data with SQL, among other things. It can be used for the following functions:

- Executing SQL via the sql method
- Registering user-defined functions via the udf method
- Caching
- Creating DataFrames
- Creating Datasets

> The examples in this chapter are written in Scala as we prefer the language, but you can develop in Python, R, and Java as well. As stated previously, the SparkSession is created from the Spark context.

Using the SparkSession allows you to implicitly convert RDDs into DataFrames or Datasets. For instance, you can convert RDD into a DataFrame or Dataset by calling the toDF or toDS methods:

```
import spark.implicits._
val rdd = sc.parallelize(List(1,2,3))
val df = rdd.toDF
val ds = rdd.toDS
```

As you can see, this is very simple as the corresponding methods are on the RDD object itself.

We are making use of Scala `implicits` function here because the RDD API wasn't designed with DataFrames or Datasets in mind and is therefore lacking the `toDF` or `toDS` methods. However, by importing the respective `implicits`, this behavior is added on the fly. If you want to learn more about Scala `implicits`, the following links are recommended:

- `http://stackoverflow.com/questions/10375633/understanding-implicit-in-scala`
- `http://www.artima.com/pins1ed/implicit-conversions-and-parameters.html`
- `https://dzone.com/articles/learning-scala-implicits-with-spark`

Next, we will examine some of the supported file formats available to import and save data.

Importing and saving data

We wanted to add this section about importing and saving data here, even though it is not purely about Spark SQL, so that concepts such as Parquet and JSON file formats could be introduced. This section also allows us to cover how to access saved data in loose text as well as the CSV, Parquet, and JSON formats conveniently in one place.

Processing the text files

Using `SparkContext`, it is possible to load a text file in `RDD` using the `textFile` method. Additionally, the `wholeTextFile` method can read the contents of a directory to `RDD`. The following examples show you how a file, based on the local filesystem (`file://`) or HDFS (`hdfs://`), can be read to a Spark RDD. These examples show you that the data will be divided into six partitions for increased performance. The first two examples are the same as they both load a file from the Linux filesystem, whereas the last one resides in HDFS:

```
sc.textFile("/data/spark/tweets.txt",6)
sc.textFile("file:///data/spark/tweets.txt",6)
sc.textFile("hdfs://server1:4014/data/spark/tweets.txt",6)
```

Processing JSON files

JavaScript Object Notation (JSON) is a data interchange format developed by the JavaScript ecosystem. It is a text-based format and has the same expressiveness such as, for instance, XML. The following example uses the `SparkSession` method called `read.json` to load the HDFS-based JSON data file named `adult.json`. This uses the so-called Apache Spark DataSource API to read and parse JSON files, but we will come back to that later.

```
val dframe = spark.read.json("hdfs:///data/spark/adult.json")
```

The result is a DataFrame.

Data can be saved in the `JSON` format using the DataSource API as well, as shown by the following example:

```
import spark.implicits._
val df = sc.parallelize(Array(1,2,3)).toDF
df.write.json("hdfs://localhost:9000/tmp/test.json")
```

So, the resulting data can be seen on HDFS; the Hadoop filesystem `ls` command shows you that the data resides in the target directory as a success file and eight part files. This is because even though small, the underlying RDD was set to have eight partitions, therefore those eight partitions have been written. This is shown in the following image:

```
Romeos-MacBook-Pro:~ romeokienzler$ hdfs dfs -ls /tmp/test.json
17/01/09 22:28:54 WARN util.NativeCodeLoader: Unable to load native-hadoop library for your platform... using builtin-java classes where applicable
Found 9 items
-rw-r--r--   3 romeokienzler supergroup          0 2017-01-09 22:28 /tmp/test.json/_SUCCESS
-rw-r--r--   3 romeokienzler supergroup          0 2017-01-09 22:28 /tmp/test.json/part-r-00000-cd2d2d53-969b-4ad9-9700-62740dfd1779.json
-rw-r--r--   3 romeokienzler supergroup          0 2017-01-09 22:28 /tmp/test.json/part-r-00001-cd2d2d53-969b-4ad9-9700-62740dfd1779.json
-rw-r--r--   3 romeokienzler supergroup         12 2017-01-09 22:28 /tmp/test.json/part-r-00002-cd2d2d53-969b-4ad9-9700-62740dfd1779.json
-rw-r--r--   3 romeokienzler supergroup          0 2017-01-09 22:28 /tmp/test.json/part-r-00003-cd2d2d53-969b-4ad9-9700-62740dfd1779.json
-rw-r--r--   3 romeokienzler supergroup          0 2017-01-09 22:28 /tmp/test.json/part-r-00004-cd2d2d53-969b-4ad9-9700-62740dfd1779.json
-rw-r--r--   3 romeokienzler supergroup         12 2017-01-09 22:28 /tmp/test.json/part-r-00005-cd2d2d53-969b-4ad9-9700-62740dfd1779.json
-rw-r--r--   3 romeokienzler supergroup          0 2017-01-09 22:28 /tmp/test.json/part-r-00006-cd2d2d53-969b-4ad9-9700-62740dfd1779.json
-rw-r--r--   3 romeokienzler supergroup         12 2017-01-09 22:28 /tmp/test.json/part-r-00007-cd2d2d53-969b-4ad9-9700-62740dfd1779.json
```

What if we want to obtain a single file? This can be accomplished by repartition to a single partition:

```
val df1 =df.repartition(1)
df1.write.json("hdfs://localhost:9000/tmp/test_single_partition.json")
```

If we now have a look at the folder, it is a single file:

```
Romeos-MacBook-Pro:~ romeokienzler$ hdfs dfs -ls /tmp/test_single_partition.json
17/01/09 22:32:15 WARN util.NativeCodeLoader: Unable to load native-hadoop library for your platform... using builtin-java classes where applicable
Found 2 items
-rw-r--r--   3 romeokienzler supergroup          0 2017-01-09 22:31 /tmp/test_single_partition.json/_SUCCESS
```

There are two important things to know. First, we still get the file wrapped in a subfolder, but this is not a problem as HDFS treats folders equal to files and as long as the containing files stick to the same format, there is no problem. So, if you refer to `/tmp/test_single_partition.json`, which is a folder, you can also use it similarly to a single file.

In addition, all files starting with _ are ignored. This brings us to the second point, the `_SUCCESS` file. This is a framework-independent way to tell users of that file that the job writing this file (or folder respectively) has been successfully completed. Using the Hadoop filesystem's `cat` command, it is possible to display the contents of the JSON data:

```
Romeos-MacBook-Pro:~ romeokienzler$ hdfs dfs -cat /tmp/test_single_partition.json/part-r-00000-f764852b-0ffa-4b58-9cdb-3fdd684c6789.json
17/01/09 22:34:44 WARN util.NativeCodeLoader: Unable to load native-hadoop library for your platform... using builtin-java classes where applicable
{"value":1}
{"value":2}
{"value":3}
```

> If you want to dive more into partitioning and what it means when using it in conjunction with HDFS, it is recommended that you start with the following discussion thread on StackOverflow: http://stackoverflow.com/questions/10666488/what-are-success-and-part-r-00000-files-in-hadoop.

Processing Parquet data is very similar, as we will see next.

Processing the Parquet files

Apache Parquet is another columnar-based data format used by many tools in the Hadoop ecosystem, such as Hive, Pig, and Impala. It increases performance using efficient compression, columnar layout, and encoding routines. The Parquet processing example is very similar to the JSON Scala code. The DataFrame is created and then saved in Parquet format using the `write` method with a `parquet` type:

```
df.write.parquet("hdfs://localhost:9000/tmp/test.parquet")
```

This results in an HDFS directory, which contains eight parquet files:

```
Romeos-MacBook-Pro:~ romeokienzler$ hdfs dfs -ls /tmp/test.parquet
17/01/09 22:36:43 WARN util.NativeCodeLoader: Unable to load native-hadoop library for your platform... using builtin-java classes where applicable
Found 9 items
-rw-r--r--   3 romeokienzler supergroup          0 2017-01-09 22:36 /tmp/test.parquet/_SUCCESS
-rw-r--r--   3 romeokienzler supergroup        252 2017-01-09 22:36 /tmp/test.parquet/part-r-00000-72743c20-e4a9-4cde-a7df-07a56615eaa6.snappy.parquet
-rw-r--r--   3 romeokienzler supergroup        252 2017-01-09 22:36 /tmp/test.parquet/part-r-00001-72743c20-e4a9-4cde-a7df-07a56615eaa6.snappy.parquet
-rw-r--r--   3 romeokienzler supergroup        343 2017-01-09 22:36 /tmp/test.parquet/part-r-00002-72743c20-e4a9-4cde-a7df-07a56615eaa6.snappy.parquet
-rw-r--r--   3 romeokienzler supergroup        252 2017-01-09 22:36 /tmp/test.parquet/part-r-00003-72743c20-e4a9-4cde-a7df-07a56615eaa6.snappy.parquet
-rw-r--r--   3 romeokienzler supergroup        252 2017-01-09 22:36 /tmp/test.parquet/part-r-00004-72743c20-e4a9-4cde-a7df-07a56615eaa6.snappy.parquet
-rw-r--r--   3 romeokienzler supergroup        343 2017-01-09 22:36 /tmp/test.parquet/part-r-00005-72743c20-e4a9-4cde-a7df-07a56615eaa6.snappy.parquet
-rw-r--r--   3 romeokienzler supergroup        252 2017-01-09 22:36 /tmp/test.parquet/part-r-00006-72743c20-e4a9-4cde-a7df-07a56615eaa6.snappy.parquet
-rw-r--r--   3 romeokienzler supergroup        343 2017-01-09 22:36 /tmp/test.parquet/part-r-00007-72743c20-e4a9-4cde-a7df-07a56615eaa6.snappy.parquet
```

For more information about possible `SparkContext` and `SparkSession` methods, check the API documentation of the classes called `org.apache.spark.SparkContext` and `org.apache.spark.sql.SparkSession`, using the Apache Spark API reference at `http://spark.apache.org/docs/latest/api/scala/index.html`.

In the next section, we will examine Apache Spark DataFrames. They were introduced in Spark 1.3 and have become one of the first-class citizens in Apache Spark 1.5 and 1.6.

Understanding the DataSource API

The DataSource API was introduced in Apache Spark 1.1, but is constantly being extended. You have already used the DataSource API without knowing when reading and writing data using SparkSession or DataFrames.

The DataSource API provides an extensible framework to read and write data to and from an abundance of different data sources in various formats. There is built-in support for Hive, Avro, JSON, JDBC, Parquet, and CSV and a nearly infinite number of third-party plugins to support, for example, MongoDB, Cassandra, ApacheCouchDB, Cloudant, or Redis.

Usually, you never directly use classes from the DataSource API as they are wrapped behind the `read` method of `SparkSession` or the `write` method of the DataFrame or Dataset. Another thing that is hidden from the user is schema discovery.

Implicit schema discovery

One important aspect of the DataSource API is implicit schema discovery. For a subset of data sources, implicit schema discovery is possible. This means that while loading the data, not only are the individual columns discovered and made available in a DataFrame or Dataset, but also the column names and types.

Take a JSON file, for example. Column names are already explicitly present in the file. Due to the dynamic schema of JSON objects per default, the complete JSON file is read to discover all the possible column names. In addition, the column types are inferred and discovered during this parsing process

If the JSON file gets very large and you want to make use of the lazy loading nature that every Apache Spark data object usually supports, you can specify a fraction of the data to be sampled in order to infer column names and types from a JSON file.

Another example is the the **Java Database Connectivity (JDBC)** data source where the schema doesn't even need to be inferred but is directly read from the source database.

Predicate push-down on smart data sources

Smart data sources are those that support data processing directly in their own engine-- where the data resides--by preventing unnecessary data to be sent to Apache Spark.

On example is a relational SQL database with a smart data source. Consider a table with three columns: column1, column2, and column3, where the third column contains a timestamp. In addition, consider an ApacheSparkSQL query using this JDBC data source but only accessing a subset of columns and rows based using projection and selection. The following SQL query is an example of such a task:

```
select column2,column3 from tab where column3>1418812500
```

Running on a smart data source, data locality is made use of by letting the SQL database do the filtering of rows based on timestamp and removal of column1.

Let's have a look at a practical example on how this is implemented in the Apache Spark MongoDB connector. First, we'll take a look at the class definition:

```
private[spark] case class MongoRelation(mongoRDD: MongoRDD[BsonDocument],
_schema: Option[StructType])(@transient val sqlContext: SQLContext)
  extends BaseRelation
  with PrunedFilteredScan
  with InsertableRelation
  with LoggingTrait {
```

As you can see, the MongoRelation class extends BaseRelation. This is all that is needed to create a new plugin to the DataSource API in order to support an additional data source. However, this class also implemented the PrunedFilteredScan trait adding the buildScan method in order to support filtering on the data source itself. So let's take a look at the implementation of this method:

```
override def buildScan(requiredColumns: Array[String], filters:
Array[Filter]): RDD[Row] = {
  // Fields that explicitly aren't nullable must also be added to the
  filters
```

```
val pipelineFilters = schema
                        .fields
                        .filter(!_.nullable)
                        .map(_.name)
                        .map(IsNotNull)
                        ++ filters

if (requiredColumns.nonEmpty || pipelineFilters.nonEmpty) {
    logInfo(s"requiredColumns: ${requiredColumns.mkString(", ")},
        filters: ${pipelineFilters.mkString(", ")}")
}
mongoRDD.appendPipeline(createPipeline(requiredColumns, pipelineFilters))
                        .map(doc => documentToRow(doc, schema,
requiredColumns))
}
```

It is not necessary to understand the complete code snippet, but you can see that two parameters are passed to the buildScan method: requiredColumns and filters. This means that the code can use this information to remove columns and rows directly using the MongoDB API.

DataFrames

We have already used DataFrames in previous examples; it is based on a columnar format. Temporary tables can be created from it but we will expand on this in the next section. There are many methods available to the data frame that allow data manipulation and processing.

Let's start with a simple example and load some JSON data coming from an IoT sensor on a washing machine. We are again using the Apache Spark DataSource API under the hood to read and parse JSON data. The result of the parser is a data frame. It is possible to display a data frame schema as shown here:

```
scala> val washing = spark.read.json("hdfs://localhost:9000/tmp/washing.json")
washing: org.apache.spark.sql.DataFrame = [_corrupt_record: string, doc: struct<_id: string, _rev: string ... 9 more fields> ... 3 more fields]

scala> washing.printSchema
root
 |-- _corrupt_record: string (nullable = true)
 |-- doc: struct (nullable = true)
 |    |-- _id: string (nullable = true)
 |    |-- _rev: string (nullable = true)
 |    |-- count: long (nullable = true)
 |    |-- flowrate: long (nullable = true)
 |    |-- fluidlevel: string (nullable = true)
 |    |-- frequency: long (nullable = true)
 |    |-- hardness: long (nullable = true)
 |    |-- speed: long (nullable = true)
 |    |-- temperature: long (nullable = true)
 |    |-- ts: long (nullable = true)
 |    |-- voltage: long (nullable = true)
 |-- id: string (nullable = true)
 |-- key: string (nullable = true)
 |-- value: struct (nullable = true)
 |    |-- rev: string (nullable = true)
```

As you can see, this is a nested data structure. So, the doc field contains all the information that we are interested in, and we want to get rid of the meta information that Cloudant/ApacheCouchDB added to the original JSON file. This can be accomplished by a call to the select method on the DataFrame:

```
scala> val washing_flat = washing.select("doc.*")
washing_flat: org.apache.spark.sql.DataFrame = [_id: string, _rev: string ... 9 more fields]

scala> washing_flat.printSchema
root
 |-- _id: string (nullable = true)
 |-- _rev: string (nullable = true)
 |-- count: long (nullable = true)
 |-- flowrate: long (nullable = true)
 |-- fluidlevel: string (nullable = true)
 |-- frequency: long (nullable = true)
 |-- hardness: long (nullable = true)
 |-- speed: long (nullable = true)
 |-- temperature: long (nullable = true)
 |-- ts: long (nullable = true)
 |-- voltage: long (nullable = true)
```

This is the first time that we are using the DataFrame API for data processing. Similar to RDDs, a set of methods is composing a relational API that is in line with, or even exceeding, the expressiveness that SQL has. It is also possible to use the select method to filter columns from the data. In SQL or relational algebra, this is called projection. Let's now look at an example to better understand the concept:

```
scala> washing_flat.select("temperature","hardness","voltage","speed").show(3)
+-----------+--------+-------+-----+
|temperature|hardness|voltage|speed|
+-----------+--------+-------+-----+
|       null|    null|   null| 1259|
|       null|    null|    237| null|
|         99|     105|   null| null|
+-----------+--------+-------+-----+
only showing top 3 rows
```

 If we want to see the contents of a DataFrame, we can call the show method on it. By default, the first 20 rows are returned. In this case, we've passed 3 as an optional parameter limiting the output to the first three rows.

Of course, the show method is only useful to debug because it is plain text and cannot be used for further downstream processing. However, we can chain calls together very easily.

 Note that the result of a method on a DataFrame returns a DataFrame again--similar to the concept of RDD methods returning RDDs. This means that method calls can be chained as we can see in the next example.

It is possible to filter the data returned from the DataFrame using the filter method. Here, we filter on voltage and select voltage and frequency:

```
scala> washing_flat.select("voltage","frequency").filter(washing_flat("voltage")>235).show(3)
+-------+---------+
|voltage|frequency|
+-------+---------+
|    237|       72|
|    244|       66|
|    253|       71|
+-------+---------+
only showing top 3 rows
```

Semantically, the preceding statement is the same independently if we first filter and then select or vice versa. However, it might make a difference on performance due to which approach we choose. Fortunately, we don't have to take care of this as DataFrames - as RDDs - are lazy. This means that until we call a materialization method such as show, no data processing can take place. In fact, ApacheSparkSQL optimizes the order of the execution under the hood. How this works is covered in the Chapter 3, *The Catalyst Optimizer.*

There is also a groupby method to determine volume counts within a Dataset. So let's check the number of rows where we had an acceptable fluidlevel:

```
scala> washing_flat.groupBy("fluidlevel").count().show()
+----------+-----+
|fluidlevel|count|
+----------+-----+
|      null| 8254|
|acceptable|15449|
+----------+-----+
```

So, SQL-like actions can be carried out against DataFrames, including select, filter, sort, groupby, and print. The next section shows you how tables can be created from DataFrames and how SQL-based actions are carried out against them.

Using SQL

After using the previous Scala example to create a data frame from a JSON input file on HDFS, we can now define a temporary table based on the data frame and run SQL against it.

The following example shows you the temporary table called `washing_flat` being defined and a row count being created using `count(*)`:

```
scala> washing_flat.createOrReplaceTempView("washing_flat")

scala> spark.sql("select count(*) from washing_flat").show
+--------+
|count(1)|
+--------+
|   23703|
+--------+
```

The schema for this data was created on the fly (inferred). This is a very nice function of the Apache Spark DataSource API that has been used when reading the JSON file from HDFS using the `SparkSession` object. However, if you want to specify the schema on your own, you can do so.

Defining schemas manually

So first, we have to `import` some classes. Follow the code to do this:

```
import org.apache.spark.sql.types._
```

So let's define a schema for some CSV file. In order to create one, we can simply write the DataFrame from the previous section to HDFS (again using the Apache Spark Datasoure API):

```
washing_flat.write.csv("hdfs://localhost:9000/tmp/washing_flat.csv")
```

Let's double-check the contents of the directory in HDFS:

```
Romeos-MacBook-Pro:~ romeokienzler$ hdfs dfs -ls /tmp/washing_flat.csv/
17/01/09 23:16:19 WARN util.NativeCodeLoader: Unable to load native-hadoop library for your platform... using builtin-java classes where applicable
Found 3 items
-rw-r--r--   3 romeokienzler supergroup          0 2017-01-09 23:16 /tmp/washing_flat.csv/_SUCCESS
-rw-r--r--   3 romeokienzler supergroup    1403285 2017-01-09 23:16 /tmp/washing_flat.csv/part-r-00000-60cc84d1-f7bb-4f3d-bf2b-b581fbbe6658.csv
-rw-r--r--   3 romeokienzler supergroup    1114646 2017-01-09 23:16 /tmp/washing_flat.csv/part-r-00001-60cc84d1-f7bb-4f3d-bf2b-b581fbbe6658.csv
```

Finally, double-check the content of one file:

```
Romeos-MacBook-Pro:~ romeokienzler$ hdfs dfs -tail /tmp/washing_flat.csv/part-r-00000-60cc84d1-f7bb-4f3d-bf2b-b581fbbe6658.csv
17/01/09 23:18:02 WARN util.NativeCodeLoader: Unable to load native-hadoop library for your platform... using builtin-java classes where applicable
23a78e72483c5f0130b42fc5323a8,12537,11,acceptable,,74,,94,1480435944176,
8fc6ac8feea61a782bf984129de154fe,1-fc1fc74a72d0322b55b501c1350b0da7,4186,,,60,,,1480435947899,230
8fc6ac8feea61a782bf984129de215af,1-14888e64d3963970bdcd36bdc84486e3,4187,,,78,,,,1480435950901,228
8fc6ac8feea61a782bf984129de3eb1f,1-3033ac666a37e9b320f80b28a6311e3f,12552,11,acceptable,,70,,91,1480435959210,
8fc6ac8feea61a782bf984129de6ea16,1-961335b72130cfb0b352e377d58749b4,4194,,,71,,,,1480435971918,243
8fc6ac8feea61a782bf984129de7206e,1-c782d2a514ef7a795c46b6804f33ffb3,12566,11,acceptable,,74,,100,1480435973233,
8fc6ac8feea61a782bf984129de8fe4c,1-67eddbfdccec30af8fb37a14f1cf1b0a,12573,11,acceptable,,78,,99,1480435980246,
8fc6ac8feea61a782bf984129dead56b,1-a7c99c2314e0787029ac45c58381b5a4,12579,11,acceptable,,74,,81,1480435986256,
8fc6ac8feea61a782bf984129deb0817,1-5649ad7f0b66dea9c55bed9abf36825b,12580,11,acceptable,,80,,83,1480435987258,
8fc6ac8feea61a782bf984129dec976c,1-3433987da79cf6b044545a708aa7a5ff,2521,,,,,1051,,1480435991874,
```

So, we are fine; we've lost the schema information but the rest of the information is preserved. We can see the following if we use the DataSource API to load this CSV again:

```
scala> val csvDF = spark.read.csv("hdfs://localhost:9000/tmp/washing_flat.csv")
csvDF: org.apache.spark.sql.DataFrame = [_c0: string, _c1: string ... 9 more fields]

scala> csvDF.printSchema
root
 |-- _c0: string (nullable = true)
 |-- _c1: string (nullable = true)
 |-- _c2: string (nullable = true)
 |-- _c3: string (nullable = true)
 |-- _c4: string (nullable = true)
 |-- _c5: string (nullable = true)
 |-- _c6: string (nullable = true)
 |-- _c7: string (nullable = true)
 |-- _c8: string (nullable = true)
 |-- _c9: string (nullable = true)
 |-- _c10: string (nullable = true)
```

This shows you that we've lost the schema information because all columns are identified as strings now and the column names are also lost. Now let's create the schema manually:

```
val schema = StructType(
    StructField("_id",StringType,true) ::
    StructField("_rev",StringType,true) ::
    StructField("count",LongType,true) ::
    StructField("flowrate",LongType,true) ::
    StructField("fluidlevel",StringType,true) ::
    StructField("frequency",LongType,true) ::
    StructField("hardness",LongType,true) ::
    StructField("speed",LongType,true) ::
    StructField("temperature",LongType,true) ::
    StructField("ts",LongType,true) ::
    StructField("voltage",LongType,true) ::
  Nil)
```

If we now load `rawRDD`, we basically get a list of strings, one string per row:

```
scala> val rawRDD = sc.textFile("hdfs://localhost:9000/tmp/washing_flat.csv")
rawRDD: org.apache.spark.rdd.RDD[String] = hdfs://localhost:9000/tmp/washing_flat.csv MapPartitionsRDD[49] at textFile at <console>:30
```

Now we have to transform this `rawRDD` into a slightly more usable RDD containing the `Row` object by splitting the row strings and creating the respective `Row` objects. In addition, we convert to the appropriate data types where necessary:

```
scala> import org.apache.spark.sql.types._
import org.apache.spark.sql.types._

scala> import org.apache.spark.sql._
import org.apache.spark.sql._

scala> val rowRDD = rawRDD.
     |     map(_.split(",")).
     |     map(p => Row(
     |         p(0),
     |         p(1),
     |         p(2).trim.toLong,
     |         p(3).trim.toLong,
     |         p(4),
     |         p(5).trim.toLong,
     |         p(6).trim.toLong,
     |         p(7).trim.toLong,
     |         p(8).trim.toLong,
     |         p(9).trim.toLong,
     |         p(10).trim.toLong
     |     )
     |   )
rowRDD: org.apache.spark.rdd.RDD[org.apache.spark.sql.Row] = MapPartitionsRDD[51] at map at <console>:46
```

Finally, we recreate our data frame object using the following code:

```
scala> val washing_flat_df = spark.createDataFrame(rowRDD, schema)
washing_flat_df: org.apache.spark.sql.DataFrame = [_id: string, _rev: string ... 9 more fields]
```

If we now print the schema, we notice that it is the same again:

```
scala> washing_flat.printSchema
root
 |-- _id: string (nullable = true)
 |-- _rev: string (nullable = true)
 |-- count: long (nullable = true)
 |-- flowrate: long (nullable = true)
 |-- fluidlevel: string (nullable = true)
 |-- frequency: long (nullable = true)
 |-- hardness: long (nullable = true)
 |-- speed: long (nullable = true)
 |-- temperature: long (nullable = true)
 |-- ts: long (nullable = true)
 |-- voltage: long (nullable = true)
```

Using SQL subqueries

It is also possible to use subqueries in ApacheSparkSQL. In the following example, a SQL query uses an anonymous inner query in order to run aggregations on Windows. The encapsulating query is making use of the virtual/temporal result of the inner query, basically removing empty columns:

```
val result = spark.sql("""
SELECT * from (
    SELECT
    min(temperature) over w as min_temperature,
    max(temperature) over w as max_temperature,
    min(voltage) over w as min_voltage,
    max(voltage) over w as max_voltage,
    min(flowrate) over w as min_flowrate,
    max(flowrate) over w as max_flowrate,
    min(frequency) over w as min_frequency,
    max(frequency) over w as max_frequency,
    min(hardness) over w as min_hardness,
    max(hardness) over w as max_hardness,
    min(speed) over w as min_speed,
    max(speed) over w as max_speed
    FROM washing_flat
    WINDOW w AS (ORDER BY ts ROWS BETWEEN CURRENT ROW AND 10 FOLLOWING)
)
WHERE min_temperature is not null
AND max_temperature is not null
AND min_voltage is not null
```

```
      AND max_voltage is not null
      AND min_flowrate is not null
      AND max_flowrate is not null
      AND min_frequency is not null
      AND max_frequency is not null
      AND min_hardness is not null
      AND min_speed is not null
      AND max_speed is not null
      """)
```

The result of the subqueries is as follows:

```
scala> result.show
17/01/09 23:45:08 WARN WindowExec: No Partition Defined for Window operation! Moving all data to a single partition, this can cause serious performance degradation.
17/01/09 23:45:08 WARN Utils: Truncated the string representation of a plan since it was too large. This behavior can be adjusted by setting 'spark.debug.maxToStringFields' in SparkEnv.conf.
+---------------+---------------+-----------+-----------+------------+------------+-------------+-------------+------------+------------+---------+---------+
|min_temperature|max_temperature|min_voltage|max_voltage|min_flowrate|max_flowrate|min_frequency|max_frequency|min_hardness|max_hardness|min_speed|max_speed|
+---------------+---------------+-----------+-----------+------------+------------+-------------+-------------+------------+------------+---------+---------+
|             84|            100|        221|        227|          11|          11|           78|           80|          71|          79|     1021|     1021|
|             84|            100|        221|        227|          11|          11|           78|           80|          71|          79|     1021|     1021|
|             84|            100|        221|        234|          11|          11|           68|           80|          71|          79|     1021|     1021|
|             84|            100|        221|        234|          11|          11|           68|           80|          71|          78|     1021|     1021|
|             84|            100|        221|        234|          11|          11|           68|           80|          71|          78|     1013|     1021|
|             84|            100|        221|        234|          11|          11|           68|           80|          71|          80|     1013|     1021|
|             84|            100|        221|        235|          11|          11|           68|           80|          71|          80|     1013|     1013|
|             84|             99|        221|        235|          11|          11|           68|           80|          71|          80|     1013|     1013|
|             84|             99|        234|        235|          11|          11|           68|           69|          71|          80|     1013|     1013|
|             81|             99|        234|        235|          11|          11|           68|           69|          71|          80|     1013|     1020|
|             81|             99|        228|        235|          11|          11|           60|           69|          71|          80|     1013|     1020|
|             81|            100|        228|        235|          11|          11|           60|           69|          71|          80|     1013|     1020|
|             81|            100|        228|        235|          11|          11|           60|           69|          71|          80|     1013|     1020|
|             81|            100|        220|        235|          11|          11|           60|           69|          71|          80|     1020|     1020|
|             81|            100|        220|        235|          11|          11|           60|           73|          71|          80|     1020|     1020|
|             81|            100|        220|        228|          11|          11|           60|           73|          71|          80|     1020|     1020|
|             81|            100|        220|        228|          11|          11|           60|           73|          72|          80|     1020|     1030|
+---------------+---------------+-----------+-----------+------------+------------+-------------+-------------+------------+------------+---------+---------+
only showing top 20 rows
```

Applying SQL table joins

In order to examine the table joins, we have created some additional test data. Let's consider banking data. We have an account table called `account_data.json` and a customer data table called `client_data.json`. So let's take a look at the two JSON files.

First, let's look at `client.json`:

```
[{"id":"1","name":"testName1","familyName":"familyName1","countryCode":"US","age":33},
{"id":"2","name":"testName2","familyName":"familyName2","countryCode":"DE","age":43},
{"id":"3","name":"testName3","familyName":"familyName3","countryCode":"US","age":53},
{"id":"4","name":"testName4","familyName":"familyName4","countryCode":"CH","age":63},
{"id":"5","name":"testName5","familyName":"familyName5","countryCode":"US","age":73},
{"id":"6","name":"testName6","familyName":"familyName6","countryCode":"DE","age":23},
{"id":"7","name":"testName7","familyName":"familyName7","countryCode":"US","age":36},
{"id":"8","name":"testName8","familyName":"familyName8","countryCode":"CH","age":38}]
```

Next, let's look at `account.json`:

```
[{"id":"1","clientId":"1","balance":1500},{"id":"2","clientId":"2","balance":500},
{"id":"3","clientId":"1","balance":1500},{"id":"4","clientId":"3","balance":500},
{"id":"5","clientId":"1","balance":1500},{"id":"6","clientId":"4","balance":500},
{"id":"7","clientId":"1","balance":1500},{"id":"8","clientId":"5","balance":500},
{"id":"9","clientId":"1","balance":1500},{"id":"10","clientId":"6","balance":500},
{"id":"11","clientId":"1","balance":1500},{"id":"12","clientId":"7","balance":500},
{"id":"13","clientId":"1","balance":1500},{"id":"14","clientId":"8","balance":500},
{"id":"15","clientId":"1","balance":1500},{"id":"16","clientId":"9","balance":500}]
```

As you can see, `clientId` of `account.json` refers to `id` of `client.json`. Therefore, we are able to join the two files but before we can do this, we have to load them:

```
var client = spark.read.json("client.json")
var account = spark.read.json("account.json")
```

Then we register these two DataFrames as temporary tables:

```
client.createOrReplaceTempView("client")
account.createOrReplaceTempView("account")
```

Let's query these individually, `client` first:

```
scala> spark.sql("select * from client").show
+---+-----------+-----------+---+---------+
|age|countryCode| familyName| id|     name|
+---+-----------+-----------+---+---------+
| 33|         US|familyName1|  1|testName1|
| 43|         DE|familyName2|  2|testName2|
| 53|         US|familyName3|  3|testName3|
| 63|         CH|familyName4|  4|testName4|
| 73|         US|familyName5|  5|testName5|
| 23|         DE|familyName6|  6|testName6|
| 36|         US|familyName7|  7|testName7|
| 38|         CH|familyName8|  8|testName8|
+---+-----------+-----------+---+---------+
```

Then follow it up with `account`:

```
scala> spark.sql("select * from account").show
+-------+--------+---+
|balance|clientId| id|
+-------+--------+---+
|   1500|       1|  1|
|    500|       2|  2|
|   1500|       1|  3|
|    500|       3|  4|
|   1500|       1|  5|
|    500|       4|  6|
|   1500|       1|  7|
|    500|       5|  8|
|   1500|       1|  9|
|    500|       6| 10|
|   1500|       1| 11|
|    500|       7| 12|
|   1500|       1| 13|
|    500|       8| 14|
|   1500|       1| 15|
|    500|       9| 16|
+-------+--------+---+
```

Now we can join the two tables:

```
scala> spark.sql("select * from account inner join client on account.clientid = client.id").show
+-------+--------+---+---+-----------+-----------+---+---------+
|balance|clientId| id|age|countryCode| familyName| id|     name|
+-------+--------+---+---+-----------+-----------+---+---------+
|   1500|       1|  1| 33|         US|familyName1|  1|testName1|
|    500|       2|  2| 43|         DE|familyName2|  2|testName2|
|   1500|       1|  3| 33|         US|familyName1|  1|testName1|
|    500|       3|  4| 53|         US|familyName3|  3|testName3|
|   1500|       1|  5| 33|         US|familyName1|  1|testName1|
|    500|       4|  6| 63|         CH|familyName4|  4|testName4|
|   1500|       1|  7| 33|         US|familyName1|  1|testName1|
|    500|       5|  8| 73|         US|familyName5|  5|testName5|
|   1500|       1|  9| 33|         US|familyName1|  1|testName1|
|    500|       6| 10| 23|         DE|familyName6|  6|testName6|
|   1500|       1| 11| 33|         US|familyName1|  1|testName1|
|    500|       7| 12| 36|         US|familyName7|  7|testName7|
|   1500|       1| 13| 33|         US|familyName1|  1|testName1|
|    500|       8| 14| 38|         CH|familyName8|  8|testName8|
|   1500|       1| 15| 33|         US|familyName1|  1|testName1|
+-------+--------+---+---+-----------+-----------+---+---------+
```

Finally, let's calculate some aggregation on the amount of money that every `client` has on all his `account`s:

```
scala> spark.sql("select sum(balance),clientId from account inner join client on account.clientid = client.id group by clientId").show
+------------+--------+
|sum(balance)|clientId|
+------------+--------+
|         500|       7|
|         500|       3|
|         500|       8|
|         500|       5|
|         500|       6|
|       12000|       1|
|         500|       4|
|         500|       2|
+------------+--------+
```

Using Datasets

This API as been introduced since Apache Spark 1.6 as experimental and finally became a first-class citizen in Apache Spark 2.0. It is basically a strongly typed version of DataFrames.

DataFrames are kept for backward compatibility and are not going to be deprecated for two reasons. First, a DataFrame since Apache Spark 2.0 is nothing else but a Dataset where the type is set to Row. This means that you actually lose the strongly static typing and fall back to a dynamic typing. This is also the second reason why DataFrames are going to stay. Dynamically typed languages such as Python or R are not capable of using Datasets because there isn't a concept of strong, static types in the language.

So what are Datasets exactly? Let's create one:

```
import spark.implicits._
case class Person(id: Long, name: String)
 val caseClassDS = Seq(Person(1,"Name1"),Person(2,"Name2")).toDS()
```

As you can see, we are defining a case class in order to determine the types of objects stored in the Dataset. This means that we have a strong, static type here that is clear at compile time already. So no dynamic type inference is taking place there. This allows for a lot of further performance optimization and also adds compile type safety to your applications. We'll cover the performance optimization aspect in more detail in the Chapter 3, *The Catalyst Optimizer*, and Chapter 4, *Project Tungsten*. As you have seen before, DataFrames can be created from an RDD containing Row objects. These also have a schema. Note that the difference between Datasets and DataFrame is that the Row objects are not static types as the schema can be created during runtime by passing it to the constructor using StructType objects (refer to the last section on DataFrames). As mentioned before, a DataFrame-equivalent Dataset would contain only elements of the Row type. However, we can do better. We can define a static case class matching the schema of our client data stored in client.json:

```
case class Client(
    age: Long,
```

```
countryCode: String,
familyName: String,
id: String,
name: String
)
```

Now we can reread our `client.json` file but this time, we convert it to a Dataset:

```
val ds =
spark.read.json("/Users/romeokienzler/Documents/romeo/Dropbox/arbeit/spark/
sparkbuch/mywork/chapter2/client.json").as[Client]
```

Now we can use it similarly to DataFrames, but under the hood, typed objects are used to represent the data:

```
scala> ds.show
+---+-----------+-----------+---+---------+
|age|countryCode| familyName| id|     name|
+---+-----------+-----------+---+---------+
| 33|         US|familyName1|  1|testName1|
| 43|         DE|familyName2|  2|testName2|
| 53|         US|familyName3|  3|testName3|
| 63|         CH|familyName4|  4|testName4|
| 73|         US|familyName5|  5|testName5|
| 23|         DE|familyName6|  6|testName6|
| 36|         US|familyName7|  7|testName7|
| 38|         CH|familyName8|  8|testName8|
+---+-----------+-----------+---+---------+
```

If we print the schema, we get the same as the formerly used DataFrame:

```
scala> ds.printSchema
root
 |-- age: long (nullable = true)
 |-- countryCode: string (nullable = true)
 |-- familyName: string (nullable = true)
 |-- id: string (nullable = true)
 |-- name: string (nullable = true)
```

The Dataset API in action

We conclude on Datasets with a final aggregation example using the relational Dataset API. Note that we now have an additional choice of methods inspired by RDDs. So we can mix in the map function known from RDDs as follows:

```scala
val dsNew = ds.filter(r => {r.age >= 18}).
    map(c => (c.age, c.countryCode)).
    groupBy($"_2").
    avg()
```

Let's understand how this works step by step:

1. This basically takes the Dataset and filters it to rows containing clients with ages over 18.
2. Then, from the `client` object *c*, we only take the `age` and `countryCode` columns. This process is again a projection and could have been done using the `select` method. The `map` method is only used here to show the capabilities of using lambda functions in conjunction with Datasets without directly touching the underlying RDD.
3. Now, we group by `countryCode`. We are using the so-called Catalyst (**DSL Domain Specific Language**) in the `groupBy` method to actually refer to the second element of the tuple that we created in the previous step.
4. Finally, we average on the groups that we previously created--basically averaging the age per country.

The result is a new strongly typed Dataset containing the average age for adults by country:

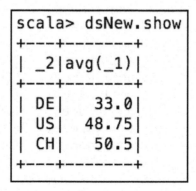

Now we have a quite complete picture of all the first-class citizens of ApacheSparkSQL, as shown in the following figure:

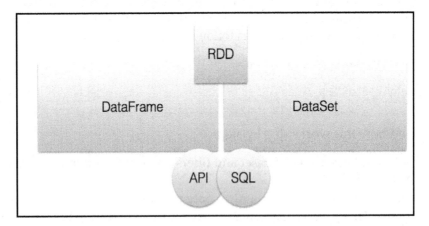

This basically shows that RDD is still the central data processing API where everything else builds on top. DataFrames allow for structured data APIs whereas Datasets bring it to the top with statically-typed domain objects, limited to Scala and Java. Both APIs are usable with SQL or a relational API as we can also run SQL queries against Datasets, as the following example illustrates:

```
scala> ds.createOrReplaceTempView("ds")

scala> spark.sql("select * from ds").show
+---+-----------+-----------+---+---------+
|age|countryCode| familyName| id|     name|
+---+-----------+-----------+---+---------+
| 33|         US|familyName1|  1|testName1|
| 43|         DE|familyName2|  2|testName2|
| 53|         US|familyName3|  3|testName3|
| 63|         CH|familyName4|  4|testName4|
| 73|         US|familyName5|  5|testName5|
| 23|         DE|familyName6|  6|testName6|
| 36|         US|familyName7|  7|testName7|
| 38|         CH|familyName8|  8|testName8|
+---+-----------+-----------+---+---------+
```

This gives us some idea of the SQL-based functionality within Apache Spark, but what if we find that the method that needed is not available? Perhaps we need a new function. This is where **user-defined functions (UDFs)** are useful. We will cover them in the next section.

User-defined functions

In order to create user-defined functions in Scala, we need to examine our data in the previous Dataset. We will use the age property on the client entries in the previously introduced `client.json`. We plan to create an UDF that will enumerate the age column. This will be useful if we need to use the data for machine learning as a lesser number of different values is sometimes useful. This process is also called **binning** or **categorization.** This is the JSON file with the age property added:

```
[{"id":"1","name":"testName1","familyName":"familyName1","countryCode":"US","age":33},
{"id":"2","name":"testName2","familyName":"familyName2","countryCode":"DE","age":43},
{"id":"3","name":"testName3","familyName":"familyName3","countryCode":"US","age":53},
{"id":"4","name":"testName4","familyName":"familyName4","countryCode":"CH","age":63},
{"id":"5","name":"testName5","familyName":"familyName5","countryCode":"US","age":73},
{"id":"6","name":"testName6","familyName":"familyName6","countryCode":"DE","age":23},
{"id":"7","name":"testName7","familyName":"familyName7","countryCode":"US","age":36},
{"id":"8","name":"testName8","familyName":"familyName8","countryCode":"CH","age":38}]
```

Now let's define a Scala enumeration that converts ages into age range codes. If we use this enumeration among all our relations, we can ensure consistent and proper coding of these ranges:

```scala
object AgeRange extends Enumeration {
  val Zero, Ten, Twenty, Thirty, Fourty, Fifty, Sixty, Seventy, Eighty,
Ninety, HundretPlus = Value
  def getAgeRange(age: Integer) = {
    age match {
      case age if 0 until 10 contains age => Zero
      case age if 11 until 20 contains age => Ten
      case age if 21 until 30 contains age => Twenty
      case age if 31 until 40 contains age => Thirty
      case age if 41 until 50 contains age => Fourty
      case age if 51 until 60 contains age => Fifty
      case age if 61 until 70 contains age => Sixty
      case age if 71 until 80 contains age => Seventy
      case age if 81 until 90 contains age => Eighty
      case age if 91 until 100 contains age => Ninety
      case _ => HundretPlus
    }
  }
}
```

```
        def asString(age: Integer) = getAgeRange(age).toString
    }
```

We can now register this function using `SparkSession` in Scala so that it can be used in a SQL statement:

```
scala> spark.udf.register("toAgeRange",AgeRange.asString _)
res12: org.apache.spark.sql.expressions.UserDefinedFunction = UserDefinedFunction(<function1>,StringType,Some(List(IntegerType)))
```

The newly registered function called `toAgeRange` can now be used in the `select` statement. It takes `age` as a parameter and returns a string for the `age` range:

```
scala> spark.sql("select *,toAgeRange(age) as ageRange from client").show
+---+-----------+-----------+---+---------+--------+
|age|countryCode| familyName| id|     name|ageRange|
+---+-----------+-----------+---+---------+--------+
| 33|         US|familyName1|  1|testName1|  Thirty|
| 43|         DE|familyName2|  2|testName2|  Fourty|
| 53|         US|familyName3|  3|testName3|   Fifty|
| 63|         CH|familyName4|  4|testName4|   Sixty|
| 73|         US|familyName5|  5|testName5| Seventy|
| 23|         DE|familyName6|  6|testName6|  Twenty|
| 36|         US|familyName7|  7|testName7|  Thirty|
| 38|         CH|familyName8|  8|testName8|  Thirty|
+---+-----------+-----------+---+---------+--------+
```

RDDs versus DataFrames versus Datasets

To make it clear, we are discouraging you from using RDDs unless there is a strong reason to do so for the following reasons:

- RDDs, on an abstraction level, are equivalent to assembler or machine code when it comes to system programming
- RDDs express how to do something and not what is to be achieved, leaving no room for optimizers
- RDDs have proprietary syntax; SQL is more widely known

Whenever possible, use Datasets because their static typing makes them faster. As long as you are using statically typed languages such as Java or Scala, you are fine. Otherwise, you have to stick with DataFrames.

Summary

This chapter started by explaining the `SparkSession` object and file I/O methods. It then showed that Spark- and HDFS-based data could be manipulated as both, DataFrames with SQL-like methods and Datasets as strongly typed version of Dataframes, and with Spark SQL by registering temporary tables. It has been shown that schema can be inferred using the DataSource API or explicitly defined using `StructType` on DataFrames or `case classes` on Datasets.

Next, user-defined functions were introduced to show that the functionality of Spark SQL could be extended by creating new functions to suit your needs, registering them as UDFs, and then calling them in SQL to process data. This lays the foundation for most of the subsequent chapters as the new DataFrame and Dataset API of Apache Spark is the way to go and RDDs are only used as fallback.

In the coming chapters, we'll discover why these new APIs are much faster than RDDs by taking a look at some internals of Apache SparkSQL in order to understand why Apache SparkSQL provides such dramatic performance improvements over the RDD API. This knowledge is important in order to write efficient SQL queries or data transformations on top of the DataFrame or Dataset relational API. So, it is of utmost importance that we take a look at the Apache Spark optimizer called **Catalyst**, which actually takes your high-level program and transforms it into efficient calls on top of the RDD API and, in later chapters, Tungsten, which is integral to the study of Apache Spark.

The Catalyst Optimizer

3

The Catalyst Optimizer is one of the most exciting developments in Apache Spark. This is because it basically frees your mind from writing effective data processing pipelines, and lets the optimizer do it for you.

In this chapter, we will like to introduce the Catalyst Optimizer of Apache Spark SQL running on top of SQL, DataFrames, and Datasets.

This chapter will cover the following topics:

- The catalog
- Abstract syntax trees
- The optimization process on logical and physical execution plans
- Code generation
- One practical code walk-through

Understanding the workings of the Catalyst Optimizer

So how does the optimizer work? The following figure shows the core components and how they are involved in a sequential optimization process:

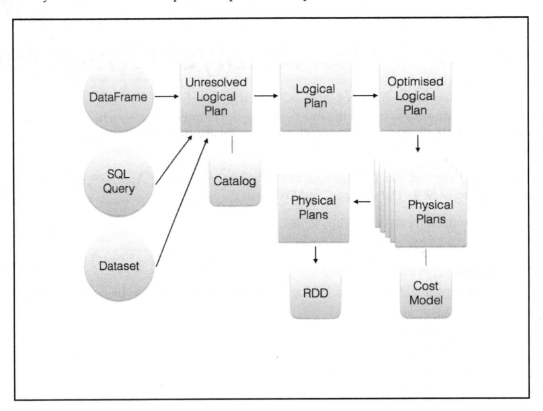

First of all, it has to be understood that it doesn't matter if a DataFrame, the Dataset API, or SQL is used. They all result in the same **Unresolved Logical Execution Plan (ULEP)**. A QueryPlan is unresolved if the column names haven't been verified and the column types haven't been looked up in the catalog. A **Resolved Logical Execution Plan (RLEP)** is then transformed multiple times, until it results in an **Optimized Logical Execution Plan**. LEPs don't contain a description of how something is computed, but only what has to be computed. The optimized LEP is transformed into multiple **Physical Execution Plans (PEP)** using so-called strategies. Finally, an optimal PEP is selected to be executed using a cost model by taking statistics about the Dataset to be queried into account. Note that the final execution takes place on RDD objects.

Managing temporary views with the catalog API

Since Apache Spark 2.0, the catalog API is used to create and remove temporary views from an internal meta store. This is necessary if you want to use SQL, because it basically provides the mapping between a virtual table name and a DataFrame or Dataset.

Internally, Apache Spark uses the `org.apache.spark.sql.catalyst.catalog.SessionCatalog` class to manage temporary views as well as persistent tables.

Temporary views are stored in the `SparkSession` object, as persistent tables are stored in an external metastore. The abstract base class `org.apache.spark.sql.catalyst.catalog.ExternalCatalog` is extended for various meta store providers. One already exists for using Apache Derby and another one for the Apache Hive metastore, but anyone could extend this class and make Apache Spark use another metastore as well.

The SQL abstract syntax tree

As explained earlier, it doesn't matter if you are using SQL, DataFrame, or Dataset, the Apache Spark SQL parser returns an abstract syntax tree. However, DataFrames or Datasets can be used as starting points. The result of all these methods is again a tree-based structure called ULEP. The following figure is an example of such an **AST (abstract syntax tree)** adding an attribute coming from a row in a table and two literals together:

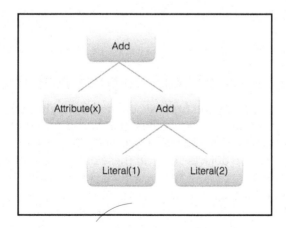

So as you can see, at the bottom of the tree (those nodes are also called leaves since they don't have any further nodes connecting to them) we have two integer literals: one and two. On top we have an operation taking those two literals and adding them together. You should note that those literals could also be loaded from a persistent data store. The **Add** operation virtually turns into another literal (three in this case), which then again is used by another **Add** operation as one of its inputs. The other input labeled as **Attribute(x)** now takes the value of **x** of that particular relation and exposes it as materialized value to the **Add** operator. So in other words, this AST does nothing else than add the number **three** to each of the values in column **x**.

How to go from Unresolved Logical Execution Plan to Resolved Logical Execution Plan

The ULEP basically reflects the structure of an AST. So again, the AST is generated from the user's code implemented either on top of the relational API of DataFrames and Datasets or using SQL, or all three. This AST can be easily transformed into a ULEP. But, of course, a ULEP can't be executed. The first thing that is checked is if the referred relations exist in the catalog. This means all table names and fields expressed in the SQL statement or relational API have to exist. If the table (or relation) exists, the column names are verified. In addition, the column names that are referred to multiple times are given an alias in order to read them only once. This is already a first stage optimization taking place here. Finally, the data types of the columns are determined in order to check if the operations expressed on top of the columns are valid. So for example taking the **sum** of a **string** doesn't work and this error is already caught at this stage. The result of this operation is a Resolved Logical Execution Plan (LEP).

Internal class and object representations of LEPs

As an unresolved plan is basically the first tree created from either SQL statements or the relational API of DataFrames and Datasets, it is mainly composed of sub-types of the LeafExpression objects, which are bound together by the Expression objects, therefore forming a tree of the TreeNode objects since all these objects are sub-types of TreeNode. Overall, this data structure is a LogicalPlan, which is therefore reflected as a LogicalPlan object. Note that LogicalPlan extends QueryPlan, and QueryPlan itself is TreeNode again. In other words, LogicalPlan is nothing else than a set of TreeNode objects.

The following two figures illustrate the inheritance tree of the different objects discussed:

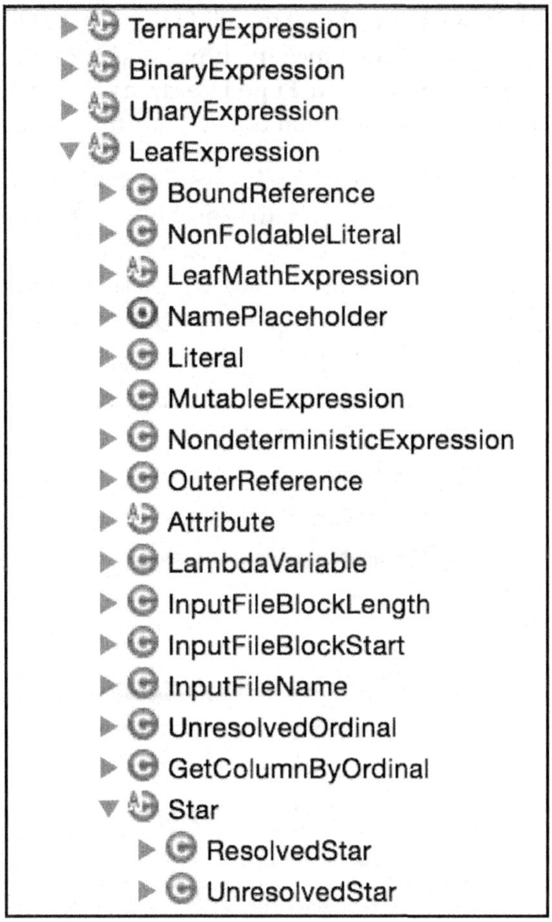

As can be seen clearly in the previous figure, `LeafExpression` is the parent of most of the functional operators. Let's take `Star` for example. `Star`, a child class of `LeafExpression`, is parent to `ResolvedStar` and `UnresolvedStar`.

An easy way to explore Java and Scala inheritance trees in **Eclipse** is by opening any particular class or interface using the `Open Type` function (**Navigate | Open Type...**) and then just type in the desired name, for example **LeafExpression**. Once the type is opened, the **Open Type Hierarchy** (**Navigate | Open Type Hierarchy...**) function can be used to generate those diagrams, as can be seen in previous figures.

Since `star` in an SQL expression denotes all columns of a particular relation, Catalyst has to query the catalog in order to determine the names and types of columns referred to. So once the tree gets transformed from `unresolved` to `resolved`, also those classes are replaced. All these classes are inherited from `TreeNode` and are used to form abstract syntax trees. The same holds true not only for abstract syntax trees, but also for execution plans, as `QueryPlan` also inherits from `TreeNode`:

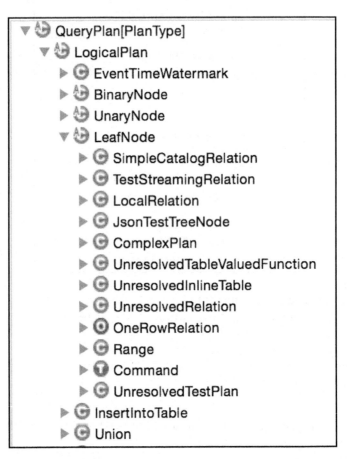

How to optimize the Resolved Logical Execution Plan

The resolved LEP can now be optimized. This is done using a set of transformation rules.

Since a LEP is just a tree, the rules transform from one tree to another. This is done iteratively until no rule fires anymore and keeps the LEP stable and the process is finished. The result of this step is an Optimized Logical Execution Plan.

Physical Execution Plan generation and selection

The Resolved and Optimized LEP is used to generate a large set of PEP candidates. PEPs are execution plans that have been completely resolved. This means that a PEP contains detailed instructions to generate the desired result. They are generated by so-called strategies. **Strategies** are used to optimize selection of join algorithms based on statistics. In addition, rules are executed for example to pipeline multiple operations on an RDD into a single, more complex operation. After a set of PEPs has been generated - they all will return the exact same result - the best one is chosen based on heuristics in order to minimize execution time.

In case the data source supports it, operations are pushed down to the source, namely for **filtering** (predicate) or selection of **attributes** (projection). This concept is explained in very detail on Chapter 2, *Apache Spark SQL,* in the section called *Predicate push-down on smart data sources.*

The main idea of predicate push-down is that parts of the AST are not executed by Apache Spark but by the data source itself. So for example filtering rows on column names can be done much more efficient by a relational or NoSQL database since it sits closer to the data and therefore can avoid data transfers between the database and Apache Spark. Also, the removal of unnecessary columns is a job done more effectively by the database.

Code generation

Finally, things can be improved even more, since Apache Spark runs on the **Java Virtual Machine (JVM)**, which allows byte code to be created and modified during runtime. Let's consider an addition of values a and b, resulting in the expression a+b. Normally, this expression had to be interpreted by the JVM for each row of the Dataset. It would be nice if we could generate the JVM ByteCode for this expression on the fly. This is possible, and Catalyst makes use of a very cool Scala feature called **Quasiquotes**, which basically allows an arbitrary string containing Scala code to be compiled into ByteCode on the fly, if it starts with q. So for example, q"row.get($a)+row.get($b)" will tell the Scala compiler to use this String to generate further JVM byte code. This way, less code has to be interpreted, which speeds things up.

Practical examples

In order to facilitate understanding of these components, we'll introduce some practical examples using Scala code. Consider data about clients and accounts according to the following schemas:

```scala
case class Client(
    age: Long,
    countryCode: String,
    familyName: String,
    id: String,
    name: String
    )
```

As you might now, a case class is somehow the Scala equivalent to JavaBeans and is meant for implementing **data transfer objects (DTOs)** without further logic built into the class. A case class is compared by value and not by reference, which is the default for all other classes. Finally, the copy method allows for easy duplications of DTOs.

This case class specifies the schema for rows of the Client relation. Let's have a look at the schema for the Account relation:

```scala
case class Account(
    balance: Long,
    id: String,
    clientId: String
    )
```

Now we can create Datasets from different files and file types in order to see how the optimizer reacts:

```
val clientDs = spark.read.json("client.json").as[Client]
val clientDsBig = spark.read.json("client_big.json").as[Client]
val accountDs = spark.read.json("account.json").as[Account]
val accountDsBig = spark.read.json("account_big.json").as[Account]
val clientDsParquet = spark.read.parquet("client.parquet").as[Client]
val clientDsBigParquet =
spark.read.parquet("client_big.parquet").as[Client]
val accountDsParquet = spark.read.parquet("account.parquet").as[Account]
val accountDsBigParquet =
spark.read.parquet("account_big.parquet").as[Account]
```

Then we register all as temporary tables, so that we can write ordinary SQL statements against them. First, we'll do this for the `json` backed DataFrames:

```
clientDs.createOrReplaceTempView("client")
clientDsBig.createOrReplaceTempView("clientbig")
accountDs.createOrReplaceTempView("account")
accountDsBig.createOrReplaceTempView("accountbig")
```

Then we also do the same for the `parquet` backed DataFrames:

```
clientDsParquet.createOrReplaceTempView("clientparquet")
 clientDsBigParquet.createOrReplaceTempView("clientbigparquet")
 accountDsParquet.createOrReplaceTempView("accountparquet")
 accountDsBigParquet.createOrReplaceTempView("accountbigparquet")
```

Using the explain method to obtain the PEP

In order to get an idea of what is happening behind the scenes, we can call the `explain` method on the Dataset. This returns (as text) an output what the Catalyst Optimizer did behind the scenes by printing a text representation of the PEP.

So let's have a look at what happens if we join two Datasets backed by the `parquet` files:

```
spark.sql("select c.familyName from clientbigparquet c inner join
accountbigparquet a on c.id=a.clientId").explain
```

The resulting execution plan (PEP) looks like this:

```
scala> spark.sql("select c.familyName from clientbigparquet c inner join accountbigparquet a on c.id=a.clientId").explain
== Physical Plan ==
*Project [familyName#79]
+- *BroadcastHashJoin [id#80], [clientId#106], Inner, BuildRight
   :- *Project [familyName#79, id#80]
   :  +- *Filter isnotnull(id#80)
   :     +- *FileScan parquet [familyName#79,id#80] Batched: true, Format: Parquet, Location: InMemoryFileIndex[file:/Users/romeokienzler/Documents/ro
meo/Dropbox/arbeit/spark/sparkbuch/mywork..., PartitionFilters: [], PushedFilters: [IsNotNull(id)], ReadSchema: struct<familyName:string,id:string>
   +- BroadcastExchange HashedRelationBroadcastMode(List(input[0, string, true]))
      +- *Project [clientId#106]
         +- *Filter isnotnull(clientId#106)
            +- *FileScan parquet [clientId#106] Batched: true, Format: Parquet, Location: InMemoryFileIndex[file:/Users/romeokienzler/Documents/romeo/
Dropbox/arbeit/spark/sparkbuch/mywork..., PartitionFilters: [], PushedFilters: [IsNotNull(clientId)], ReadSchema: struct<clientId:string>
```

Since this might be a bit hard to read for beginners, find the same plan in the following figure:

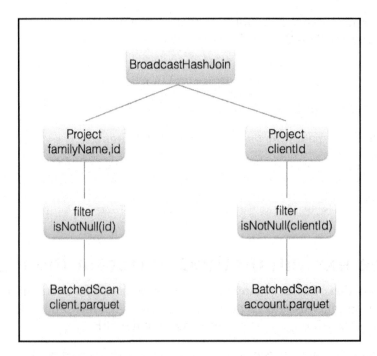

So what is done here is basically--when read from bottom to top--two read operations to `parquet` files followed by a filter operations to ensure that the columns of the join predicate are not null. This is important since otherwise the join operation fails.

 In relational databases, the `isNotNull` filter would be a redundant step, since RDBMS recognizes the notion of not nullable columns; therefore, the null check is done during insert and not during read.

Then, a projection operation is performed, which basically means that unnecessary columns are removed. We are only selecting `familyName`, but for the `join` operation, `clientId` and `id` are also necessary. Therefore, these fields are included in the set of column names to be obtained as well.

Finally, all data is available to execute the join.

Note that in the preceding diagram, `BroadCastHashJoin` is illustrated as single stage, but in reality, a join spans partitions over - potentially - multiple physical nodes. Therefore, the two tree branches are executed in parallel and the results are shuffled over the cluster using hash bucketing based on the join predicate.

As previously stated, the `Parquet` files are smart data sources, since projection and filtering can be performed at the storage level, eliminating disk reads of unnecessary data. This can be seen in the `PushedFilters` and `ReadSchema` sections in the explained plan, where the `IsNotNull` operation and the `ReadSchema` projection on `id`, `clientId`, and `familyName` is directly performed at the read level of the `Parquet` files.

How smart data sources work internally

JDBC stands for **Java Database Connectivity**. When talking about Apache Spark and JDBC there is sometimes a bit of confusion because JDBC can be used in the context of a data source as well as referred to Apache Spark's capability to serve as JDBC-compliant data source to other systems. The latter is not further covered in this book, whereas the former is only used as one particular example where the data source (in this case a relational database) can be transparently used for data pre-processing without the user of Apache SparkSQL further noticing it.

If you want to use Apache SparkSQL as a data source for other JAVA/JVM-based applications you have to start the JDBC Thrift server, as explained here: `https://developer.ibm.com/hadoop/2016/08/22/how-to-run-queries-on-spark-sql-using-jdbc-via-thrift-server/`. The following website explains how to connect to a MySQL database from Apache SparkSQL using JDBC: `https://docs.databricks.com/spark/latest/data-sources/sql-databases.html`. And more on JDBC in general can be found here: `http://www.oracle.com/technetwork/java/overview-141217.html#2`.

Now we want to show how Apache Spark internally implements smart data sources exemplified on a filter pushed down to a JDBC data source. This means that if in a PEP data has to be filtered, then this filter will be executed in the SQL statement on the RDBMS when the underlying data is read. This way, reading unnecessary data is avoided. Depending on the seductiveness of the filter predicate, the performance gain can be multiple orders of magnitude.

Let's have a look at the following trait (here's the link to the source code ht tps://github.com/apache/spark/blob/master/sql/core/src/main/scala/org/apache /spark/sql/sources/interfaces.scala):

```
trait PrunedFilteredScan {
   def buildScan(requiredColumns: Array[String], filters: Array[Filter]):
RDD[Row]
 }
```

This trait defines a method called buildScan, which takes two parameters. First, a list of column names which have to be included in the result, and second, an array of filter objects basically expressing the query predicate pushed down to the underlying smart data source. The return type is of RDD[Row]. One example is implemented in the JDBCRelation class (again, here is the link to the source code https://github.com/apache/spark/blob/maste r/sql/core/src/main/scala/org/apache/spark/sql/execution/datasources/jdbc/JDB CRelation.scala):

```
private[sql] case class JDBCRelation(
     parts: Array[Partition], jdbcOptions: JDBCOptions)(@transient val
sparkSession: SparkSession)
   extends BaseRelation
   with PrunedFilteredScan
   with InsertableRelation {
```

JDBCRelation implemented the buildScan method in the following way:

```
   override def buildScan(requiredColumns: Array[String], filters:
Array[Filter]): RDD[Row] = {
      // Rely on a type erasure hack to pass RDD[InternalRow] back as
RDD[Row]
      JDBCRDD.scanTable(
        sparkSession.sparkContext,
        schema,
        requiredColumns,
        filters,
        parts,
        jdbcOptions).asInstanceOf[RDD[Row]]
   }
```

As we can see, this method is just a `delegate`. Therefore, we have to have a look at the `scanTable` method of the `JDBCRDD` class. It is interesting to note that, in case of `JDBCRDD`, support for predicate push-down is implemented directly in the `RDD` class. But we'll skip the `scanTable` method for now, since it just parameterizes and creates a new `JDBCRDD` object. So the most interesting method in `JDBCRDD` is `compute`, which it inherits from the abstract `RDD` class. Through the `compute` method, Apache Spark tells this RDD to get out of lazy mode and materialize itself whenever it is appropriate during computation of a data processing job. We'll show you two important fractions of this method after we have had a look at the method signature:

```
override def compute(thePart: Partition, context: TaskContext):
Iterator[InternalRow] = {
```

Here you can see that the return type is of `Iterator`, which allows a lazy underlying data source to be read lazily as well. As we can see, this is the case for this particular implementation as well:

```
    val sqlText = s"SELECT $columnList FROM ${options.table}
$myWhereClause"
    stmt = conn.prepareStatement(sqlText,
        ResultSet.TYPE_FORWARD_ONLY, ResultSet.CONCUR_READ_ONLY)
    stmt.setFetchSize(options.fetchSize)
    rs = stmt.executeQuery()
```

 Note that the SQL statement created and stored in the `sqlText` constant is referencing two interesting variables: `columnList` and `myWhereClause`. Both are derived from the `requiredColumns` and `filter` arguments passed to the `JDBCRelation` class.

Therefore, this data source can be called a smart source, because the underlying storage technology (an SQL database in this case) can be told to only return columns and rows which are actually requested. And as already mentioned, the data source supports passing lazy data access patterns to be pushed to the underlying database as well. Here you can see that the JDBC result set is wrapped into a typed `InternalRow` iterator, `Iterator[InternalRow]`). Since this matches the return type of the `compute` method, we are done upon execution of the following code:

```
    val rowsIterator = JdbcUtils.resultSetToSparkInternalRows(rs, schema,
    inputMetrics) CompletionIterator[InternalRow,
    Iterator[InternalRow]](rowsIterator, close())
```

Note that `ResultSet rs` obtained from the JDBC database query is passed to (wrapped into) a `delegate` object. Therefore, the JDBC connection stays open, and the RDBMS courser doesn't get destroyed and can be used to return subsequent data once requested from Apache Spark.

Summary

This chapter basically was a sales pitch for using DataFrames, Datasets, and SQL over RDDs, because in the majority of cases, the optimizer does such a great job that the performance is nearly equal to hand-optimized code on RDDs. You now know the internals of the optimizer, which will give you a solid foundation in using all components that are based on it and that are introduced in the subsequent chapters.

The next chapter is dedicated to Tungsten Phase I and Phase II, which is a mind-blowing technology that accelerates computations by a factor of 100, so stay tuned!

4
Project Tungsten

This chapter introduces Project Tungsten. CPU and main memory performance became the new bottlenecks in big data processing after the massive increase in I/O performance due to the usage of **solid state disks** (**SSDs**) and 10 Gbps Ethernet. Therefore, Project Tungsten, the core of the Apache Spark execution engine, aims at improving performance at the CPU and main memory level. This chapter will cover the following topics:

- Memory management beyond the **Java Virtual Machine** (**JVM**) **Garbage Collector** (**GC**)
- Cache-friendly layout of data in memory
- Code generation

We will have an in-depth look at all these three topics now.

Memory management beyond the Java Virtual Machine Garbage Collector

 The JVM Garbage Collector is in support of the whole object's life cycle management the JVM provides. Whenever you see the word new in Java code, memory is allocated in a JVM memory segment called heap.

Java completely takes care of memory management and it is impossible to overwrite memory segments that do not belong to you (or your object). So if you write something to an object's memory segment on the heap (for example by updating a class property value of type `Integer`, you are changing 32 bit on the heap) you don't use the actual heap memory address for doing so but you use the reference to the object and either access the object's property or use a setter method.

So we've learned about `new` allocated memory on the heap, but how does it ever get freed? This is where the Java Garbage collector kicks in. It continuously monitors how many active references to a certain object on the heap exist and once no more references exist those objects are destroyed and the allocated memory is freed.

References to an object can either exist within objects on the heap itself or in the stack. The stack is a memory segment where variables in method calls and variables defined within methods reside. They are usually short lived whereas data on the heap might live for longer.

This topic would be worth a book on it's own, because there are a lot of catches, for example circular references of objects which are not used anymore but kind of dead-lock themselves and many more. Therefore we stop there on explaining how exactly this works but let's conclude with the following statement: The Garbage Collector is a highly complex component and has been optimized to support **Online Transaction Processing (OLTP)** workloads whereas Apache Spark concentrates on **Online Analytical Processing (OLAP)**. There is a clash between optimizing a garbage collector for both disciplines at the same time since the object life cycle is very different between those two disciplines.

The main idea behind Tungsten is to get rid of the JVM Garbage Collector. Although for the general purpose bytecode, the GC does a pretty awesome job of predicting object life cycles, and the resulting frequency and bearing of GC cycles. But Apache Spark knows better which data has to be kept and which data can be removed from the memory. Therefore, Tungsten bypasses the managed (and safe) memory management system which the JVM provides and uses the classes from the `sun.misc.Unsafe` package, which allows Tungsten to manage memory layout on its behalf.

Understanding the UnsafeRow object

At its core, since Apache Spark V1.4 Tungsten uses `org.apache.spark.sql.catalyst.expressions.UnsafeRow`, which is a binary representation of a row object. An `UnsafeRow` object consists of three regions, as illustrated in the following figure:

Note that all regions, and also the contained fields within the regions, are 8-byte aligned. Therefore, individual chunks of data perfectly fit into 64 bit CPU registers. This way, a compare operation can be done in a single machine instruction only. In addition, 8-byte stride memory access patterns are very cache-friendly, but more on this will be explained later.

Please note that although the technology is called **unsafe** it is perfectly safe, for you as user, since Tungsten takes care of the memory management. This is just a technology allowing people other than the JVM creators to implement memory management. Another success story for the openness of the JVM. In the following sections, we'll explain the purpose of each memory region of the `UnsafeRow` object.

The null bit set region

In this region, for each field contained in the row, a bit is reserved to indicate whether it contains a null value or not. This is very useful for filtering, because only the bit set has to be read from memory, omitting the actual values. The number of fields and the size of this region are reflected as individual properties in the `org.apache.spark.sql.catalyst.expressions.UnsafeRow` object. Therefore, this region can be of variable size as well, which is an implicit requirement since the number of fields varies as well.

The fixed length values region

The **fixed length values** region stores two things. Either values fitting into the 8 bytes - called fixed length values like `long`, `double`, or `int` - or in the event the value of a particular field doesn't fit into that chunk only a pointer or a reference is stored. This reference points to a byte offset in the **variable length values** region. In addition to the pointer, the length (in bytes) of that field is also stored. Both integer values are combined into a long value. This way, two 4-byte integer values are stored in one 8-byte field. Again, since the number of fields is known, this region is of variable length and reserves 8 bytes for each field.

The variable length values region

Finally, the variable length values region, the last region of an UnsafeRow object, contains variable-sized fields like strings. As mentioned earlier, a pointer containing the offset to the position in the variable length values region is stored in the fixed length values region. Since offset and length are known to be stored in the fixed length values region, a variable sized value can be easily addressed.

For those of you interested in getting a better idea about how these offsets are calculated, let's have a look at some code. Note that this code is Java code, since UnsafeRow has been implemented in Java instead of Scala:

```java
private long getFieldOffset(int ordinal) {
    return baseOffset + bitSetWidthInBytes + ordinal * 8L;
}
```

The method getFieldOffset returns the byte offset of a fixed size field by using baseOffset of the UnsafeRow object itself, adding the size of the first region to it (bitSetWidthInBytes) and finally jumping right to the start of the correct slot by using ordinal, which stores the number/id of the field multiplied by eight. We multiply by eight because all slots are 8-byte aligned.

Slightly more complicated is addressing variable sized fields. Let's have a look at the corresponding Java code:

```java
public UTF8String getUTF8String(int ordinal) {
    if (isNullAt(ordinal)) return null;
    final long offsetAndSize = getLong(ordinal);
    final int offset = (int) (offsetAndSize >> 32);
    final int size = (int) offsetAndSize;
    return UTF8String.fromAddress(baseObject, baseOffset + offset, size);
}
```

First, we check in the fixed size region if the value is null, because then we can already stop here and return null. Then, offsetAndSize is obtained by reading an ordinary Long from the fixed size region, which stores the offset and length of variable size objects in the variable sized objects area. Next, this Long value has to be split into two int values, containing offset and size separately, therefore offsetAndSize, right-shifted 32 bits and cast to int to resemble the offset value, whereas only casting offsetAndSize to int resembles the size value. Finally, using all these address values, a String object is created from the raw bytes within the UnsafeRow object.

Understanding the BytesToBytesMap

A very common data structure in Java is `java.util.HashMap`. The advantage of such a data structure is fast, but more importantly, convenient data access since only a key, which can be any sort of Java object, has to be provided to obtain the value; again, any type of Java object is supported as the key. While convenient for the programmer, `java.util.HashMap` has some drawbacks. The most important are:

- Memory overhead due to usage of objects as keys and values
- Very cache-unfriendly memory layout
- Impossible to directly address fields by calculating offsets

This means that simple but important things, such as sequential scans, result in very random and cache-unfriendly memory access patterns. Therefore, Tungsten has introduced a new data structure called `BytesToBytesMap`, which has improved the memory locality and has led to less space overhead by avoiding the usage of heavyweight Java objects, which has improved performance. Sequential scans are very cache friendly, since they access the memory in sequence.

A practical example on memory usage and performance

So let's have a look at how Tungsten actually saves a lot of memory when using DataFrames or Datasets in contrast to RDDs. Let's have a look at the following code:

```
//create 10^6 integers and store it in intList
 val intList = 0 to math.pow(10, 6).toInt
//create a RDD out of intList
 val rdd = sc.parallelize(intList)
//..and count it
 rdd.cache.count
```

Here we create a Scala list containing 1,000,000 integers, create a RDD out of it, cache it, and finally count the number of entries. We can do the same using a DataFrame:

```
//create a DataFrame out of intList
 val df = intList.toDF
//..and count it
 df.cache.count
```

Again, we take the list of integers, but this time we create a DataFrame out of it. And again, we cache and count.

Luckily Apache Spark provides very detailed insights into its internals. We can access the management UI of Apache Spark on port 4040. Besides job-and task-related information, the **Storage** tab provides information on each RDD currently existing on the cluster. Let's have a look at memory usage:

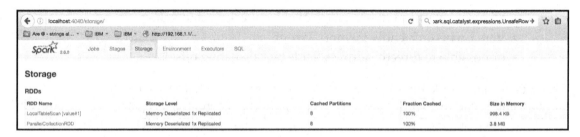

We can see that the RDD takes nearly 4 megabytes of memory, whereas DataFrame (which is backed by a RDD[Row] object) takes only 1 megabyte. Unfortunately, while the wrapping of values into the Row objects has advantages for memory consumption, it has disadvantages for execution performance. Therefore, we give it another try using a Dataset:

```
//create a Dataset out of DataFrame df
case class Ints(value: Int)
val ds = df.as[Ints]
//..and count it
ds.cache.count
```

First, we create a case class for the Dataset's content, since Datasets are strongly (and statically) typed. Then we use the existing DataFrame object df in order to create a Dataset ds out of it. And then, again, we count. Now we ran three Apache Spark jobs on the three different data types and we can take a look at their execution times:

As we can see, the first job on the RDD took only 500 ms, whereas the second job on the DataFrame took two seconds. This means that saving memory actually caused an increase in execution time.

Fortunately, when using Datasets, this performance loss is mitigated and we can take advantage of both the fast execution time and the efficient usage of memory.

Why are we using DataFrames and Datasets at all if RDDs are faster? We could also just put additional memory to the cluster. Note that although this particular execution on an RDD runs faster, Apache Spark jobs are very rarely composed only out of a single operation on an RDD. In theory you could write very efficient Apache Spark jobs on RDDs only, but actually re-writing your Apache Spark application for performance tuning will take a lot of time. So the best way is to use DataFrames and Datasets, to make use of the Catalyst optimizer, in order to get efficient calls to the RDD operations generated.

Cache-friendly layout of data in memory

In order to understand how data structures can be laid out in a cache-friendly manner, let's have a brief look at how caches work in general. Memory on a modern computer system is addressed using 64 bit addresses pointing to 64 bit memory blocks. Remember, Tungsten tries to always use 8-byte Datasets which perfectly fit into these 64-bit memory blocks.

So between your CPU cores and main memory, there is a hierarchical list of L1, L2, and L3 caches-with increasing size. Usually, L3 is shared among all the cores. If your CPU core requests a certain main memory address to be loaded into the CPU core's register (a register is a memory area in your CPU core) - this happens by an explicit machine code (assembler) instruction - then first the L1-3 cache hierarchy is checked to see if it contains the requested memory address.

We call data associated with such an address a **memory page**. If this is the case, then main memory access is omitted and the page is directly loaded from the L1, L2, or L3 cache. Otherwise, the page is loaded from main memory, resulting in higher latency. The latency is so high that the CPU core is waiting (or executing other work) for multiple CPU clock cycles, until the main memory page is transferred into the CPU core's register. In addition, the page is also put into all caches, and in case they are full, less frequently accessed memory pages are deleted from the caches.

This brings us to the following two conclusions:

- Caching only makes sense if memory pages are accessed multiple times during a computation.
- Since caches are far smaller than main memory, they only contain subsets of the main memory pages. Therefore, a temporally close access pattern is required in order to benefit from the caches, because if the same page is accessed at a very late stage of the computation, it might have already gotten evicted from the cache.

Cache eviction strategies and pre-fetching

Of course, modern computer systems not only use **least recently used** (LRU) memory page eviction strategies to delete cached memory pages from the caches, they also try to predict the access pattern in order to keep the memory pages that are old but have a high probability of being requested again. In addition, modern CPUs also try to predict future memory page requests and try to pre-fetch them. Nevertheless, random memory access patterns should always be avoided and the more sequential memory access patterns are, usually the faster they are executed.

So how can we avoid random memory access patterns? Let's have a look at `java.util.HashMap` again. As the name suggests, the hash codes of the key objects are used in order to group contained objects into buckets. A side-effect of hashing is that even close by key values, such as subsequent integer numbers, result in different hash codes and therefore end up in different buckets. Each bucket can be seen as a pointer pointing to a linked list of key-value pairs stored in the map. These pointers point to random memory regions. Therefore, sequential scans are impossible. The following figure tries to illustrate this, as you can see pointers pointing to objects which are located at random regions in the main memory (the Java Heap to be precise):

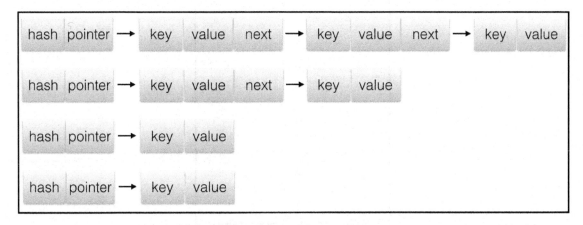

In order to improve sequential scans, Tungsten does the following trick: the pointer not only stores the target memory address of the value, but also the key.

We have learned about this concept already, where an 8-byte memory region is used to store two integer values, for example, in this case the key and the pointer to the value. This way, one can run a sorting algorithm with sequential memory access patterns (for example, quick-sort). The following figure illustrates this layout:

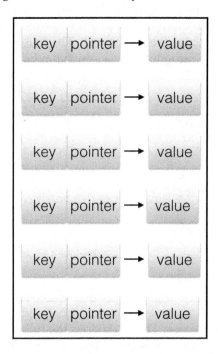

This way, when sorting, the key and pointer combination memory region must be moved around but the memory region where the values are stored can be kept constant. While the values can still be randomly spread around the memory, the key and pointer combination are sequentially laid out, as the following figure tries to illustrate:

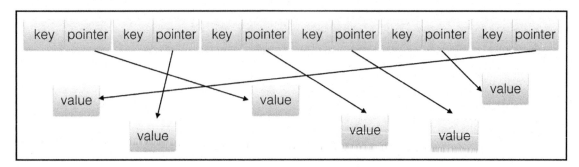

This optimization was introduced in Apache Spark V1.5 and requested in the SPARK-7082 feature request (`https://issues.apache.org/jira/browse/SPARK-7082`).

Code generation

Apache Spark V1.5 introduced code generation for expression evaluation. In order to understand this, let's start with an example. Let's have a look at the following expression:

```
val i = 23
val j = 5
var z = i*x+j*y
```

Imagine x and y are data coming from a row in a table. Now, consider that this expression is applied for every row in a table of, let's say, one billion rows. Now the Java Virtual Machine has to execute (interpret) this expression one billion times, which is a huge overhead. So what Tungsten actually does is transform this expression into byte-code and have it shipped to the executor thread.

As you might know, every class executed on the JVM is byte-code. This is an intermediate abstraction layer to the actual machine code specific for each different micro-processor architecture. This was one of the major selling points of Java decades ago. So the basic workflow is:

1. Java source code gets compiled into Java byte-code.
2. Java byte-code gets interpreted by the JVM.
3. The JVM translates this byte-code and issues platform specific-machine code instructions to the target CPU.

These days nobody ever thinks of creating byte-code on the fly, but this is what's happening in code generation. Apache Spark Tungsten analyzes the task to be executed and instead of relying on chaining pre-compiled components it generates specific, high-performing byte code as written by a human to be executed by the JVM.

Another thing Tungsten does is to accelerate the serialization and deserialization of objects, because the native framework that the JVM provides tends to be very slow. Since the main bottleneck on every distributed data processing system is the shuffle phase (used for sorting and grouping similar data together), where data gets sent over the network in Apache Spark, object serialization and deserialization are the main contributor to the bottleneck (and not I/O bandwidth), also adding to the CPU bottleneck. Therefore increasing performance here reduces the bottleneck.

All things introduced until now are known as **Tungsten Phase 1 improvements**. With Apache Spark V2.0, **Tungsten Phase 2 improvements** went live, which are the following:

- Columnar storage
- Whole stage code generation

Understanding columnar storage

With Apache Spark V2.0, columnar storage was introduced. Many on-disk technologies, such as parquet, or relational databases, such as IBM DB2 BLU or dashDB, support it. So it was an obvious choice to add this to Apache Spark as well. So what is it all about? Consider the following figure:

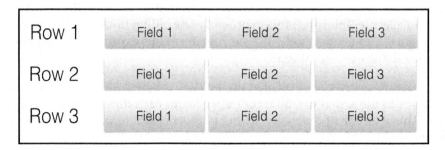

If we now transpose, we get the following column-based layout:

In contrast to row-based layouts, where fields of individual records are memory-aligned close together, in columnar storage values from similar columns of different records are residing close together in memory. This changes performance significantly. Not only can columnar data such as parquet be read faster by an order of magnitude, columnar storage also benefits when it comes to indexing individual columns or projection operations.

Understanding whole stage code generation

To understand whole stage code generation, we have to understand the Catalyst Optimizer as well, because whole stage code generation is nothing but a set of rules during the optimization of a **Logical Execution Plan (LEP)**. The object called `CollapseCodegenStages`, extending `Rule[SparkPlan]`, is the object used by Apache Spark for transforming a LEP, by fusing supported operators together. This is done by creating byte code of a new custom operator with the same functionality of the original operators which has been fused together.

A practical example on whole stage code generation performance

So let's actually run a little test. We join one billion integers. Once with whole stage code generation turned off and once with it turned on. So let's first have a look at the corresponding explained outputs:

```
scala> spark.range(1000L * 1000 * 1000).join(spark.range(1000L).toDF(),"id").explain()
== Physical Plan ==
*Project [id#140L]
+- *BroadcastHashJoin [id#140L], [id#143L], Inner, BuildRight
   :- *Range (0, 1000000000, step=1, splits=Some(8))
   +- BroadcastExchange HashedRelationBroadcastMode(List(input[0, bigint, false]))
      +- *Range (0, 1000, step=1, splits=Some(8))
```

An asterisk symbol, in the explained output, indicates that these operations are executed as a single thread with whole stage generated code. Note that the `BroadcastExchange` operation, which belongs to `BroadcastHashJoin`, is not part of this, since it might run on another machine.

 Operator fusing: Other data processing systems call this technique operator fusing. In Apache Spark whole stage code generation is actually the only means for doing so.

Now, let's actually turn off this feature:

scala> spark.conf.set("spark.sql.codegen.wholeStage",false)

If we now explain the preceding statement again, we get the following output:

```
scala> spark.range(1000L * 1000 * 1000).join(spark.range(1000L).toDF(),"id").explain()
== Physical Plan ==
Project [id#151L]
+- BroadcastHashJoin [id#151L], [id#154L], Inner, BuildRight
   :- Range (0, 1000000000, step=1, splits=Some(8))
   +- BroadcastExchange HashedRelationBroadcastMode(List(input[0, bigint, false]))
      +- Range (0, 1000, step=1, splits=Some(8))
```

The only difference is the missing asterisk symbol in front of some operators, and this actually means that each operator is executed as a single thread or at least as different code fragments, passing data from one to another.

So let's actually materialize this query by calling the `count` method, once with and once without whole stage code generation, and have a look at the performance differences:

```
scala> spark.range(1000L * 1000 * 1000).join(spark.range(1000L).toDF(),"id").count()
res13: Long = 1000
```

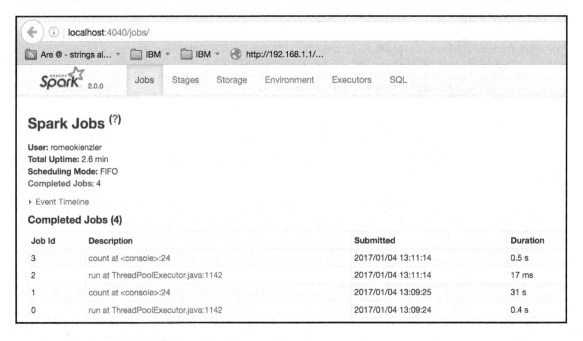

As we can see, without whole stage code generation, the operations (composed of job 0 and job 1) take nearly 32 seconds, whereas with whole stage code generation enabled, it takes only slightly more than half a second (job id 2 and 3).

If we now click on the job's description, we can obtain a DAG visualization, where **DAG** stands for **directed acyclic graph** - another way of expressing a data processing workflow:

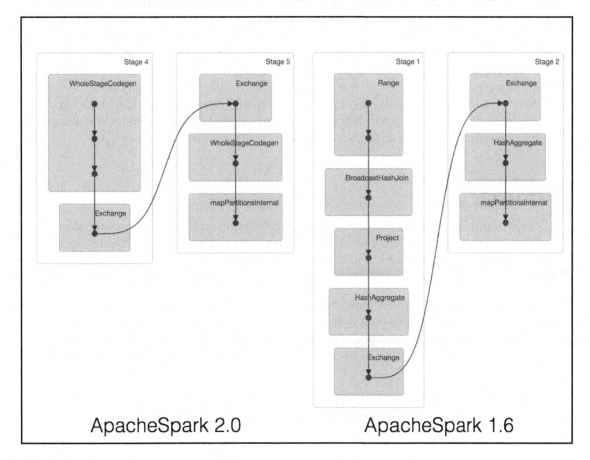

 DAG visualization is a very important tool when it comes to manual performance optimization. This is a very convenient way to find out how Apache Spark translates your queries into a physical execution plan. And therefore a convenient way of discovering performance bottlenecks.

By the way, RDBMS administrators use a similar visualization mechanism in relational database tooling which is called **visual explain**. As we can see in Apache Spark V2.0, with the whole stage code generation enabled, multiple operators get fused together.

Operator fusing versus the volcano iterator model

The volcano iterator model is an internal data processing model. Nearly every relational database system makes use of it. It basically says that each atomic operation is only capable to processing one row at a time. By expressing a database query as a **directed acyclic graph (DAG)**, which connects individual operators together, data flows in the opposite direction of the edge direction of the graph. Again, one row at a time, which means that multiple operators run in parallel, but every operator processes a different, and only one, row at a time. When fusing operators together (this is what whole stage code generation does), the volcano iterator model is violated. It is interesting to see that such a violation was done after decades of database research and actually leads to better performance.

Summary

This chapter and the preceding chapter on Catalyst Optimizer have been quite challenging. However, it makes sense to cover so many Apache Spark internals, as in the subsequent chapters we will always refer back to the functionalities provided by Catalyst and Tungsten.

We've learned that many features the JVM provides are far from optimal for massive parallel data processing. This starts with the Garbage Collectors, includes inefficient data structures and ends with the introduction of columnar storage and the removal of the volcano iterator model by fusing individual operators together using whole stage code generation.

In the next chapter we'll have a look at a more practical function of Apache Spark. We'll take a look at how to process data in real-time using Apache Spark Streaming.

5
Apache Spark Streaming

The Apache Streaming module is a stream processing-based module within Apache Spark. It uses the Spark cluster to offer the ability to scale to a high degree. Being based on Spark, it is also highly fault tolerant, having the ability to rerun failed tasks by checkpointing the data stream that is being processed. The following topics will be covered in this chapter after an introductory section, which will provide a practical overview of how Apache Spark processes stream-based data:

- Error recovery and checkpointing
- TCP-based stream processing
- File streams
- Kafka stream source

For each topic, we will provide a worked example in Scala and show how the stream-based architecture can be set up and tested.

Overview

The following diagram shows potential data sources for Apache Streaming, such as Kafka, Flume, and HDFS:

These feed into the Spark Streaming module and are processed as Discrete Streams. The diagram also shows that other Spark module functionality, such as machine learning, can be used to process stream-based data.

The fully processed data can then be an output for HDFS, databases, or dashboards. This diagram is based on the one at the Spark streaming website, but we wanted to extend it to express the Spark module functionality:

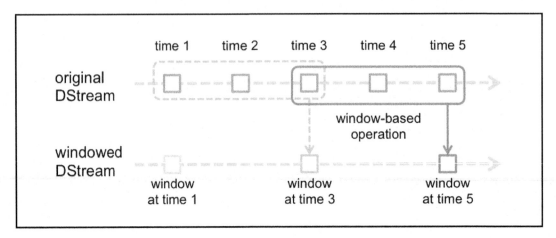

When discussing Spark Discrete Streams, the previous figure, taken from the Spark website at http://spark.apache.org/, is the diagram that we would like to use.

The green boxes in the previous figure show the continuous data stream sent to Spark being broken down into a **Discrete Stream (DStream)**.

 A DStream is nothing other than an ordered set of RDDs. Therefore, Apache Spark Streaming is not real streaming, but micro-batching. The size of the RDDs backing the DStream determines the batch size. This way DStreams can make use of all the functionality provided by RDDs including fault tolerance and the capability of being spillable to disk. The size of each element in the stream is then based on a batch time, which might be two seconds.

It is also possible to create a window, expressed as the previous red box, over the DStream. For instance, when carrying out trend analysis in real time, it might be necessary to determine the top ten Twitter-based hashtags over a ten-minute window.

So, given that Spark can be used for stream processing, how is a stream created? The following Scala-based code shows how a Twitter stream can be created. This example is simplified because Twitter authorization has not been included, but you get the idea. (The full example code is in the *Checkpointing* section.)

The **Spark Stream Context (SSC)** is created using the Spark Context, sc. A **batch time** is specified when it is created; in this case, 5 seconds. A Twitter-based DStream, called stream, is then created from Streamingcontext using a window of 60 seconds:

```
val ssc    = new StreamingContext(sc, Seconds(5) )
val stream = TwitterUtils.createStream(ssc,None) .window( Seconds(60) )
```

Stream processing can be started with the stream context start method (shown next), and the awaitTermination method indicates that it should process until stopped. So, if this code is embedded in a library-based application, it will run until the session is terminated, perhaps with *Crtl + C*:

```
ssc.start()
ssc.awaitTermination()
```

This explains what Spark Streaming is and what it does, but it does not explain error handling or what to do if your stream-based application fails. The next section will examine Spark Streaming error management and recovery.

Errors and recovery

Generally, the question that needs to be asked for your application is: is it critical that you receive and process all the data? If not, then on failure, you might just be able to restart the application and discard the missing or lost data. If this is not the case, then you will need to use checkpointing, which will be described in the next section.

It is also worth noting that your application's error management should be robust and self-sufficient. What we mean by this is that if an exception is non-critical, then manage the exception, perhaps log it, and continue processing. For instance, when a task reaches the maximum number of failures (specified by `spark.task.maxFailures`), it will terminate processing.

 This property, among others can be set during creation of the `SparkContext` object or as additional command line parameters when invoking `spark-shell` or `spark-submit`.

Checkpointing

On batch processing we are used to having fault tolerance. This means, in case a node crashed, the job doesn't loose its state and the lost tasks are rescheduled on other workers. Intermediate results are written to persistent storage (which of course has to be fault tolerant as well which is the case for HDFS, GPFS or Cloud Object Storage). Now we want to achieve the same guarantees in streaming as well, since it might be crucial that the data stream we are processing is not lost.

It is possible to set up an HDFS-based checkpoint directory to store Apache Spark-based streaming information. In this Scala example, data will be stored in HDFS under `/data/spark/checkpoint`. The following HDFS filesystem `ls` command shows that before starting, the directory does not exist:

```
[hadoop@hc2nn stream]$ hdfs dfs -ls /data/spark/checkpoint
ls: `/data/spark/checkpoint': No such file or directory
```

For replicating the following example, Twitter API credentials are used in order to connect to the Twitter API and obtain a stream of tweets. The following link explains how such credentials are created within the Twitter UI: `https://dev.twitter.com/oauth/overview/application-owner-access-tokens`.

The following Scala code sample starts by importing Spark Streaming Context and Twitter-based functionality. It then defines an application object named `stream1`:

```
import org.apache.spark._
import org.apache.spark.SparkContext._
import org.apache.spark.streaming._
import org.apache.spark.streaming.twitter._
import org.apache.spark.streaming.StreamingContext._

object stream1 {
```

Next, a method is defined called `createContext`, which will be used to create both the Spark and Streaming contexts. It will also checkpoint the stream to the HDFS-based directory using the streaming context checkpoint method, which takes a directory path as a parameter. The directory path the value (`cpDir`) that was passed to the `createContext` method:

```
def createContext( cpDir : String ) : StreamingContext = {
  val appName = "Stream example 1"
  val conf    = new SparkConf()
  conf.setAppName(appName)
  val sc = new SparkContext(conf)
  val ssc    = new StreamingContext(sc, Seconds(5) )
  ssc.checkpoint( cpDir )
  ssc
}
```

Now, the main method is defined as is the HDFS directory, as well as Twitter access authority and parameters. The Spark Streaming context `ssc` is either retrieved or created using the HDFS checkpoint directory via the `StreamingContext` method--`checkpoint`. If the directory doesn't exist, then the previous method called `createContext` is called, which will create the context and `checkpoint`. Obviously, we have truncated our own Twitter `auth.keys` in this example for security reasons:

```
def main(args: Array[String]) {
  val hdfsDir = "/data/spark/checkpoint"
  val consumerKey       = "QQpxx"
  val consumerSecret    = "0HFzxx"
  val accessToken       = "323xx"
  val accessTokenSecret = "IlQxx"

  System.setProperty("twitter4j.oauth.consumerKey", consumerKey)
  System.setProperty("twitter4j.oauth.consumerSecret", consumerSecret)
  System.setProperty("twitter4j.oauth.accessToken", accessToken)
  System.setProperty("twitter4j.oauth.accessTokenSecret",
accessTokenSecret)
```

```
    val ssc = StreamingContext.getOrCreate(hdfsDir,
        () => { createContext( hdfsDir ) })
    val stream = TwitterUtils.createStream(ssc,None).window(   Seconds(60) )
    // do some processing
    ssc.start()
    ssc.awaitTermination()
  } // end main
```

Having run this code, which has no actual processing, the HDFS `checkpoint` directory can be checked again. This time, it is apparent that the `checkpoint` directory has been created and the data has been stored:

```
[hadoop@hc2nn stream]$ hdfs dfs -ls /data/spark/checkpoint
Found 1 items
drwxr-xr-x   - hadoop supergroup          0 2015-07-02 13:41
/data/spark/checkpoint/0fc3d94e-6f53-40fb-910d-1eef044b12e9
```

This example, taken from the Apache Spark website, shows you how checkpoint storage can be set up and used. How often is checkpointing carried out? The metadata is stored during each stream batch. The actual data is stored with a period, which is the maximum of the batch interval, or ten seconds. This might not be ideal for you, so you can reset the value using the following method:

```
DStream.checkpoint( newRequiredInterval )
```

Here, `newRequiredInterval` is the new checkpoint interval value that you require; generally, you should aim for a value that is five to ten times your batch interval. Checkpointing saves both the stream batch and metadata (data about the data).

 If the application fails, then, when it restarts, the check pointed data is used when processing is started. The batch data that was being processed at the time of failure is reprocessed along with the batched data since the failure. Remember to monitor the HDFS disk space being used for the checkpointing.

In the next section, we will examine the streaming sources and provide some examples of each type.

Streaming sources

We will not be able to cover all the stream types with practical examples in this section, but where this chapter is too small to include code, we will at least provide a description. In this chapter, we will cover the TCP and file streams and the Flume, Kafka, and Twitter streams. Apache Spark tends only to support this limited set out of the box, but this is not a problem since 3rd party developers provide connectors to other sources as well. We will start with a practical TCP-based example. This chapter examines stream processing architecture.

> For instance, what happens in cases where the stream data delivery rate exceeds the potential data processing rate? Systems such as Kafka provide the possibility of solving this issue by caching data until it is requested with the additional ability to use multiple data topics and consumers (publish-subscribe model).

TCP stream

There is a possibility of using the Spark Streaming Context method called `socketTextStream` to stream data via TCP/IP, by specifying a hostname and port number. The Scala-based code example in this section will receive data on port `10777` that was supplied using the `netcat` Linux command.

> The `netcat` command is a Linux/Unix command which allows you to send and receive data to or from local or remote IP destinations using TCP or UDP. This way every shell script can play the role of a full network client or server. The following is a good tutorial on how to use `netcat`: ht tp://www.binarytides.com/netcat-tutorial-for-beginners/.

The code sample starts by importing Spark, the context, and the streaming classes. The object class named `stream2` is defined as it is the main method with arguments:

```
import org.apache.spark._
import org.apache.spark.SparkContext._
import org.apache.spark.streaming._
import org.apache.spark.streaming.StreamingContext._

object stream2 {
  def main(args: Array[String]) {
```

The number of arguments passed to the class is checked to ensure that it is the hostname and port number. A Spark configuration object is created with an application name defined. The Spark and streaming contexts are then created. Then, a streaming batch time of 10 seconds is set:

```
if ( args.length < 2 ) {
 System.err.println("Usage: stream2 <host> <port>")
 System.exit(1)
}

val hostname = args(0).trim
val portnum  = args(1).toInt
val appName  = "Stream example 2"
val conf     = new SparkConf()
conf.setAppName(appName)
val sc  = new SparkContext(conf)
val ssc = new StreamingContext(sc, Seconds(10) )
```

A DStream called `rawDstream` is created by calling the `socketTextStream` method of the streaming context using the `hostname` and port name parameters:

```
val rawDstream = ssc.socketTextStream( hostname, portnum )
```

A top-ten word count is created from the raw stream data by splitting words with spacing. Then, a (key,value) pair is created as (word,1), which is reduced by the key value, this being the word. So now, there is a list of words and their associated counts. The key and value are swapped so the list becomes (count and word). Then, a sort is done on the key, which is now the count. Finally, the top 10 items in the RDD within the DStream are taken and printed out:

```
val wordCount = rawDstream
  .flatMap(line => line.split(" "))
  .map(word => (word,1))
  .reduceByKey(_+_)
  .map(item => item.swap)
  .transform(rdd => rdd.sortByKey(false))
  .foreachRDD( rdd =>
    { rdd.take(10).foreach(x=>println("List : " + x)) }
  )
```

The code closes with the Spark Streaming `start` and `awaitTermination` methods being called to start the stream processing and await process termination:

```
ssc.start()
  ssc.awaitTermination()
} // end main
} // end stream2
```

The data for this application is provided, as we stated previously, by the Linux Netcat (`nc`) command. The Linux `cat` command dumps the contents of a log file, which is piped to `nc`. The `lk` options force Netcat to listen for connections and keep on listening if the connection is lost. This example shows that the port being used is `10777`:

```
[root@hc2nn log]# pwd
/var/log
[root@hc2nn log]# cat ./anaconda.storage.log | nc -lk 10777
```

The output from this TCP-based stream processing is shown here. The actual output is not as important as the method demonstrated. However, the data shows, as expected, a list of 10 log file words in descending count order. Note that the top word is empty because the stream was not filtered for empty words:

```
List : (17104,)
List : (2333,=)
List : (1656,:)
List : (1603,;)
List : (1557,DEBUG)
List : (564,True)
List : (495,False)
List : (411,None)
List : (356,at)
List : (335,object)
```

This is interesting if you want to stream data using Apache Spark Streaming based on TCP/IP from a host and port. However, what about more exotic methods? What if you wish to stream data from a messaging system or via memory-based channels? What if you want to use some of the big data tools available today such as Flume and Kafka? The next sections will examine these options, but, first, we will demonstrate how streams can be based on files.

File streams

We have modified the Scala-based code example in the last section to monitor an HDFS-based directory by calling the Spark Streaming Context method called `textFileStream`. We will not display all of the code, given this small change. The application class is now called `stream3`, which takes a single parameter--the HDFS directory. The directory path could be on another storage system as well (all the code samples will be available with this book):

```
val rawDstream = ssc.textFileStream( directory )
```

The stream processing is the same as before. The stream is split into words and the top-ten word list is printed. The only difference this time is that the data must be put in the HDFS directory while the application is running. This is achieved with the HDFS filesystem `put` command here:

```
[root@hc2nn log]# hdfs dfs -put ./anaconda.storage.log /data/spark/stream
```

As you can see, the HDFS directory used is /data/spark/stream/, and the text-based source log file is anaconda.storage.log (under /var/log/). As expected, the same word list and count is printed:

```
List : (17104,)
List : (2333,=)
...
List : (564,True)
List : (495,False)
List : (411,None)
List : (356,at)
List : (335,object)
```

These are simple streaming methods based on TCP and filesystem data. What if we want to use some of the built-in streaming functionality in Spark Streaming? This will be examined next. The Spark Streaming Flume library will be used as an example.

Flume

Flume is an Apache open source project and product, which is designed to move large amounts of data at a big data scale. It is highly scalable, distributed, and reliable, working on the basis of data source, data sink, and data channels, as shown in the following diagram taken from http://flume.apache.org/:

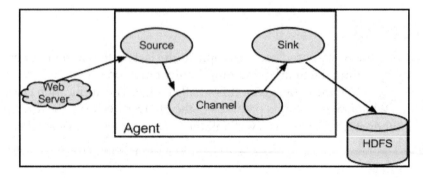

Flume uses agents to process data streams. As can be seen in the previous figure, an agent has a data source, data processing channel, and data sink. A clearer way to describe this flow is via the figure we just saw. The channel acts as a queue for the sourced data and the sink passes the data to the next link in the chain.

Flume agents can form Flume architectures; the output of one agent's sink can be the input to a second agent. Apache Spark allows two approaches to using Apache Flume. The first is an Avro push-based in-memory approach, whereas the second one, still based on Avro, is a pull-based system using a custom Spark sink library. We are using Flume version 1.5 for this example:

```
[root@hc2nn ~]# flume-ng version
Flume 1.5.0-cdh5.3.3
Source code repository: https://git-wip-us.apache.org/repos/asf/flume.git
Revision: b88ce1fd016bc873d817343779dfff6aeea07706
Compiled by jenkins on Wed Apr  8 14:57:43 PDT 2015
From source with checksum 389d91c718e03341a2367bf4ef12428e
```

The Flume-based Spark example that we will initially implement here is the Flume-based push approach, where Spark acts as a receiver and Flume pushes the data to Spark. The following figure represents the structure that we will implement on a single node:

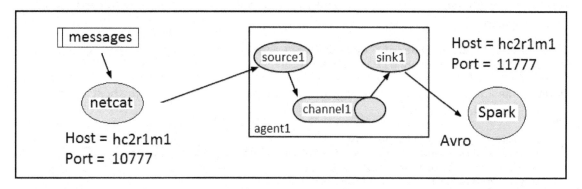

The message data will be sent to port 10777 on a host called hc2r1m1 using the Linux netcat (nc) command. This will act as a source (source1) for the Flume agent (agent1), which will have an in-memory channel called channel1. The sink used by agent1 will be Apache Avro-based, again on a host called hc2r1m1, but this time, the port number will be 11777. The Apache Spark Flume application stream4 (which we will describe shortly) will listen for Flume stream data on this port.

We start the streaming process by executing the `nc` command against the `10777` port. Now, when we type text in this window, it will be used as a Flume source and the data will be sent to the Spark application:

```
[hadoop@hc2nn ~]$ nc  hc2r1m1.semtech-solutions.co.nz  10777
```

In order to run the Flume agent, `agent1`, we have created a Flume configuration file called `agent1.flume.cfg`, which describes the agent's source, channel, and sink. The contents of the file are as follows. The first section defines the `agent1` source, channel, and sink names.

```
agent1.sources  = source1
agent1.channels = channel1
agent1.sinks    = sink1
```

The next section defines `source1` to be netcat-based, running on the host called `hc2r1m1` and the `10777` port:

```
agent1.sources.source1.channels=channel1
agent1.sources.source1.type=netcat
agent1.sources.source1.bind=hc2r1m1.semtech-solutions.co.nz
agent1.sources.source1.port=10777
```

The `agent1` channel, `channel1`, is defined as a memory-based channel with a maximum event capacity of `1000` events:

```
agent1.channels.channel1.type=memory
agent1.channels.channel1.capacity=1000
```

Finally, the `agent1` sink, `sink1`, is defined as an Apache Avro sink on the host called `hc2r1m1` and the `11777` port:

```
agent1.sinks.sink1.type=avro
agent1.sinks.sink1.hostname=hc2r1m1.semtech-solutions.co.nz
agent1.sinks.sink1.port=11777
agent1.sinks.sink1.channel=channel1
```

We have created a Bash script called `flume.bash` to run the Flume agent, `agent1`. It looks as follows:

```
[hadoop@hc2r1m1 stream]$ more flume.bash
#!/bin/bash
# run the bash agent
flume-ng agent \
    --conf /etc/flume-ng/conf \
    --conf-file ./agent1.flume.cfg \
    -Dflume.root.logger=DEBUG,INFO,console  \
    -name agent1
```

The script calls the Flume executable `flume-ng`, passing the `agent1` configuration file. The call specifies the agent named `agent1`. It also specifies the Flume configuration directory to be `/etc/flume-ng/conf/`, the default value. Initially, we will use a `netcat` Flume source with a Scala-based example to show how data can be sent to an Apache Spark application. Then, we will show how an RSS-based data feed can be processed in a similar way. So initially, the Scala code that will receive the `netcat` data looks like this. The application class name is defined. The necessary classes for Spark and Flume are imported. Finally, the main method is defined:

```
import org.apache.spark._
import org.apache.spark.SparkContext._
import org.apache.spark.streaming._
import org.apache.spark.streaming.StreamingContext._
import org.apache.spark.streaming.flume._

object stream4 {
  def main(args: Array[String]) {
  //The host and port name arguments for the data stream are checked and
extracted:
      if ( args.length < 2 ) {
        System.err.println("Usage: stream4 <host> <port>")
        System.exit(1)
      }
      val hostname = args(0).trim
      val portnum  = args(1).toInt
      println("hostname : " + hostname)
      println("portnum  : " + portnum)
```

The Spark and Streaming contexts are created. Then, the Flume-based data stream is created using the stream context host and port number. The Flume-based class, `FlumeUtils`, has been used to do this by calling its `createStream` method:

```
val appName = "Stream example 4"
val conf    = new SparkConf()
conf.setAppName(appName)
val sc  = new SparkContext(conf)
val ssc = new StreamingContext(sc, Seconds(10) )
val rawDstream = FlumeUtils.createStream(ssc,hostname,portnum)
```

Finally, a stream event count is printed and (for debug purposes while we test the stream) the stream content is dumped. After this, the stream context is started and configured to run until terminated via the application:

```
rawDstream.count()
        .map(cnt => ">>>> Received events : " + cnt )
        .print()
```

```
        rawDstream.map(e => new String(e.event.getBody.array() ))
              .print
      ssc.start()
      ssc.awaitTermination()
    } // end main
  } // end stream4
```

Having compiled it, we will run this application using `spark-submit`. In some of the other chapters of this book, we will use a Bash-based script called `run_stream.bash` to execute the job. The script looks as follows:

```
[hadoop@hc2r1m1 stream]$ more run_stream.bash
#!/bin/bash
SPARK_HOME=/usr/local/spark
SPARK_BIN=$SPARK_HOME/bin
SPARK_SBIN=$SPARK_HOME/sbin
JAR_PATH=/home/hadoop/spark/stream/target/scala-2.10/streaming_2.10-1.0.jar
CLASS_VAL=$1
CLASS_PARAMS="${*:2}"
STREAM_JAR=/usr/local/spark/lib/spark-examples-1.3.1-hadoop2.3.0.jar
cd $SPARK_BIN
./spark-submit \
    --class $CLASS_VAL \
    --master spark://hc2nn.semtech-solutions.co.nz:7077   \
    --executor-memory 100M \
    --total-executor-cores 50 \
    --jars $STREAM_JAR \
    $JAR_PATH \
    $CLASS_PARAMS
```

So, this script sets some Spark-based variables and a JAR library path for this job. It takes the Spark class to run as its first parameter. It passes all the other variables as parameters to the Spark application class job. So, the execution of the application looks as follows:

```
[hadoop@hc2r1m1 stream]$ ./run_stream.bash stream4 hc2r1m1 11777
```

This means that the Spark application is ready and is running as a Flume sink on port `11777`. The Flume input is ready, running as a `netcat` task on port `10777`. Now, the Flume agent, `agent1`, can be started using the Flume script called `flume.bash` to send the `netcat` source-based data to the Apache Spark Flume-based sink:

```
[hadoop@hc2r1m1 stream]$ ./flume.bash
```

Now, when the text is passed to the `netcat` session, it should flow through Flume and be processed as a stream by Spark. Let's try it:

```
[hadoop@hc2nn ~]$ nc  hc2r1m1.semtech-solutions.co.nz 10777
```

```
I hope that Apache Spark will print this
OK
I hope that Apache Spark will print this
OK
I hope that Apache Spark will print this
OK
```

Three simple pieces of text have been added to the `netcat` session and acknowledged with an `OK` so that they can be passed to Flume. The debug output in the Flume session shows that the events (one per line) have been received and processed:

```
2015-07-06 18:13:18,699 (netcat-handler-0) [DEBUG -
org.apache.flume.source.NetcatSource$NetcatSocketHandler.run(NetcatSource.j
ava:318)] Chars read = 41
 2015-07-06 18:13:18,700 (netcat-handler-0) [DEBUG -
org.apache.flume.source.NetcatSource$NetcatSocketHandler.run(NetcatSource.j
ava:322)] Events processed = 1
 2015-07-06 18:13:18,990 (netcat-handler-0) [DEBUG -
org.apache.flume.source.NetcatSource$NetcatSocketHandler.run(NetcatSource.j
ava:318)] Chars read = 41
 2015-07-06 18:13:18,991 (netcat-handler-0) [DEBUG -
org.apache.flume.source.NetcatSource$NetcatSocketHandler.run(NetcatSource.j
ava:322)] Events processed = 1
 2015-07-06 18:13:19,270 (netcat-handler-0) [DEBUG -
org.apache.flume.source.NetcatSource$NetcatSocketHandler.run(NetcatSource.j
ava:318)] Chars read = 41
 2015-07-06 18:13:19,271 (netcat-handler-0) [DEBUG -
org.apache.flume.source.NetcatSource$NetcatSocketHandler.run(NetcatSource.j
ava:322)] Events processed = 1
```

Finally, in the Spark `stream4` application session, three events have been received and processed; in this case, they have been dumped to the session to prove the point that the data arrived. Of course, this is not what you would normally do, but we wanted to prove data transit through this configuration:

```
-----------------------------------------------
Time: 1436163210000 ms
-----------------------------------------------
>>> Received events : 3
-----------------------------------------------
Time: 1436163210000 ms
-----------------------------------------------
I hope that Apache Spark will print this
I hope that Apache Spark will print this
I hope that Apache Spark will print this
```

This is interesting, but it is not really a production-worthy example of Spark Flume data processing. So, in order to demonstrate a potentially real data processing approach, we will change the Flume configuration file source details so that it uses a Perl script, which is executable as follows:

```
agent1.sources.source1.type=exec
agent1.sources.source.command=./rss.perl
```

The Perl script, which has been referenced previously, `rss.perl`, just acts as a source of Reuters science news. It receives the news as XML and converts it into JSON format. It also cleans the data of unwanted noise. First, it imports packages such as LWP and `XML::XPath` to enable XML processing. Then, it specifies a science-based Reuters news data source and creates a new LWP agent to process the data, similar to the following:

```perl
#!/usr/bin/perl
use strict;
use LWP::UserAgent;
use XML::XPath;
my $urlsource="http://feeds.reuters.com/reuters/scienceNews" ;
my  $agent = LWP::UserAgent->new;
#Then an infinite while loop is opened, and an HTTP GET request is carried
out against  the URL. The request is configured, and the agent makes the
request via  a call to the request method:
while()
{
  my  $req = HTTP::Request->new(GET => ($urlsource));
  $req->header('content-type' => 'application/json');
  $req->header('Accept'       => 'application/json');
  my $resp = $agent->request($req);
```

If the request is successful, then the XML data returned is defined as the decoded content of the request. Title information is extracted from the XML via an XPath call using the path called `/rss/channel/item/title`:

```perl
    if ( $resp->is_success )
    {
      my $xmlpage = $resp -> decoded_content;
      my $xp = XML::XPath->new( xml => $xmlpage );
      my $nodeset = $xp->find( '/rss/channel/item/title' );
      my @titles = () ;
      my $index = 0 ;
```

For each node in the extracted title data XML string, data is extracted. It is cleaned of unwanted XML tags and added to a Perl-based array called titles:

```perl
      foreach my $node ($nodeset->get_nodelist) {
        my $xmlstring = XML::XPath::XMLParser::as_string($node) ;
```

```
        $xmlstring =~ s/<title>//g;
        $xmlstring =~ s/<\/title>//g;
        $xmlstring =~ s/"//g;
        $xmlstring =~ s/,//g;
        $titles[$index] = $xmlstring ;
        $index = $index + 1 ;
    } # foreach find node
```

The same process is carried out for description-based data in the request response XML. The XPath value used this time is `/rss/channel/item/description/`. There are many more tags to be cleaned from the description data, so there are many more Perl searches and line replacements that act on this data (`s///g`):

```
    my $nodeset = $xp->find( '/rss/channel/item/description' );
    my @desc = () ;
    $index = 0 ;
    foreach my $node ($nodeset->get_nodelist) {
        my $xmlstring = XML::XPath::XMLParser::as_string($node) ;
        $xmlstring =~ s/<img.+\/img>//g;
        $xmlstring =~ s/href=".+"//g;
        $xmlstring =~ s/src=".+"//g;
        $xmlstring =~ s/src='.+'//g;
        $xmlstring =~ s/<br.+\/>//g;
        $xmlstring =~ s/<\/div>//g;
        $xmlstring =~ s/<\/a>//g;
        $xmlstring =~ s/<a >\n//g;
        $xmlstring =~ s/<img >//g;
        $xmlstring =~ s/<img \/>//g;
        $xmlstring =~ s/<div.+>//g;
        $xmlstring =~ s/<title>//g;
        $xmlstring =~ s/<\/title>//g;
        $xmlstring =~ s/<description>//g;
        $xmlstring =~ s/<\/description>//g;
        $xmlstring =~ s/&lt;.+>//g;
        $xmlstring =~ s/"//g;
        $xmlstring =~ s/,//g;
        $xmlstring =~ s/\r|\n//g;
        $desc[$index] = $xmlstring ;
        $index = $index + 1 ;
    } # foreach find node
```

Finally, the XML-based title and description data is output in the RSS JSON format using a `print` command. The script then sleeps for 30 seconds and requests more RSS news information to process:

```
    my $newsitems = $index ;
    $index = 0 ;
```

```
for ($index=0; $index < $newsitems; $index++) {
  print "{"category": "science","
              . " "title": "" . $titles[$index] . "","
              . " "summary": "" . $desc[$index] . """
              . "}\n";
  } # for rss items
 } # success ?
 sleep(30) ;
} # while
```

We have created a second Scala-based stream processing code example called stream5. It is similar to the stream4 example, but it now processes the rss item data from the stream. Next, case class is defined to process the category, title, and summary from the XML RSS information. An HTML location is defined to store the resulting data that comes from the Flume channel:

```
case class RSSItem(category : String, title : String, summary : String) {
  val now: Long = System.currentTimeMillis
  val hdfsdir = "hdfs://hc2nn:8020/data/spark/flume/rss/"
```

The RSS stream data from the Flume-based event is converted to a string. It is then formatted using the case class called RSSItem. If there is event data, it is then written to an HDFS directory using the previous hdfsdir path:

```
rawDstream.map(record => {
implicit val formats = DefaultFormats
read[RSSItem](new String(record.event.getBody().array()))
}).foreachRDD(rdd => {
      if (rdd.count() > 0) {
        rdd.map(item => {
          implicit val formats = DefaultFormats
          write(item)
          }).saveAsTextFile(hdfsdir+"file_"+now.toString())
      }
  })
```

Running this code sample, it is possible to see that the Perl RSS script is producing data, because the Flume script output indicates that 80 events have been accepted and received:

```
2015-07-07 14:14:24,017 (agent-shutdown-hook) [DEBUG -
org.apache.flume.source.ExecSource.stop(ExecSource.java:219)] Exec source
with command:./news_rss_collector.py stopped.
Metrics:SOURCE:source1{src.events.accepted=80, src.events.received=80,
src.append.accepted=0, src.append-batch.accepted=0, src.open-
connection.count=0, src.append-batch.received=0, src.append.received=0}
The Scala Spark application stream5 has processed 80 events in two batches:
>>>> Received events : 73
```

```
>>>> Received events : 7
```

The events have been stored on HDFS under the expected directory, as the Hadoop filesystem `ls` command shows here:

```
[hadoop@hc2r1m1 stream]$ hdfs dfs -ls /data/spark/flume/rss/
 Found 2 items
 drwxr-xr-x   - hadoop supergroup          0 2015-07-07 14:09
/data/spark/flume/rss/file_1436234439794
 drwxr-xr-x   - hadoop supergroup          0 2015-07-07 14:14
/data/spark/flume/rss/file_1436235208370
```

Also, using the Hadoop filesystem `cat` command, it is possible to prove that the files on HDFS contain `rss` feed news-based data, as shown here:

```
[hadoop@hc2r1m1 stream]$  hdfs dfs -cat
/data/spark/flume/rss/file_1436235208370/part-00000 | head -1
{"category":"healthcare","title":"BRIEF-Aetna CEO says has not had specific
conversations with DOJ on Humana - CNBC","summary":"* Aetna CEO Says Has
Not Had Specific Conversations With Doj About Humana Acquisition - CNBC"}
```

This Spark stream-based example has used Apache Flume to transmit data from an `rss` source, through Flume, to HDFS via a Spark consumer. This is a good example, but what if you want to publish data to a group of consumers? In the next section, we will examine Apache Kafka--a publish/subscribe messaging system--and determine how it can be used with Spark.

Kafka

Apache Kafka (`http://kafka.apache.org/`) is a top-level open source project in Apache. It is a big data publish/subscribe messaging system that is fast and highly scalable. It uses message brokers for data management and ZooKeeper for configuration so that data can be organized into consumer groups and topics.

Data in Kafka is split into partitions. In this example, we will demonstrate a receiverless Spark-based Kafka consumer so that we don't need to worry about configuring Spark data partitions when compared to our Kafka data. In order to demonstrate Kafka-based message production and consumption, we will use the Perl RSS script from the last section as a data source. The data passing into Kafka and to Spark will be Reuters RSS news data in the JSON format. As topic messages are created by message producers, they are placed in partitions in message order sequence. The messages in the partitions are retained for a configurable time period. Kafka then stores the offset value for each consumer, which is that consumer's position (in terms of message consumption) in that partition.

We are currently using Kafka 0.10.1.0. We have used Kafka message brokers on the Hortonworks HDP 2.6 Sandbox virtual machine. We then set the Kafka broker ID values for each Kafka broker server, giving them a `broker.id` number of 1 through 4. As Kafka uses ZooKeeper for cluster data configuration, we wanted to keep all the Kafka data in a top-level node called kafka in ZooKeeper. In order to do this, we set the Kafka ZooKeeper root value, called `zookeeper.chroot`, to `/kafka`. After making these changes, we restarted the Kafka servers for the changes to take effect.

With Kafka installed, we can check the scripts available to test. The following list shows Kafka-based scripts for message producers and consumers as well as scripts to manage topics and check consumer offsets. These scripts will be used in this section in order to demonstrate Kafka functionality:

```
[hadoop@hc2nn ~]$ ls /usr/bin/kafka*
/usr/bin/kafka-console-consumer          /usr/bin/kafka-run-class
/usr/bin/kafka-console-producer          /usr/bin/kafka-topics
/usr/bin/kafka-consumer-offset-checker
```

In order to run the installed Kafka servers, we need to have the broker server ID's (`broker.id`) values set; otherwise, an error will occur. Once Kafka is running, we will need to prepare a message producer script. The simple Bash script given next, called `kafka.bash`, defines a comma-separated broker list of hosts and ports. It also defines a topic called `rss`. It then calls the Perl script `rss.perl` to generate the RSS-based data. This data is then piped into the Kafka producer script called kafka-console-producer to be sent to Kafka.

```
[hadoop@hc2r1m1 stream]$ more kafka.bash
#!/bin/bash
#BROKER_LIST="hc2r1m1:9092,hc2r1m2:9092,hc2r1m3:9092,hc2r1m4:9092"
BROKER_LIST="hc2r1m1:9092"
TOPIC="rss"
./rss.perl | /usr/bin/kafka-console-producer --broker-list $BROKER_LIST --
topic $TOPIC
```

Notice that we are only running against a single broker, but a link how to use multiple brokers has been provided as well. Also notice that we have not mentioned Kafka topics at this point. When a topic is created in Kafka, the number of partitions can be specified. In the following example, the kafka-topics script has been called with the create option. The number of partitions have been set to 5, and the data replication factor has been set to 3. The ZooKeeper server string has been defined as hc2r1m2-4 with a port number of 2181. Also note that the top level ZooKeeper Kafka node has been defined as /kafka in the ZooKeeper string:

```
/usr/bin/kafka-topics \
```

```
--create  \
--zookeeper hc2r1m1:2181:2181/kafka \
--replication-factor 3  \
--partitions 5  \
--topic rss
```

We have also created a Bash script called `kafka_list.bash` for use during testing, which checks all the Kafka topics that have been created, and also the Kafka consumer offsets. It calls the Kafka-topics commands with a list option, and a ZooKeeper string to get a list of created topics. It then calls the Kafka script called Kafka-consumer-offset-checker with a ZooKeeper string--the topic name and a group name to get a list of consumer offset values. Using this script, we can check that our topics are created, and the topic data is being consumed correctly:

```
[hadoop@hc2r1m1 stream]$ cat kafka_list.bash
#!/bin/bash
ZOOKEEPER="hc2r1m1:2181:2181/kafka"
TOPIC="rss"
GROUP="group1"
echo ""
echo "==============================="
echo " Kafka Topics "
echo "==============================="
/usr/bin/kafka-topics --list --zookeeper $ZOOKEEPER
echo ""
echo "==============================="
echo " Kafka Offsets "
echo "==============================="
/usr/bin/kafka-consumer-offset-checker \
    --group $GROUP \
    --topic $TOPIC \
    --zookeeper $ZOOKEEPER
```

Next, we need to create the Apache Spark Scala-based Kafka consumer code. As we said, we will create a receiver-less example, so that the Kafka data partitions match in both, Kafka and Spark. The example is called `stream6`. First, the classes are imported for Kafka, spark, context, and streaming. Then, the object class called `stream6`, and the main method are defined. The code looks like this:

```
import kafka.serializer.StringDecoder
import org.apache.spark._
import org.apache.spark.SparkContext._
import org.apache.spark.streaming._
import org.apache.spark.streaming.StreamingContext._
import org.apache.spark.streaming.kafka._

object stream6 {
```

```
def main(args: Array[String]) {
```

Next, the class parameters (broker's string, group ID, and topic) are checked and processed. If the class parameters are incorrect, then an error is printed, and execution stops, else the parameter variables are defined:

```
if ( args.length < 3 ) {
    System.err.println("Usage: stream6 <brokers> <groupid> <topics>\n")
    System.err.println("<brokers> = host1:port1,host2:port2\n")
    System.err.println("<groupid> = group1\n")
    System.err.println("<topics>  = topic1,topic2\n")
    System.exit(1)
}
val brokers = args(0).trim
val groupid = args(1).trim
val topics  = args(2).trim
println("brokers : " + brokers)
println("groupid : " + groupid)
println("topics  : " + topics)
```

The Spark context is defined in terms of an application name. The Spark URL has again been left as the default. The streaming context has been created using the Spark context. We have left the stream batch interval at 10 seconds, which is the same as the last example. However, you can set it using a parameter of your choice:

```
val appName = "Stream example 6"
val conf    = new SparkConf()
conf.setAppName(appName)
val sc  = new SparkContext(conf)
val ssc = new StreamingContext(sc, Seconds(10) )
```

Next, the broker list and group ID are set up as parameters. These values are then used to create a Kafka-based Spark Stream called rawDstream:

```
val topicsSet = topics.split(",").toSet
val kafkaParams : Map[String, String] =
  Map("metadata.broker.list" -> brokers,
    "group.id" -> groupid )
val rawDstream = KafkaUtils.createDirectStream[
  String,
  String,
  StringDecoder,
  StringDecoder](ssc, kafkaParams, topicsSet)
```

We have again printed the stream event count for debugging purposes so that we know when the application is receiving and processing the data:

```
rawDstream.count().map(cnt => ">>>>>>>>>>>>>>> Received events : " + cnt
).print()
```

The HDFS location for the Kafka data has been defined as `/data/spark/kafka/rss/`. It has been mapped from the `DStream` into the variable lines. Using the `foreachRDD` method, a check on the data count is carried out on the `lines` variable before saving the data in HDFS using the `saveAsTextFile` method:

```
val now: Long = System.currentTimeMillis
val hdfsdir = "hdfs://hc2nn:8020/data/spark/kafka/rss/"
val lines = rawDstream.map(record => record._2)
lines.foreachRDD(rdd => {
        if (rdd.count() > 0) {
          rdd.saveAsTextFile(hdfsdir+"file_"+now.toString())
        }
    })
```

Finally, the Scala script closes by starting the stream processing and setting the application class to run until terminated with `awaitTermination`:

```
    ssc.start()
      ssc.awaitTermination()
  } // end main
} // end stream6
```

With all of the scripts explained and the Kafka brokers running, it is time to examine the Kafka configuration, which, if you remember, is maintained by Apache ZooKeeper. (All of the code samples that have been described so far will be released with the book.) We will use the `zookeeper-client` tool and connect to the ZooKeeper server on the host called `hc2r1m2` on the `2181` port. As you can see here, we have received a connected message from the client session:

```
[hadoop@hc2r1m1 stream]$ /usr/bin/zookeeper-client -server hc2r1m2:2181
[zk: hc2r1m2:2181(CONNECTED) 0]
```

If you remember, we specified the top-level ZooKeeper directory for Kafka to be `/kafka`. If we examine this now via a client session, we can see the Kafka ZooKeeper structure. We will be interested in brokers (the Kafka broker servers) and consumers (the previous Spark Scala code). The ZooKeeper `ls` command shows that the four Kafka servers are registered with ZooKeeper and are listed by their `broker.id` configuration values, one to four:

```
[zk: hc2r1m2:2181(CONNECTED) 2] ls /kafka
 [consumers, config, controller, admin, brokers, controller_epoch]
[zk: hc2r1m2:2181(CONNECTED) 3] ls /kafka/brokers
 [topics, ids]
[zk: hc2r1m2:2181(CONNECTED) 4] ls /kafka/brokers/ids
```

```
[3, 2, 1, 4]
```

We will create the topic that we want to use for this test using the Kafka script, `kafka-topics`, with a `create` flag. We do this manually because we want to demonstrate the definition of the data partitions while we do it. Note that we have set the partitions in the Kafka topic `rss` to 5, as shown in the following piece of code. Note also that the ZooKeeper connection string for the command has a comma-separated list of ZooKeeper servers, terminated by the top-level ZooKeeper Kafka directory called /kafka. This means that the command puts the new topic in the proper place:

```
[hadoop@hc2nn ~]$ /usr/bin/kafka-topics \
>    --create \
>    --zookeeper hc2r1m2:2181,hc2r1m3:2181,hc2r1m4:2181/kafka \
>    --replication-factor 3 \
>    --partitions 5 \
>    --topic rss
Created topic "rss".
```

Now, when we use the ZooKeeper client to check the Kafka topic configuration, we can see the correct topic name and the expected number of the partitions:

```
[zk: hc2r1m2:2181(CONNECTED) 5] ls /kafka/brokers/topics
[rss]
[zk: hc2r1m2:2181(CONNECTED) 6] ls /kafka/brokers/topics/rss
[partitions]
[zk: hc2r1m2:2181(CONNECTED) 7] ls /kafka/brokers/topics/rss/partitions
[3, 2, 1, 0, 4]
```

This describes the configuration for the Kafka broker servers in ZooKeeper, but what about the data consumers? Well, the following list shows where the data will be held. Remember that, at this time, there is no consumer running, so it is not represented in ZooKeeper:

```
[zk: hc2r1m2:2181(CONNECTED) 9]  ls /kafka/consumers
[]
[zk: hc2r1m2:2181(CONNECTED) 10] quit
```

In order to start this test, we will run our Kafka data producer and consumer scripts. We will also check the output of the Spark application class and check the Kafka partition offsets and HDFS to make sure that the data has arrived. This is quite complicated, so we will add a diagram here to explain the test architecture:

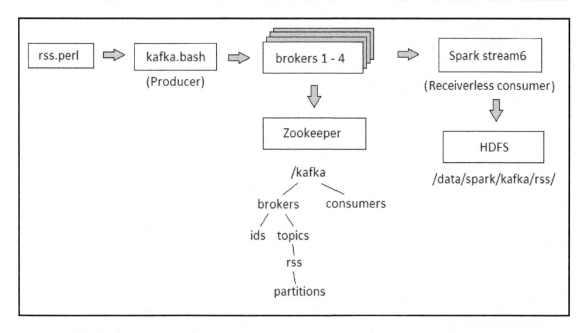

The Perl script called `rss.perl` will be used to provide a data source for a Kafka data producer, which will feed data to the Hortonworks Kafka broker servers. The data will be stored in ZooKeeper, in the structure that has just been examined, under the top-level node called `/kafka`. The Apache Spark Scala-based application will then act as a Kafka consumer and read the data that it will store under HDFS.

In order to try and explain the complexity here, we will examine our method of running the Apache Spark class. It will be started via the `spark-submit` command. Remember that all of these scripts will be released with this book, so you can examine them in your own time. We always use scripts for server test management so that we encapsulate complexity, and command execution is quickly repeatable. The script, `run_stream.bash`, is like many example scripts that have already been used in this chapter and in this book. It accepts a class name and class parameters, and runs the class via `spark-submit`:

```
[hadoop@hc2r1m1 stream]$ more run_stream.bash
#!/bin/bash
SPARK_HOME=/usr/local/spark
SPARK_BIN=$SPARK_HOME/bin
SPARK_SBIN=$SPARK_HOME/sbin
JAR_PATH=/home/hadoop/spark/stream/target/scala-2.10/streaming_2.10-1.0.jar
CLASS_VAL=$1
CLASS_PARAMS="${*:2}"
STREAM_JAR=/usr/local/spark/lib/spark-examples-1.3.1-hadoop2.3.0.jar
cd $SPARK_BIN
```

```
./spark-submit \
   --class $CLASS_VAL \
   --master spark://hc2nn.semtech-solutions.co.nz:7077  \
   --executor-memory 100M \
   --total-executor-cores 50 \
   --jars $STREAM_JAR \
   $JAR_PATH \
   $CLASS_PARAMS
```

We then used a second script, which calls the run_kafka_example.bash script to execute the Kafka consumer code in the previous stream6 application class. Note that this script sets up the full application class name--the broker server list. It also sets up the topic name, called RSS, to use for data consumption. Finally, it defines a consumer group called group1. Remember that Kafka is a publish/subscribe message brokering system. There may be many producers and consumers organized by topic, group, and partition:

```
[hadoop@hc2r1m1 stream]$ more run_kafka_example.bash
#!/bin/bash
RUN_CLASS=nz.co.semtechsolutions.stream6
BROKERS="hc2r1m1:9092,hc2r1m2:9092,hc2r1m3:9092,hc2r1m4:9092"
GROUPID=group1
TOPICS=rss
# run the Apache Spark Kafka example
./run_stream.bash $RUN_CLASS \
                  $BROKERS \
                  $GROUPID \
                  $TOPICS
```

So, we will start the Kafka consumer by running the run_kafka_example.bash script, which, in turn, will run the previous stream6 Scala code using spark-submit. While monitoring Kafka data consumption using the script called kafka_list.bash, we were able to get the kafka-consumer-offset-checker script to list the Kafka-based topics, but for some reason, it will not check the correct path (under /kafka in ZooKeeper) when checking the offsets, as shown here:

```
[hadoop@hc2r1m1 stream]$ ./kafka_list.bash
===============================
  Kafka Topics
===============================
 __consumer_offsets
 rss
===============================
  Kafka Offsets
===============================
Exiting due to: org.apache.zookeeper.KeeperException$NoNodeException:
KeeperErrorCode = NoNode for /consumers/group1/offsets/rss/4.
```

By starting the Kafka producer `rss` feed using the `kafka.bash` script, we can now start feeding the RSS-based data through Kafka into Spark, and then into HDFS. Periodically checking the `spark-submit` session output, it can be seen that events are passing through the Spark-based Kafka DStream. The following output comes from the stream count in the Scala code and shows that, at that point, `28` events were processed:

```
------------------------------------------
Time: 1436834440000 ms
------------------------------------------
>>>>>>>>>>>>>>>> Received events : 28
```

By checking HDFS under the `/data/spark/kafka/rss/` directory via the Hadoop filesystem `ls` command, it can be seen that there is now data stored on HDFS:

```
[hadoop@hc2r1m1 stream]$ hdfs dfs -ls /data/spark/kafka/rss
 Found 1 items
 drwxr-xr-x   - hadoop supergroup          0 2015-07-14 12:40
/data/spark/kafka/rss/file_1436833769907
```

By checking the contents of this directory, it can be seen that an HDFS part data file exists, which should contain the RSS-based data from Reuters:

```
[hadoop@hc2r1m1 stream]$ hdfs dfs -ls
/data/spark/kafka/rss/file_1436833769907
 Found 2 items
 -rw-r--r--   3 hadoop supergroup          0 2015-07-14 12:40
/data/spark/kafka/rss/file_1436833769907/_SUCCESS
 -rw-r--r--   3 hadoop supergroup       8205 2015-07-14 12:40
/data/spark/kafka/rss/file_1436833769907/part-00001
```

Using the Hadoop filesystem `cat` Command, we can dump the contents of this HDFS-based file to check its contents. We have used the Linux head command to limit the data to save space. Clearly, this is RSS Reuters science-based information that the Perl script `rss.perl` has converted from XML to RSS JSON format.

```
[hadoop@hc2r1m1 stream]$ hdfs dfs -cat
/data/spark/kafka/rss/file_1436833769907/part-00001 | head -2
{"category": "science", "title": "Bear necessities: low metabolism lets
pandas survive on bamboo", "summary": "WASHINGTON (Reuters) - Giant pandas
eat vegetables even though their bodies are better equipped to eat meat. So
how do these black-and-white bears from the remote misty mountains of
central China survive on a diet almost exclusively of a low-nutrient food
like bamboo?"}
{"category": "science", "title": "PlanetiQ tests sensor for commercial
weather satellites", "summary": "CAPE CANAVERAL (Reuters) - PlanetiQ a
privately owned company is beginning a key test intended to pave the way
for the first commercial weather satellites."}
```

This ends this Kafka example. It can be seen that Kafka brokers have been configured. It shows that an RSS data-based Kafka producer has fed data to the brokers. It has been proved, using the ZooKeeper client, that the Kafka architecture matching the brokers, topics, and partitions has been set up in ZooKeeper. Finally, it has been shown using the Apache Spark-based Scala code in the `stream6` application, that the Kafka data has been consumed and saved to HDFS.

Summary

We could have provided streaming examples for other systems as well, but there was no room in this chapter. Twitter streaming has been examined by example in the *Checkpointing* section. This chapter has provided practical examples of data recovery via checkpointing in Spark Streaming. It has also touched on the performance limitations of checkpointing and shown that the checkpointing interval should be set at five to ten times the Spark stream batch interval.

Checkpointing provides a stream-based recovery mechanism in the case of Spark application failure. This chapter has provided some stream-based worked examples for TCP, File, Flume, and Kafka-based Spark stream coding. All the examples here are based on Scala and compiled with `sbt`. In case you are more familiar with **Maven** the following tutorial explains how to set up a Maven based Scala project: `http://www.scala-lang.org /old/node/345`.

All of the code will be released with this book. Where the example architecture has become overcomplicated, we have provided an architecture diagram (the Kafka example). It is clear to us that the Apache Spark streaming module contains a rich source of functionality that should meet most of your needs and will grow as future releases of Spark are delivered. Apache Spark Streaming was introduced before Catalyst and Tungsten. So let's have a look how Apache Spark Structured Streaming can make use of those in the next chapter.

6
Structured Streaming

As you might already have understood from the previous chapters, Apache Spark is currently in transition from RDD-based data processing to a more structured one, backed by DataFrames and Datasets in order to let Catalyst and Tungsten kick in for performance optimizations. This means that the community currently uses a double-tracked approach. While the unstructured APIs are still supported--they haven't even been marked as deprecated yet ,and it is questionable if they ever will--a new set of structured APIs has been introduced for various components with Apache Spark V 2.0, and this is also true for Spark Streaming. Structured Steaming was marked stable in Apache Spark V 2.2. Note that, as of Apache Spark V 2.1 when we started writing this chapter, Structured Streaming is was marked as *alpha*. This is another example of the extreme pace at which Apache Spark is developing.

The following topics will be covered in this chapter:

- The concept of continuous applications
- Unification of batch and stream processing
- Windowing
- Event versus processing time and how to handle late arriving data
- How Catalyst and Tungsten support streaming
- How fault tolerance and end-to-end exactly-once delivery guarantee is achieved
- An example of subscribing to a stream on a message hub
- Stream life cycle management

The concept of continuous applications

Streaming apps tend to grow in complexity. Streaming computations don't run in isolation; they interact with storage systems, batch applications, and machine learning libraries. Therefore, the notion of continuous applications--in contrast to batch processing--emerged, and basically means the composite of batch processing and real-time stream processing with a clear focus of the streaming part being the main driver of the application, and just accessing the data created or processed by batch processes for further augmentation. Continuous applications never stop and continuously produce data as new data arrives.

True unification - same code, same engine

So a continuous application could also be implemented on top of RDDs and DStreams but would require the use of use two different APIs. In Apache Spark Structured Streaming the APIs are unified. This unification is achieved by seeing a structured stream as a relational table without boundaries where new data is continuously appended to the bottom of it. In batch processing on DataFrames using the relational API or SQL, intermediate DataFrames are created. As stream and batch computing are unified on top of the Apache SparkSQL engine, when working with structured streams, intermediate relational tables without boundaries are created.

 It is important to note that one can mix (join) static and incremental data within the same query called a continuous application, which is an application taking static and dynamic data into account and never stops, producing output all the time or, at least when new data arrives. A continuous application doesn't necessarily need access to static data, it can also process streaming data only. But an example for using static data on streams is when getting GPS locations in as a stream and matching those GPS locations to addresses stored in persistent storage. The output of such an operation is a stream of addresses.

Windowing

Open source and commercial streaming engines such as IBM Streams, Apache Storm, or Apache Flink are using the concept of windows.

Windows specify the granularity or number of subsequent records, which are taken into account when executing aggregation functions on streams.

How streaming engines use windowing

There exist five different properties in two dimensions, which is how windows can be defined, where each window definition needs to use one property of each dimension.

The first property is the mode in which subsequent windows of a continuous stream of tuples can be created: sliding and tumbling.

The second is that the number of tuples that fall into a window has to be specified: either count-based, time-based or session-based.

Let's take a look at what they mean:

- **Sliding windows**: A sliding window removes a tuple from it whenever a new tuple is eligible to be included.
- **Tumbling windows**: A tumbling window removes all tuples from it whenever there are enough tuples arriving to create a new window.
- **Count-based windows**: Such windows always have the n newest elements in it. Note that this can be achieved either by a sliding or tumbling tuple update policy.
- **Time-based windows**: This window takes the timestamp of a tuple into account in order to determine whether it belongs to a certain window or not. Such a window can contain the latest n seconds worth of data, for example. Such a window can be sliding and tumbling as well.
  Time-based windows especially are eligible for late arriving data, which is a very interesting concept that Apache Spark Structured Streaming makes possible.
- **Session-based windows**: This window takes a session ID of a tuple into account in order to determine whether it belongs to a certain window or not. Such a window eventually contains all data from a user interaction with an online shop, for example. Such a window can be sliding and tumbling as well, although this notion doesn't make really sense here because you want eventually act on/react to all data belonging to a specific session.

Time-based and Session-based windows especially are eligible for late arriving data, which is a very interesting concept that Apache Spark Structured Streaming makes possible.

Let's take a look at the following figure, which illustrates tumbling windows:

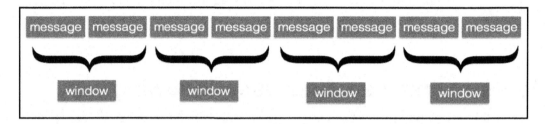

As can be observed, every tuple (or message respectively) ends up in one single window. Now let's have a look at sliding windows:

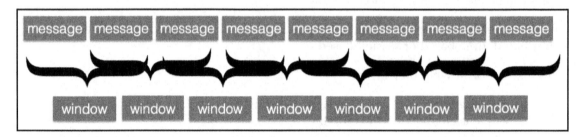

Sliding windows are meant to share tuples among their neighbors. This means that for every tuple arriving, a new window is issued. One example of such a paradigm is the calculation of a moving average once a tuple arrives for the last 100 data points. Now let's consider time based windows:

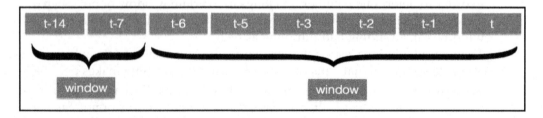

Finally, this last illustration shows time-based windows. It's important to notice that the number of tuples per window can be different as it only depends on how many messages in a certain time frame have arrived; only those will be included in the respective window. So for example consider an HTTP server log file to be streamed into Apache Spark Structured Streaming (using Flume as a possible solution). We are grouping tuples (which are the individual lines of the log file) together on a minute basis. Since the number of concurrent users are different at each point in time during the day the size of the minute windows will also vary depending on it.

How Apache Spark improves windowing

Apache Spark structured streaming is significantly more flexible in the window-processing model. As streams are virtually treated as continuously appended tables, and every row in such a table has a timestamp, operations on windows can be specified in the query itself and each query can define different windows. In addition, if there is a timestamp present in static data, window operations can also be defined, leading to a very flexible stream-processing model.

In other words, Apache Spark windowing is just a sort of special type of grouping on the timestamp column. This makes it really easy to handle late arriving data as well because Apache Spark can include it in the appropriate window and rerun the computation on that window when a certain data item arrives late. This feature is highly configurable.

Event time versus processing time: In time series analysis and especially in stream computing, each record is assigned to a particular timestamp. One way of creating such a timestamp is the arrival time at the stream-processing engine. Often, this is not what you want. Usually, you want to assign an event time for each record at that particular point in time when it was created, for example, when a measurement on an IoT device took place. This allows coping with latency between creating and processing of an event, for example, when an IoT sensor was offline for a certain amount of time, or network congestion caused a delay of data delivery.

The concept of late data is interesting when using event time instead of processing time to assign a unique timestamp to each tuple. Event time is the timestamp when a particular measurement took place, for example. Apache Spark structured streaming can automatically cope with subsets of data arriving at a later point in time transparently.

Late data: If a record arrives at any streaming engine, it is processed immediately. Here, Apache Spark streaming doesn't differ from other engines. However, Apache Spark has the capability of determining the corresponding windows a certain tuple belongs to at any time. If, for whatever reason, a tuple arrives late, all affected windows will be updated and all affected aggregate operations based on these updated windows are rerun. This means that results are allowed to change over time in case late data arrives. This is supported out of the box without the programmer worrying about it. Finally, since Apache Spark V2.1, it is possible to specify the amount of time that the system accepts late data using the `withWatermark` method.

The watermark is basically the threshold used to define how old a late arriving data point is allowed to be in order to still be included in the respective window. Again, consider the HTTP server log file working over a minute length window. If, for whatever reason, a data tuple arrives which is more than 4 hours old it might not make sense to include it in the windows if, for example, this application is used to create a time-series forecast model on an hourly basis to provision or de-provision additional HTTP servers to a cluster. A four-hour-old data point just wouldn't make sense to process, even if it could change the decision, as the decision has already been made.

Increased performance with good old friends

As in Apache SparkSQL for batch processing and, as Apache Spark structured streaming is part of Apache SparkSQL, the Planner (Catalyst) creates incremental execution plans as well for mini batches. This means that the whole streaming model is based on batches. This is the reason why a unified API for streams and batch processing could be achieved. The price we pay is that Apache Spark streaming sometimes has drawbacks when it comes to very low latency requirements (sub-second, in the range of tens of ms). As the name Structured Streaming and the usage of DataFrames and Datasets implies, we are also benefiting from performance improvements due to project Tungsten, which has been introduced in a previous chapter. To the Tungsten engine itself, a mini batch doesn't look considerably different from an ordinary batch. Only Catalyst is aware of the incremental nature of streams. Therefore, as of Apache Spark V2.2, the following operations are *not* (yet) supported, but they are on the roadmap to be supported eventually:

- Chain of aggregations
- Taking first *n* rows
- Distinct
- Sorting before aggregations
- Outer joins between streaming and static data (only limited support)

As this is constantly changing; it is best to refer to the latest documentation: `http://spark.apache.org/docs/latest/structured-streaming-programming-guide.html`.

How transparent fault tolerance and exactly-once delivery guarantee is achieved

Apache Spark structured streaming supports full crash fault tolerance and exactly-once delivery guarantee without the user taking care of any specific error handling routines. Isn't this amazing? So how is this achieved?

 Full crash fault tolerance and exactly-once delivery guarantee are terms of systems theory. Full crash fault tolerance means that you can basically pull the power plug of the whole data center at any point in time, and no data is lost or left in an inconsistent state. Exactly-once delivery guarantee means, even if the same power plug is pulled, it is guaranteed that each tuple- end-to-end from the data source to the data sink - is delivered - only, and exactly, once. Not zero times and also not more than one time. Of course those concepts must also hold in case a single node fails or misbehaves (for example- starts throttling).

First of all, states between individual batches and offset ranges (position in a source stream) are kept in-memory but are backed by a **Write Ahead Log (WAL)** in a fault-tolerant filesystem such as HDFS. A WAL is basically a log file reflecting the overall stream processing state in a pro-active fashion. This means, before data is transformed though an operator, it is first persistently stored in the WAL in a way it can be recovered after a crash. So, in other words, during the processing of an individual mini batch, the regions of the worker memory, as well as the position offset of the streaming source, are persisted to disk. In case the system fails and has to recover, it can re-request chunks of data from the source. Of course, this is only possible if the source supports these semantics.

Replayable sources can replay streams from a given offset

End-to-end exactly-once delivery guarantee requires the streaming source to support some sort of stream replay at a requested position. This is true for file sources and Apache Kafka, for example, as well as the IBM Watson Internet of Things platform, where the following example in this chapter will be based on.

Idempotent sinks prevent data duplication

Another key to end-to-end exactly-once delivery guarantee is idempotent sinks. This basically means that sinks are aware of which particular write operation has succeeded in the past. This means that such a smart sink can re-request data in case of a failure and also drop data in case the same data has been sent multiple times.

State versioning guarantees consistent results after reruns

What about state? Imagine that a machine learning algorithm maintains a count variable on all the workers. If you replay the exact same data twice, you will end up counting the data multiple times. Therefore, the query planner also maintains a versioned key-value map within the workers, which are persisting their state in turn to HDFS--which is by design fault tolerant.

So, in case of a failure, if data has to be replayed, the planner makes sure that the correct version of the key-value map is used by the workers.

Example - connection to a MQTT message broker

So, let's start with a sample use case. Let's connect to an **Internet of Things (IoT)** sensor data stream. As we haven't covered machine learning so far, we don't analyze the data, we just showcase the concept.

We are using the IBM Watson IoT platform as a streaming source. At its core, the Watson IoT platform is backed by an **MQTT (Message Queue Telemetry Transport)** message broker. MQTT is a lightweight telemetry protocol invented by IBM in 1999 and became-- an **OASIS (Organization for the Advancement of Structured Information Standards**, a global nonprofit consortium that works on the development, convergence, and adoption of standards for security, Internet of Things, energy, content technologies, emergency management, and other areas) standard in 2013--the de facto standard for IoT data integration.

Messaging between applications can be backed by a message queue which is a middleware system supporting asynchronous point to point channels in various delivery modes like **first-in first-out (FIFO)**, **last-in first-out (LIFO)** or **Priority Queue** (where each message can be re-ordered by certain criteria).

This is already a very nice feature but still couples applications in a certain way because, once a message is read, it is made unavailable to others.

This way N to N communication is hard (but not impossible) to achieve. In a publish/subscribe model applications are completely de-coupled. There doesn't exists any queues anymore but the notion of topics is introduced. Data providers publish messages on specific topics and data consumers subscribe to those topics. This way N to N communication is very straightforward to achieve since it is reflected by the underlying message delivery model. Such a middleware is called a Message Broker in contrast to a Message Queue.

As cloud services tend to change constantly, and cloud in general is introduced later in this book, the following tutorial explains how to set up the test data generator in the cloud and connect to the remote MQTT message broker. In this example, we will use the IBM Watson IoT Platform, which is an MQTT message broker available in the cloud. Alternatively one can install an open source message broker like MOSQUITTO which also provides a publicly available test installation on the following URL: `http://test.mosquitto.org/`.

In order to replicate the example, the following steps (1) and (2) are necessary as described in the following tutorial: `https://www.ibm.com/developerworks/library/iot-cognitive-iot-app-machine-learning/index.html`. Please make sure to note down `http_host`, `org`, `apiKey`, and `apiToken` during execution of the tutorial. Those are needed later in order to subscribe to data using Apache Spark Structured Streaming.

As the IBM Watson IoT platform uses the open MQTT standard, no special IBM component is necessary to connect to the platform. Instead, we are using MQTT and Apache Bahir as a connector between MQTT and Apache Spark structured streaming.

 The goal of the Apache Bahir project is to provide a set of source and sink connectors for various data processing engines including Apache Spark and Apache Flink since they are lacking those connectors. In this case we will use the Apache Bahir MQTT data source for MQTT.

In order to use Apache Bahir, we need to add two dependencies to our local maven repository. A complete pom.xml file is provided in the download section of this chapter. Let's have a look at the dependency section of pom.xml:

```
<dependency>
    <groupId>org.apache.bahir</groupId>
    <artifactId>spark-sql-streaming-mqtt_2.11</artifactId>
    <version>2.1.0-SNAPSHOT</version>
</dependency>
<dependency>
        <groupId>org.eclipse.paho</groupId>
        <artifactId>org.eclipse.paho.client.mqttv3</artifactId>
        <version>1.1.0</version>
</dependency>
```

We are basically getting the MQTT Apache structured streaming adapter of Apache Bahir and a dependent package for low-level MQTT processing. A simple mvn dependency:resolve command in the directory of the pom.xml file pulls the required dependencies into our local maven repository, where they can be accessed by the Apache Spark driver and transferred to the Apache Spark workers automatically.

Another way of resolving the dependencies is when using the following command in order to start a spark-shell (spark-submit works the same way); the necessary dependencies are automatically distributed to the workers:

```
Romeos-MacBook-Pro:chapter6 romeokienzler$ spark-shell --packages org.apache.bahir:spark-sql-streaming-mqtt_2.11:2.1.0,org.eclipse.paho:org.eclipse.paho.client.mqttv3:1.1.0
Ivy Default Cache set to: /Users/romeokienzler/.ivy2/cache
The jars for the packages stored in: /Users/romeokienzler/.ivy2/jars
:: loading settings :: url = jar:file:/Users/romeokienzler/Documents/runtimes/spark-2.1.0-bin-hadoop2.7/jars/ivy-2.4.0.jar!/org/apache/ivy/core/settings/ivysettings.xml
org.apache.bahir#spark-sql-streaming-mqtt_2.11 added as a dependency
org.eclipse.paho#org.eclipse.paho.client.mqttv3 added as a dependency
:: resolving dependencies :: org.apache.spark#spark-submit-parent;1.0
        confs: [default]
        found org.apache.bahir#spark-sql-streaming-mqtt_2.11;2.1.0 in local-m2-cache
        found org.apache.spark#spark-tags_2.11;2.1.0 in local-m2-cache
        found org.scalatest#scalatest_2.11;2.2.6 in local-m2-cache
        found org.scala-lang#scala-reflect;2.11.8 in local-m2-cache
        found org.scala-lang.modules#scala-xml_2.11;1.0.2 in local-m2-cache
        found org.spark-project.spark#unused;1.0.0 in local-m2-cache
        found org.eclipse.paho#org.eclipse.paho.client.mqttv3;1.1.0 in central
:: resolution report :: resolve 7237ms :: artifacts dl 8ms
        :: modules in use:
        org.apache.bahir#spark-sql-streaming-mqtt_2.11;2.1.0 from local-m2-cache in [default]
        org.apache.spark#spark-tags_2.11;2.1.0 from local-m2-cache in [default]
        org.eclipse.paho#org.eclipse.paho.client.mqttv3;1.1.0 from central in [default]
        org.scala-lang#scala-reflect;2.11.8 from local-m2-cache in [default]
        org.scala-lang.modules#scala-xml_2.11;1.0.2 from local-m2-cache in [default]
        org.scalatest#scalatest_2.11;2.2.6 from local-m2-cache in [default]
        org.spark-project.spark#unused;1.0.0 from local-m2-cache in [default]
        ---------------------------------------------------------------------
        |                  |            modules            ||   artifacts   |
        |       conf       | number| search|dwnlded|evicted|| number|dwnlded|
        ---------------------------------------------------------------------
        |      default     |   7   |   1   |   1   |   0   ||   7   |   0   |
        ---------------------------------------------------------------------
:: retrieving :: org.apache.spark#spark-submit-parent
        confs: [default]
        0 artifacts copied, 7 already retrieved (0kB/9ms)
Using Spark's default log4j profile: org/apache/spark/log4j-defaults.properties
Setting default log level to "WARN".
To adjust logging level use sc.setLogLevel(newLevel). For SparkR, use setLogLevel(newLevel).
17/07/10 08:37:49 WARN NativeCodeLoader: Unable to load native-hadoop library for your platform... using builtin-java classes where applicable
17/07/10 08:38:08 WARN ObjectStore: Failed to get database global_temp, returning NoSuchObjectException
Spark context Web UI available at http://192.168.0.100:4040
Spark context available as 'sc' (master = local[*], app id = local-1499668675824).
Spark session available as 'spark'.
Welcome to
      ____              __
     / __/__  ___ _____/ /__
    _\ \/ _ \/ _ `/ __/  '_/
   /___/ .__/\_,_/_/ /_/\_\   version 2.1.0
      /_/

Using Scala version 2.11.8 (Java HotSpot(TM) 64-Bit Server VM, Java 1.8.0_65)
Type in expressions to have them evaluated.
Type :help for more information.

scala>
```

Now we need the MQTT credentials that we've obtained earlier. Let's set the values here:

```
val mqtt_host = "pcoyha.messaging.internetofthings.ibmcloud.com"
val org = "pcoyha"
val apiKey = "a-pcoyha-oaigc1k8ub"
val apiToken = "&wuypVX2yNgVLAcLr8"
var randomSessionId = scala.util.Random.nextInt(10000)
```

Now we can start creating a stream connecting to an MQTT message broker. We are telling Apache Spark to use the Apache Bahir MQTT streaming source:

```
val df =
spark.readStream.format("org.apache.bahir.sql.streaming.mqtt.MQTTStreamSour
ceProvider")
```

We need to specify credentials such as "username", "password", and "clientId" in order to pull data from the MQTT message broker; the link to the tutorial mentioned earlier explains how to obtain these:

```
.option("username",apiKey)
.option("password",apiToken)
.option("clientId","a:"+org+":"+apiKey)
```

As we are using a publish/subscribe messaging model, we have to provide the topic that we are subscribing to--this topic is used by the test data generator that you've deployed to the cloud before:

```
.option("topic",
"iot-2/type/WashingMachine/id/Washer01/evt/voltage/fmt/json")
```

Once everything is set on the configuration side, we have to provide the endpoint host and port in order to create the stream:

```
.load("tcp://"+mqtt_host+":1883")
```

Interestingly, as can be seen in the following screenshot, this leads to the creation of a DataFrame:

```
scala> :paste
// Entering paste mode (ctrl-D to finish)

val df = spark.readStream
    .format("org.apache.bahir.sql.streaming.mqtt.MQTTStreamSourceProvider")
    .option("username","a-vy0z2s-zfzzckrnqf")
    .option("password","jbusSUaLM5a7v3I-7x")
    .option("clientId","a:vy0z2s:a-vy0z2s-zfzzckrnqf")
    .option("topic", "iot-2/type/TestDeviceType517/id/TestDevice517/evt/lorenz/fmt/json")
    .load("tcp://vy0z2s.messaging.internetofthings.ibmcloud.com:1883")

// Exiting paste mode, now interpreting.

df: org.apache.spark.sql.DataFrame = [value: string, timestamp: timestamp]
```

Note that the schema is fixed to [String, Timestamp] and cannot be changed during stream creation--this is a limitation of the Apache Bahir library. However, using the rich DataFrame API, you can parse the value, a JSON string for example, and create new columns.

As discussed before, this is one of the powerful features of Apache Spark structured streaming, as the very same DataFrame (and Dataset) API now can be used to process historic and real-time data. So let's take a look at the contents of this stream by writing it to the console:

```
val query = df.writeStream.
outputMode("append").
format("console").
start()
```

As output mode, we choose `append` to enforce incremental display and avoid having the complete contents of the historic stream being written to the console again and again. As `format`, we specify `console` as we just want to debug what's happening on the stream:

```
scala> val query = df.writeStream.
     |   outputMode("append").
     |   format("console").
     |   start()
query: org.apache.spark.sql.streaming.StreamingQuery = Streaming Query [id = a2377c24-c274-476e-bc2b-07d57bab1877, runId = 387ca22f-138c-4456-9243-9218766a6f13] [state = ACTIVE]
```

Finally, the `start` method initiates query processing, as can be seen here:

```
-------------------------------------------
Batch: 332
-------------------------------------------
+--------------------+--------------------+
|               value|           timestamp|
+--------------------+--------------------+
|{"d":{"voltage":2...|2017-04-26 05:31:...|
|{"d":{"voltage":2...|2017-04-26 05:31:...|
|{"d":{"voltage":2...|2017-04-26 05:31:...|
|{"d":{"voltage":2...|2017-04-26 05:31:...|
|{"d":{"voltage":2...|2017-04-26 05:31:...|
|{"d":{"voltage":2...|2017-04-26 05:31:...|
|{"d":{"voltage":2...|2017-04-26 05:31:...|
|{"d":{"voltage":2...|2017-04-26 05:31:...|
|{"d":{"voltage":2...|2017-04-26 05:31:...|
+--------------------+--------------------+


-------------------------------------------
Batch: 333
-------------------------------------------
+--------------------+--------------------+
|               value|           timestamp|
+--------------------+--------------------+
|{"d":{"voltage":2...|2017-04-26 05:31:...|
|{"d":{"voltage":2...|2017-04-26 05:31:...|
|{"d":{"voltage":2...|2017-04-26 05:31:...|
|{"d":{"voltage":2...|2017-04-26 05:31:...|
|{"d":{"voltage":2...|2017-04-26 05:31:...|
|{"d":{"voltage":2...|2017-04-26 05:31:...|
+--------------------+--------------------+


-------------------------------------------
Batch: 334
-------------------------------------------
+--------------------+--------------------+
|               value|           timestamp|
+--------------------+--------------------+
|{"d":{"voltage":2...|2017-04-26 05:31:...|
|{"d":{"voltage":2...|2017-04-26 05:31:...|
|{"d":{"voltage":2...|2017-04-26 05:31:...|
|{"d":{"voltage":2...|2017-04-26 05:31:...|
|{"d":{"voltage":2...|2017-04-26 05:31:...|
|{"d":{"voltage":2...|2017-04-26 05:31:...|
+--------------------+--------------------+
```

Controlling continuous applications

Once a continuous application (even a simple one, not taking historic data into account) is started and running, it has to be controlled somehow as the call to the `start` method immediately starts processing, but also returns without blocking. In case you want your program to block at this stage until the application has finished, one can use the `awaitTermination` method as follows:

```
query.awaitTermination()
```

This is particularly important when precompiling code and using the `spark-submit` command. When using `spark-shell`, the application is not terminated anyway.

More on stream life cycle management

Streaming tends to be used in the creation of continuous applications. This means that the process is running in the background and, in contrast to batch processing, doesn't have a clear stop time; therefore, DataFrames and Datasets backed by a streaming source, support various methods for stream life cycle management, which are explained as follows:

- `start`: This starts the continuous application. This method doesn't block. If this is not what you want, use `awaitTermination`.
- `stop` : This terminates the continuous application.
- `awaitTermination` : As mentioned earlier, starting a stream using the `start` method immediately returns, which means that the call is not blocking. Sometimes you want to wait until the stream is terminated, either by someone else calling `stop` on it or by an error.
- `exception`: In case a stream stopped because of an error, the cause can be read using this method.
- `sourceStatus`: This is to obtain real-time meta information on the streaming source.
- `sinkStatus` : This is to obtain real-time meta information on the streaming sink.

Sinks in Apache Spark streaming are smart in the sense that they support fault tolerance and end-to-end exactly-once delivery guarantee as mentioned before. In addition, Apache Spark needs them to support different output methods. Currently, the following three output methods, append, update, and complete, significantly change the underlying semantics. The following paragraph contains more details about the different output methods.

Different output modes on sinks: Sinks can be specified to handle output in different ways. This is known as `outputMode`. The naive choice would use an incremental approach as we are processing incremental data with streaming anyway. This mode is referred to as `append`. However, there exist requirements where data already processed by the sink has to be changed. One example is the late arrival problem of missing data in a certain time window, which can lead to changing results once the computation for that particular time window is recomputed. This mode is called `complete`.

> Since Version 2.1 of Apache Spark, the `update` mode was introduced that behaves similarly to the `complete` mode but only changes rows that have been altered, therefore saving processing resources and improving speed. Some types of modes do not support all query types. As this is constantly changing, it is best to refer to the latest documentation at `http://spark.apache.org/docs/latest/streaming-programming-guide.html`.

Summary

So why do we have two different streaming engines within the same data processing framework? We hope that after reading this chapter, you'll agree that the main pain points of the classical DStream based engine have been addressed. Formerly, event time-based processing was not possible and only the arrival time of data was considered. Then, late data has simply been processed with the wrong timestamp as only processing time could be used. Also, batch and stream processing required using two different APIs: RDDs and DStreams. Although the API is similar, it is not exactly the same; therefore, the rewriting of code when going back and forth between the two paradigms was necessary. Finally, end-to-end delivery guarantee was hard to achieve and required lots of user intervention and thinking.

This fault-tolerant end-to-end exactly-once delivery guarantee is achieved through offset tracking and state management in a fault-tolerant Write Ahead Log in conjunction with fault-tolerant sources and sinks. Finally, the unification of batch and streaming APIs on top of Catalyst and Tungsten is one of the most important innovations in Apache Spark since version 2.0.

Now let's examine the very interesting topic of machine learning in the next chapter.

7
Apache Spark MLlib

MLlib is the original machine learning library that is provided with Apache Spark, the in-memory cluster-based open source data processing system. This library is still based on the RDD API. In a later chapter, we'll also learn how machine learning on the newer DataFrame and Dataset API works. In this chapter, we will examine the functionality provided with the MLlib library in terms of areas such as regression, classification, and neural network processing. We will examine the theory behind each algorithm before providing working examples that tackle real problems. The example code and documentation on the web can be sparse and confusing.

We will take a step-by-step approach in describing how the following algorithms can be used and what they are capable of doing:

- Architecture
- Classification with Naive Bayes
- Clustering with K-Means
- Image classification with **artificial neural networks**

Architecture

Remember that, although Spark is used for the speed of its in-memory distributed processing, it doesn't provide storage. You can use the Host (local) filesystem to read and write your data, but if your data volumes are big enough to be described as big data, then it makes sense to use a cloud-based distributed storage system such as OpenStack Swift Object Storage, which can be found in many cloud environments and can also be installed in private data centers.

In case very high I/O is needed, HDFS would also be an option. More information on HDFS can be found here: http://hadoop.apache.org/doc s/current/hadoop-project-dist/hadoop-hdfs/HdfsDesign.html.

The development environment

The Scala language will be used for the coding samples in this book. This is because, as a scripting language, it produces less code than Java. It can also be used from the Spark shell as well as compiled with Apache Spark applications. We will be using the **sbt tool** to compile the Scala code, which we have installed into Hortonworks HDP 2.6 Sandbox as follows:

```
[hadoop@hc2nn ~]# sudo su -
[root@hc2nn ~]# cd /tmp
[root@hc2nn ~]#wget
http://repo.scala-sbt.org/scalasbt/sbt-native-packages/org/scala-sbt/sbt/0.
13.1/sbt.rpm
[root@hc2nn ~]# rpm -ivh sbt.rpm
```

The following URL provides instructions to install sbt on other operating systems including Windows, Linux and macOS: http://www.scala-sbt.org/0.13/docs/Setup.html.

We used a generic Linux account called **Hadoop**. As the previous commands show, we need to install sbt as the root account, which we have accessed via sudo su -l (switch user). We then downloaded the sbt.rpm file to the /tmp directory from the web-based server called repo.scala-sbt.org using wget. Finally, we installed the rpm file using the rpm command with the options i for install, v for verify, and h to print the hash marks while the package is being installed.

We developed all of the Scala code for Apache Spark in this chapter on the Linux server, using the Linux Hadoop account. We placed each set of code within a subdirectory under /home/hadoop/spark. For instance, the following sbt structure diagram shows that the MLlib Naive Bayes code is stored in a subdirectory called nbayes under the Spark directory. What the diagram also shows is that the Scala code is developed within a subdirectory structure named src/main/scala under the nbayes directory. The files called bayes1.scala and convert.scala contain the Naive Bayes code that will be used in the next section:

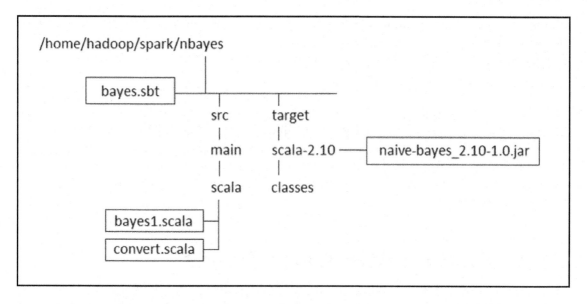

The `bayes.sbt` file is a configuration file used by the `sbt` tool, which describes how to compile the Scala files within the Scala directory. (Note that if you were developing in Java, you would use a path of the `nbayes/src/main/java` form .) The contents of the `bayes.sbt` file are shown next. The `pwd` and `cat` Linux commands remind you of the file location and also remind you to dump the file contents.

The `name`, `version`, and `scalaVersion` options set the details of the project and the version of Scala to be used. The `libraryDependencies` options define where the Hadoop and Spark libraries can be located.

```
[hadoop@hc2nn nbayes]$ pwd
/home/hadoop/spark/nbayes
[hadoop@hc2nn nbayes]$ cat bayes.sbt
name := "Naive Bayes"
version := "1.0"
scalaVersion := "2.11.2"
libraryDependencies += "org.apache.hadoop" % "hadoop-client" % "2.8.1"
libraryDependencies += "org.apache.spark" %% "spark-core" % "2.6.0"
libraryDependencies += "org.apache.spark" %% "spark-mllib" % "2.1.1"
```

The Scala `nbayes` project code can be compiled from the `nbayes` subdirectory using this command:

```
[hadoop@hc2nn nbayes]$ sbt compile
```

The `sbt compile` command is used to compile the code into classes. The classes are then placed in the `nbayes/target/scala-2.10/classes` directory. The compiled classes can be packaged in a JAR file with this command:

```
[hadoop@hc2nn nbayes]$ sbt package
```

The `sbt package` command will create a JAR file under the `nbayes/target/scala-2.10` directory. As we can see in the example in the **sbt structure diagram**, the JAR file named `naive-bayes_2.10-1.0.jar` has been created after a successful compile and package. This JAR file, and the classes that it contains, can then be used in a `spark-submit` command. This will be described later as the functionality in the Apache Spark MLlib module is explored.

Classification with Naive Bayes

This section will provide a working example of the Apache Spark MLlib Naive Bayes algorithm. It will describe the theory behind the algorithm and will provide a step-by-step example in Scala to show how the algorithm may be used.

Theory on Classification

In order to use the Naive Bayes algorithm to classify a dataset, the data must be linearly divisible; that is, the classes within the data must be linearly divisible by class boundaries. The following figure visually explains this with three datasets and two class boundaries shown via the dotted lines:

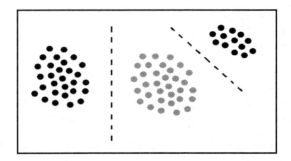

Naive Bayes assumes that the features (or dimensions) within a dataset are independent of one another; that is, they have no effect on each other. The following example considers the classification of e-mails as spam. If you have 100 e-mails, then perform the following:

```
60% of emails are spam
80% of spam emails contain the word buy
20% of spam emails don't contain the word buy
40% of emails are not spam
10% of non spam emails contain the word buy
90% of non spam emails don't contain the word buy
```

Let's convert this example into conditional probabilities so that a Naive Bayes classifier can pick it up:

```
P(Spam) = the probability that an email is spam = 0.6
P(Not Spam) = the probability that an email is not spam = 0.4
P(Buy|Spam) = the probability that an email that is spam has the word buy =
0.8
P(Buy|Not Spam) = the probability that an email that is not spam has the
word buy = 0.1
```

What is the probability that an e-mail that contains the word buy is spam? Well, this would be written as *P (Spam | Buy)*. Naive Bayes says that it is described by the equation in the following figure:

$$P(\text{Spam}|\text{Buy}) = \frac{P(\text{Buy}|\text{Spam}) * P(\text{Spam})}{P(\text{Buy}|\text{Spam}) * P(\text{Spam}) + P(\text{Buy}|\text{Not Spam}) * P(\text{Not Spam})}$$

So, using the previous percentage figures, we get the following:

P(Spam | Buy) = (0.8 * 0.6) / ((0.8 * 0.6) + (0.1 * 0.4)) = (.48) / (.48 + .04)

= .48 / .52 = .923

This means that it is *92* percent more likely that an e-mail that contains the word buy is spam. That was a look at the theory; now it's time to try a real-world example using the Apache Spark MLlib Naive Bayes algorithm.

Naive Bayes in practice

The first step is to choose some data that will be used for classification. We have chosen some data from the UK Government data website at http://data.gov.uk/dataset/road-accidents-safety-data.

The dataset is called **Road Safety - Digital Breath Test Data 2013**, which downloads a zipped text file called DigitalBreathTestData2013.txt. This file contains around half a million rows. The data looks as follows:

```
Reason,Month,Year,WeekType,TimeBand,BreathAlcohol,AgeBand,Gender
Suspicion of Alcohol,Jan,2013,Weekday,12am-4am,75,30-39,Male
Moving Traffic Violation,Jan,2013,Weekday,12am-4am,0,20-24,Male
Road Traffic Collision,Jan,2013,Weekend,12pm-4pm,0,20-24,Female
```

In order to classify the data, we have modified both the column layout and the number of columns. We have simply used Excel, given the data volume. However, if our data size had been in the big data range, we would have had to run some Scala code on top of Apache Spark for **ETL (Extract Transform Load)**. As the following commands show, the data now resides in HDFS in the directory named /data/spark/nbayes. The file name is called DigitalBreathTestData2013- MALE2.csv. The line count from the Linux wc command shows that there are 467,000 rows. Finally, the following data sample shows that we have selected the columns, Gender, Reason, WeekType, TimeBand, BreathAlcohol, and AgeBand to classify. We will try to classify on the Gender column using the other columns as features:

```
[hadoop@hc2nn ~]$ hdfs dfs -cat
/data/spark/nbayes/DigitalBreathTestData2013-MALE2.csv | wc -l
467054
[hadoop@hc2nn ~]$ hdfs dfs -cat
/data/spark/nbayes/DigitalBreathTestData2013-MALE2.csv | head -5
Male,Suspicion of Alcohol,Weekday,12am-4am,75,30-39
Male,Moving Traffic Violation,Weekday,12am-4am,0,20-24
Male,Suspicion of Alcohol,Weekend,4am-8am,12,40-49
Male,Suspicion of Alcohol,Weekday,12am-4am,0,50-59
Female,Road Traffic Collision,Weekend,12pm-4pm,0,20-24
```

The Apache Spark MLlib classification function uses a data structure called LabeledPoint, which is a general purpose data representation defined at http://spark.apache.org/docs/1.0.0/api/scala/index.html#org.apache.spark.mllib.regression.LabeledPoint and https://spark.apache.org/docs/latest/mllib-data-types.html#labeled-point.

This structure only accepts double values, which means that the text values in the previous data need to be classified numerically. Luckily, all of the columns in the data will convert to numeric categories, and we have provided a program in the software package with this book under the `chapter2\naive bayes` directory to do just that. It is called `convert.scala`. It takes the contents of the `DigitalBreathTestData2013- MALE2.csv` file and converts each record into a double vector.

The directory structure and files for an `sbt` Scala-based development environment have already been described earlier. We are developing our Scala code on the Linux server using the Linux account, Hadoop. Next, the Linux `pwd` and `ls` commands show our top-level `nbayes` development directory with the `bayes.sbt` configuration file, whose contents have already been examined:

```
[hadoop@hc2nn nbayes]$ pwd
/home/hadoop/spark/nbayes
[hadoop@hc2nn nbayes]$ ls
bayes.sbt      target    project    src
```

The Scala code to run the Naive Bayes example is in the `src/main/scala` subdirectory under the `nbayes` directory:

```
[hadoop@hc2nn scala]$ pwd
/home/hadoop/spark/nbayes/src/main/scala
[hadoop@hc2nn scala]$ ls
bayes1.scala convert.scala
```

We will examine the `bayes1.scala` file later, but first, the text-based data on HDFS must be converted into numeric double values. This is where the `convert.scala` file is used. The code is as follows:

```
import org.apache.spark.SparkContext
import org.apache.spark.SparkContext._
import org.apache.spark.SparkConf
```

These lines import classes for the Spark context, the connection to the Apache Spark cluster, and the Spark configuration. The object that is being created is called `convert1`. It is an application as it extends the `App` class:

```
object convert1 extends App
{
```

The next line creates a function called `enumerateCsvRecord`. It has a parameter called `colData`, which is an array of `Strings` and returns `String`:

```
def enumerateCsvRecord( colData:Array[String]): String =
{
```

The function then enumerates the text values in each column, so, for instance, Male becomes 0. These numeric values are stored in values such as `colVal1`:

```
val colVal1 =
  colData(0) match
  {
    case "Male"                        => 0
    case "Female"                      => 1
    case "Unknown"                     => 2
    case _                             => 99
  }

val colVal2 =
  colData(1) match
  {
    case "Moving Traffic Violation"    => 0
    case "Other"                       => 1
    case "Road Traffic Collision"      => 2
    case "Suspicion of Alcohol"        => 3
    case _                             => 99
  }

val colVal3 =
  colData(2) match
  {
    case "Weekday"                     => 0
    case "Weekend"                     => 0
    case _                             => 99
  }

val colVal4 =
  colData(3) match
  {
    case "12am-4am"                    => 0
    case "4am-8am"                     => 1
    case "8am-12pm"                    => 2
    case "12pm-4pm"                    => 3
    case "4pm-8pm"                     => 4
    case "8pm-12pm"                    => 5
    case _                             => 99
  }
```

```
val colVal5 = colData(4)
val colVal6 =
  colData(5) match
  {
    case "16-19"                          => 0
    case "20-24"                          => 1
    case "25-29"                          => 2
    case "30-39"                          => 3
    case "40-49"                          => 4
    case "50-59"                          => 5
    case "60-69"                          => 6
    case "70-98"                          => 7
    case "Other"                          => 8
    case _                                => 99
  }
```

 A comma-separated string called `lineString` is created from the numeric column values and is then returned. The function closes with the final brace character. Note that the data line created next starts with a label value at column one and is followed by a vector, which represents the data.

The vector is space-separated while the label is separated from the vector by a comma. Using these two separator types allows us to process both--the label and vector--in two simple steps:

```
val lineString = colVal1+","+colVal2+" "+colVal3+" "+colVal4+"
"+colVal5+" "+colVal6
    return lineString
}
```

The main script defines the HDFS server name and path. It defines the input file and the output path in terms of these values. It uses the Spark URL and application name to create a new configuration. It then creates a new context or connection to Spark using these details:

```
val hdfsServer = "hdfs://localhost:8020"
val hdfsPath   = "/data/spark/nbayes/"
val inDataFile = hdfsServer + hdfsPath + "DigitalBreathTestData2013-
MALE2.csv"
val outDataFile = hdfsServer + hdfsPath + "result"
val sparkMaster = "spark://localhost:7077"
val appName = "Convert 1"
val sparkConf = new SparkConf()
sparkConf.setMaster(sparkMaster)
sparkConf.setAppName(appName)
val sparkCxt = new SparkContext(sparkConf)
```

The CSV-based raw data file is loaded from HDFS using the Spark context `textFile` method. Then, a data row count is printed:

```
val csvData = sparkCxt.textFile(inDataFile)
println("Records in : "+ csvData.count() )
```

The CSV raw data is passed line by line to the `enumerateCsvRecord` function. The returned string-based numeric data is stored in the `enumRddData` variable:

```
val enumRddData = csvData.map
{
  csvLine =>
    val colData = csvLine.split(',')
    enumerateCsvRecord(colData)
}
```

Finally, the number of records in the `enumRddData` variable is printed, and the enumerated data is saved to HDFS:

```
println("Records out : "+ enumRddData.count() )
  enumRddData.saveAsTextFile(outDataFile)
} // end object
```

In order to run this script as an application against Spark, it must be compiled. This is carried out with the `sbt package` command, which also compiles the code. The following command is run from the `nbayes` directory:

```
[hadoop@hc2nn nbayes]$ sbt package
Loading /usr/share/sbt/bin/sbt-launch-lib.bash
. . . .
[info] Done packaging.
[success] Total time: 37 s, completed Feb 19, 2015 1:23:55 PM
```

This causes the compiled classes that are created to be packaged into a JAR library, as shown here:

```
[hadoop@hc2nn nbayes]$ pwd
/home/hadoop/spark/nbayes
[hadoop@hc2nn nbayes]$ ls -l target/scala-2.10
total 24
drwxrwxr-x 2 hadoop hadoop 4096 Feb 19 13:23 classes
-rw-rw-r-- 1 hadoop hadoop 17609 Feb 19 13:23 naive-bayes_2.10-1.0.jar
```

The `convert1` application can now be run against Spark using the application name, Spark URL, and full path to the JAR file that was created. Some extra parameters specify memory and the maximum cores that are supposed to be used:

```
spark-submit \
 --class convert1 \
 --master spark://localhost:7077 \
 --executor-memory 700M \
 --total-executor-cores 100 \
 /home/hadoop/spark/nbayes/target/scala-2.10/naive-bayes_2.10-1.0.jar
```

This creates a data directory on HDFS called /data/spark/nbayes/ followed by the result, which contains part files with the processed data:

```
[hadoop@hc2nn nbayes]$ hdfs dfs -ls /data/spark/nbayes
Found 2 items
-rw-r--r--   3 hadoop supergroup   24645166 2015-01-29 21:27
/data/spark/nbayes/DigitalBreathTestData2013-MALE2.csv
drwxr-xr-x   - hadoop supergroup          0 2015-02-19 13:36
/data/spark/nbayes/result
[hadoop@hc2nn nbayes]$ hdfs dfs -ls /data/spark/nbayes/result
Found 3 items
-rw-r--r--   3 hadoop supergroup          0 2015-02-19 13:36
/data/spark/nbayes/result/_SUCCESS
-rw-r--r--   3 hadoop supergroup    2828727 2015-02-19 13:36
/data/spark/nbayes/result/part-00000
-rw-r--r--   3 hadoop supergroup    2865499 2015-02-19 13:36
/data/spark/nbayes/result/part-00001
```

In the following HDFS cat command, we concatenated the part file data into a file called DigitalBreathTestData2013-MALE2a.csv. We then examined the top five lines of the file using the head command to show that it is numeric. Finally, we loaded it in HDFS with the put command:

```
[hadoop@hc2nn nbayes]$ hdfs dfs -cat /data/spark/nbayes/result/part* >
./DigitalBreathTestData2013-MALE2a.csv
[hadoop@hc2nn nbayes]$ head -5 DigitalBreathTestData2013-MALE2a.csv
0,3 0 0 75 3
0,0 0 0 0 1
0,3 0 1 12 4
0,3 0 0 0 5
1,2 0 3 0 1
[hadoop@hc2nn nbayes]$ hdfs dfs -put ./DigitalBreathTestData2013-MALE2a.csv
/data/spark/nbayes
```

The following HDFS ls command now shows the numeric data file stored on HDFS in the nbayes directory:

```
[hadoop@hc2nn nbayes]$ hdfs dfs -ls /data/spark/nbayes
Found 3 items
-rw-r--r--   3 hadoop supergroup   24645166 2015-01-29 21:27
```

```
/data/spark/nbayes/DigitalBreathTestData2013-MALE2.csv
-rw-r--r--    3 hadoop supergroup    5694226 2015-02-19 13:39
/data/spark/nbayes/DigitalBreathTestData2013-MALE2a.csv
drwxr-xr-x - hadoop supergroup         0 2015-02-19 13:36
/data/spark/nbayes/result
```

Now that the data has been converted into a numeric form, it can be processed with the MLlib Naive Bayes algorithm; this is what the Scala file, bayes1.scala, does. This file imports the same configuration and context classes as before. It also imports MLlib classes for Naive Bayes, vectors, and the LabeledPoint structure. The application class that is created this time is called bayes1:

```
import org.apache.spark.SparkContext
import org.apache.spark.SparkContext._
import org.apache.spark.SparkConf
import org.apache.spark.mllib.classification.NaiveBayes
import org.apache.spark.mllib.linalg.Vectors
import org.apache.spark.mllib.regression.LabeledPoint

object bayes1 extends App {
```

The HDFS data file is again defined, and a Spark context is created as before:

```
val hdfsServer = "hdfs://localhost:8020"
val hdfsPath   = "/data/spark/nbayes/"
val dataFile = hdfsServer+hdfsPath+"DigitalBreathTestData2013-MALE2a.csv"
val sparkMaster = "spark://loclhost:7077"
val appName = "Naive Bayes 1"
val conf = new SparkConf()
conf.setMaster(sparkMaster)
conf.setAppName(appName)
val sparkCxt = new SparkContext(conf)
```

The raw CSV data is loaded and split by the separator characters. The first column becomes the label (Male/Female) that the data will be classified on. The final columns separated by spaces become the classification features:

```
val csvData = sparkCxt.textFile(dataFile)
val ArrayData = csvData.map {
  csvLine =>
    val colData = csvLine.split(',')
    LabeledPoint(colData(0).toDouble,
                 Vectors.dense(colData(1)
                   .split('')
                   .map(_.toDouble)
                 )
    )
}
```

```
}
```

The data is then randomly divided into training (70%) and testing (30%) datasets:

```
val divData = ArrayData.randomSplit(Array(0.7, 0.3), seed = 13L)
val trainDataSet = divData(0)
val testDataSet = divData(1)
```

The Naive Bayes MLlib function can now be trained using the previous training set. The trained Naive Bayes model, held in the `nbTrained` variable, can then be used to predict the Male/Female result labels against the testing data:

```
val nbTrained = NaiveBayes.train(trainDataSet)
val nbPredict = nbTrained.predict(testDataSet.map(_.features))
```

Given that all of the data already contained labels, the original and predicted labels for the test data can be compared. An accuracy figure can then be computed to determine how accurate the predictions were, by comparing the original labels with the prediction values:

```
val predictionAndLabel = nbPredict.zip(testDataSet.map(_.label))
val accuracy = 100.0 * predictionAndLabel.filter(x => x._1 ==
x._2).count() /
    testDataSet.count()
println( "Accuracy : " + accuracy );
}
```

So, this explains the Scala Naive Bayes code example. It's now time to run the compiled `bayes1` application using `spark-submit` and determine the classification accuracy. The parameters are the same. It's just the class name that has changed:

```
spark-submit \
  --class bayes1 \
  --master spark://hc2nn.semtech-solutions.co.nz:7077 \
  --executor-memory 700M \
  --total-executor-cores 100 \
  /home/hadoop/spark/nbayes/target/scala-2.10/naive-bayes_2.10-1.0.jar
```

The resulting accuracy given by the Spark cluster is just 43 percent, which seems to imply that this data is not suitable for Naive Bayes:

```
Accuracy: 43.30
```

Luckily we'll introduce artificial neural networks later in the chapter, a more powerful classifier. In the next example, we will use K-Means to try to determine what clusters exist within the data. Remember, Naive Bayes needs the data classes to be linearly separable along the class boundaries. With K-Means, it will be possible to determine both: the membership and centroid location of the clusters within the data.

Clustering with K-Means

This example will use the same test data from the previous example, but we will attempt to find clusters in the data using the MLlib K-Means algorithm.

Theory on Clustering

The K-Means algorithm iteratively attempts to determine clusters within the test data by minimizing the distance between the mean value of cluster center vectors, and the new candidate cluster member vectors. The following equation assumes dataset members that range from *X1* to *Xn*; it also assumes *K* cluster sets that range from *S1* to *Sk*, where *K <= n*.

$$\underset{S}{\arg\min} \sum_{i=1}^{K} \sum_{x \in S_i} \left\| X - B_i \right\|^2$$

where B_i is the mean of members of S_i

K-Means in practice

The K-Means MLlib functionality uses the `LabeledPoint` structure to process its data and so it needs numeric input data. As the same data from the last section is being reused, we will not explain the data conversion again. The only change that has been made in data terms in this section, is that processing in HDFS will now take place under the `/data/spark/kmeans/` directory. Additionally, the conversion Scala script for the K-Means example produces a record that is all comma-separated.

The development and processing for the K-Means example has taken place under the /home/hadoop/spark/kmeans directory to separate the work from other development. The sbt configuration file is now called kmeans.sbt and is identical to the last example, except for the project name:

```
name := "K-Means"
```

The code for this section can be found in the software package under chapter7\K-Means. So, looking at the code for kmeans1.scala, which is stored under kmeans/src/main/scala, some similar actions occur. The import statements refer to the Spark context and configuration. This time, however, the K-Means functionality is being imported from MLlib. Additionally, the application class name has been changed for this example to kmeans1:

```
import org.apache.spark.SparkContext
import org.apache.spark.SparkContext._
import org.apache.spark.SparkConf
import org.apache.spark.mllib.linalg.Vectors
import org.apache.spark.mllib.clustering.{KMeans,KMeansModel}

object kmeans1 extends App {
```

The same actions are being taken as in the last example to define the data file--to define the Spark configuration and create a Spark context:

```
val hdfsServer = "hdfs://localhost:8020"
val hdfsPath   = "/data/spark/kmeans/"
val dataFile   = hdfsServer + hdfsPath + "DigitalBreathTestData2013-
MALE2a.csv"
val sparkMaster = "spark://localhost:7077"
val appName = "K-Means 1"
val conf = new SparkConf()
conf.setMaster(sparkMaster)
conf.setAppName(appName)
val sparkCxt = new SparkContext(conf)
```

Next, the CSV data is loaded from the data file and split by comma characters into the VectorData variable:

```
val csvData = sparkCxt.textFile(dataFile)
val VectorData = csvData.map {
  csvLine =>
    Vectors.dense( csvLine.split(',').map(_.toDouble))
}
```

A `KMeans` object is initialized, and the parameters are set to define the number of clusters and the maximum number of iterations to determine them:

```
val kMeans = new KMeans
val numClusters        = 3
val maxIterations      = 50
```

Some default values are defined for the initialization mode, number of runs, and Epsilon, which we needed for the K-Means call but did not vary for the processing. Finally, these parameters were set against the `KMeans` object:

```
val initializationMode = KMeans.K_MEANS_PARALLEL
val numRuns            = 1
val numEpsilon         = 1e-4
kMeans.setK( numClusters )
kMeans.setMaxIterations( maxIterations )
kMeans.setInitializationMode( initializationMode )
kMeans.setRuns( numRuns )
kMeans.setEpsilon( numEpsilon )
```

We cached the training vector data to improve the performance and trained the `KMeans` object using the vector data to create a trained K-Means model:

```
VectorData.cache
val kMeansModel = kMeans.run( VectorData )
```

We have computed the K-Means cost and number of input data rows, and have output the results via `println` statements. The cost value indicates how tightly the clusters are packed and how separate the clusters are:

```
val kMeansCost = kMeansModel.computeCost( VectorData )
println( "Input data rows : " + VectorData.count() )
println( "K-Means Cost    : " + kMeansCost )
```

Next, we have used the K-Means Model to print the cluster centers as vectors for each of the three clusters that were computed:

```
kMeansModel.clusterCenters.foreach{ println }
```

Finally, we use the K-Means model predict function to create a list of cluster membership predictions. We then count these predictions by value to give a count of the data points in each cluster. This shows which clusters are bigger and whether there really are three clusters:

```
val clusterRddInt = kMeansModel.predict( VectorData )
val clusterCount = clusterRddInt.countByValue
  clusterCount.toList.foreach{ println }
```

```
} // end object kmeans1
```

So, in order to run this application, it must be compiled and packaged from the kmeans
subdirectory as the Linux pwd command shows here:

```
[hadoop@hc2nn kmeans]$ pwd
/home/hadoop/spark/kmeans
[hadoop@hc2nn kmeans]$ sbt package
Loading /usr/share/sbt/bin/sbt-launch-lib.bash
[info] Set current project to K-Means (in build
file:/home/hadoop/spark/kmeans/)
[info] Compiling 2 Scala sources to
/home/hadoop/spark/kmeans/target/scala-2.10/classes...
[info] Packaging /home/hadoop/spark/kmeans/target/scala-2.10/k-
means_2.10-1.0.jar ...
[info] Done packaging.
[success] Total time: 20 s, completed Feb 19, 2015 5:02:07 PM
```

Once this packaging is successful, we check HDFS to ensure that the test data is ready. As in
the last example, we convert our data to numeric form using the convert.scala file,
provided in the software package. We will process the DigitalBreathTestData2013-
MALE2a.csv data file in the HDFS directory, /data/spark/kmeans, as follows:

```
[hadoop@hc2nn nbayes]$ hdfs dfs -ls /data/spark/kmeans
Found 3 items
-rw-r--r--   3 hadoop supergroup   24645166 2015-02-05 21:11
/data/spark/kmeans/DigitalBreathTestData2013-MALE2.csv
-rw-r--r--   3 hadoop supergroup    5694226 2015-02-05 21:48
/data/spark/kmeans/DigitalBreathTestData2013-MALE2a.csv
drwxr-xr-x   - hadoop supergroup          0 2015-02-05 21:46
/data/spark/kmeans/result
```

The spark-submit tool is used to run the K-Means application. The only change in this
command is that the class is now kmeans1:

```
spark-submit \
  --class kmeans1 \
  --master spark://localhost:7077 \
  --executor-memory 700M \
  --total-executor-cores 100 \
  /home/hadoop/spark/kmeans/target/scala-2.10/k-means_2.10-1.0.jar
```

The output from the Spark cluster run is shown to be as follows:

```
Input data rows : 467054
K-Means Cost    : 5.40312223450789E7
```

The previous output shows the input data volume, which looks correct; it also shows the K-Means cost value. The cost is based on the **Within Set Sum of Squared Errors (WSSSE)** which basically gives a measure how well the found cluster centroids are matching the distribution of the data points. The better they are matching, the lower the cost. The following link https://datasciencelab.wordpress.com/2013/12/27/finding-the-k-in-k-means-clustering/ explains WSSSE and how to find a good value for **k** in more detail.

Next come the three vectors, which describe the data cluster centers with the correct number of dimensions. Remember that these cluster centroid vectors will have the same number of columns as the original vector data:

```
[0.24698249738061878,1.3015883142472253,0.005830116872250263,2.917374778855
5207,1.156645130895448,3.4400290524342454]
[0.3321793984152627,1.784137241326256,0.007615970459266097,2.58319870759289
17,119.58366028156011,3.8379106085083468]
[0.25247226760684494,1.702510963969387,0.006384899819416975,2.2314042480006
88,52.202897927594805,3.551509158139135]
```

Finally, cluster membership is given for clusters 1 to 3 with cluster 1 (index 0) having the largest membership at 407539 member vectors:

```
(0,407539)
(1,12999)
(2,46516)
```

So, these two examples show how data can be classified and clustered using Naive Bayes and K-Means. What if I want to classify images or more complex patterns, and use a black box approach to classification? The next section examines Spark-based classification using **ANNs**, or **artificial neural networks**.

Artificial neural networks

The following figure shows a simple biological neuron to the left. The neuron has dendrites that receive signals from other neurons. A cell body controls activation, and an axon carries an electrical impulse to the dendrites of other neurons. The artificial neuron to the right has a series of weighted inputs: a summing function that groups the inputs and a **firing mechanism (F(Net))**, which decides whether the inputs have reached a threshold, and, if so, the neuron will fire:

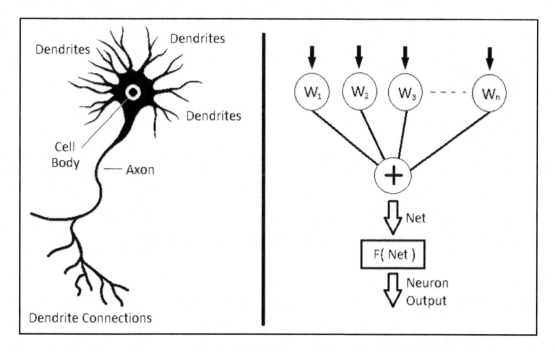

Neural networks are tolerant of noisy images and distortion, and so are useful when a black box classification method is needed for potentially degraded images. The next area to consider is the summation function for the neuron inputs. The following diagram shows the summation function called **Net** for neuron **i**. The connections between the neurons that have the weighting values, contain the stored knowledge of the network. Generally, a network will have an input layer, output layer, and a number of hidden layers. A neuron will fire if the sum of its inputs exceeds a threshold:

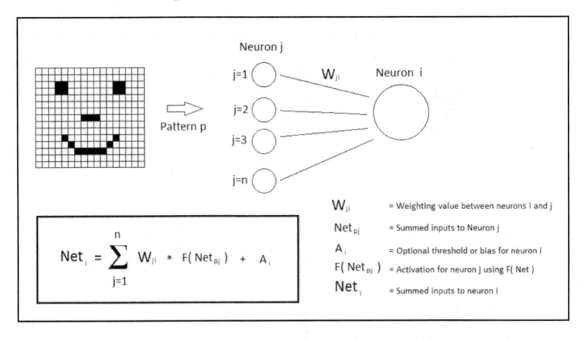

In the previous equation, the diagram and key show that the input values from a pattern **P** are passed to neurons in the input layer of a network. These values become the input layer neuron activation values; they are a special case. The inputs to neuron **i** are the sum of the weighting value for neuron connection **i-j**, multiplied by the activation from neuron **j**. The activation at neuron **j** (if it is not an input layer neuron) is given by **F(Net)**, the squashing function, which will be described next.

A simulated neuron needs a firing mechanism, which decides whether the inputs to the neuron have reached a threshold. Then, it fires to create the activation value for that neuron. This `firing` or `squashing` function can be described by the generalized `sigmoid` function shown in the following figure:

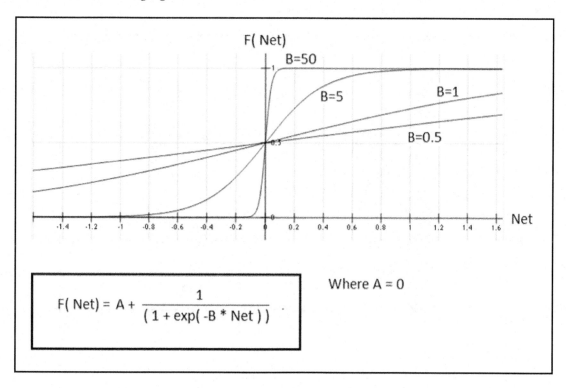

This function has two constants: **A** and **B**; **B** affects the shape of the activation curve as shown in the previous graph. The bigger the value, the more similar a function becomes to an on/off step. The value of **A** sets a minimum for the returned activation. In the previous graph, it is zero.

So, this provides a mechanism to simulate a neuron, create weighting matrices as the neuron connections, and manage the neuron activation. How are the networks organized? The next diagram shows a suggested architecture--the neural network has an input layer of neurons, an output layer, and one or more hidden layers. All neurons in each layer are connected to each neuron in the adjacent layers:

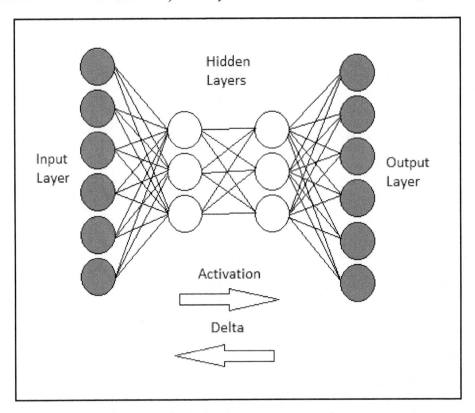

During the training, activation passes from the input layer through the network to the output layer. Then, the error or difference between the expected or actual output causes error deltas to be passed back through the network, altering the weighting matrix values. Once the desired output layer vector is achieved, then the knowledge is stored in the weighting matrices and the network can be further trained or used for classification.

So, the theory behind neural networks has been described in terms of back propagation. Now is the time to obtain some practical knowledge.

ANN in practice

In order to begin ANN training, test data is needed. Given that this type of classification method is supposed to be good at classifying distorted or noisy images, we decided to attempt to classify the images here:

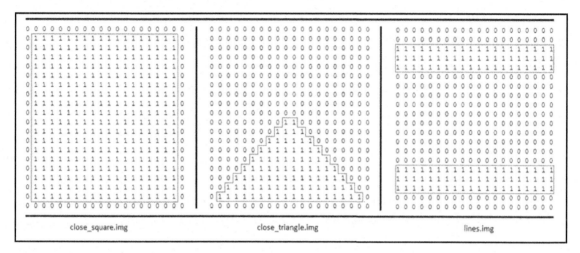

They are hand-crafted text files that contain shaped blocks, created from the characters 1 and 0. When they are stored on HDFS, the carriage return characters are removed so that the image is presented as a single line vector. So, the ANN will be classifying a series of shape images and then will be tested against the same images with noise added to determine whether the classification will still work. There are six training images, and they will each be given an arbitrary training label from 0.1 to 0.6. So, if the ANN is presented with a closed square, it should return a label of 0.1. The following image shows an example of a testing image with noise added.

The noise, created by adding extra zero (0) characters within the image, has been highlighted:

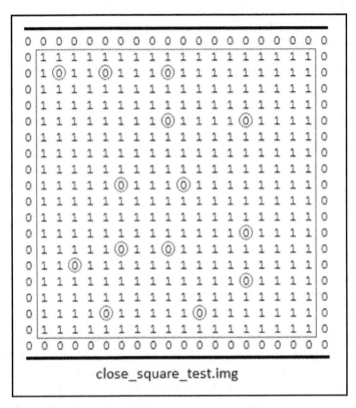

close_square_test.img

As before, the ANN code is developed using the Linux Hadoop account in a subdirectory called spark/ann. The ann.sbt file exists in the ann directory:

```
[hadoop@hc2nn ann]$ pwd
/home/hadoop/spark/ann

[hadoop@hc2nn ann]$ ls
ann.sbt    project src target
```

The contents of the ann.sbt file have been changed to use full paths of JAR library files for the Spark dependencies:

```
name := "A N N"
version := "1.0"
scalaVersion := "2.11.2"
libraryDependencies += "org.apache.hadoop" % "hadoop-client" % "2.8.1"
```

```
libraryDependencies += "org.apache.spark" % "spark-core" % "2.6.0"
libraryDependencies += "org.apache.spark" % "spark-mllib" % "2.1.1"
libraryDependencies += "org.apache.spark" % "akka" % "2.5.3"
```

As in the previous examples, the actual Scala code to be compiled exists in a subdirectory named src/main/scala. We have created two Scala programs. The first trains using the input data and then tests the ANN model with the same input data. The second tests the trained model with noisy data to test the distorted data classification:

```
[hadoop@hc2nn scala]$ pwd
/home/hadoop/spark/ann/src/main/scala
[hadoop@hc2nn scala]$ ls
test_ann1.scala test_ann2.scala
```

We will examine the first Scala file and then we will just show the extra features of the second file, as the two examples are very similar up to the point of training the ANN. The code examples shown here can be found in the software package provided with this book under the path, chapter2\ANN. So, to examine the first Scala example, the import statements are similar to the previous examples. The Spark context, configuration, vectors, and LabeledPoint are being imported. The RDD class for RDD processing is being imported this time, along with the new ANN class, ANNClassifier. Note that the MLlib/classification routines widely use the LabeledPoint structure for input data, which will contain the features and labels that are supposed to be trained against:

```
import org.apache.spark.SparkContext
import org.apache.spark.SparkContext._
import org.apache.spark.SparkConf
import org.apache.spark.mllib.classification.ANNClassifier
import org.apache.spark.mllib.regression.LabeledPoint
import org.apache.spark.mllib.linalg.Vectors
import org.apache.spark.mllib.linalg._
import org.apache.spark.rdd.RDD

object testann1 extends App {
```

The application class in this example has been called testann1. The HDFS files to be processed have been defined in terms of the HDFS server, path, and file name:

```
val server = "hdfs://localhost:8020"
val path   = "/data/spark/ann/"

val data1 = server + path + "close_square.img"
val data2 = server + path + "close_triangle.img"
val data3 = server + path + "lines.img"
val data4 = server + path + "open_square.img"
val data5 = server + path + "open_triangle.img"
```

```
val data6 = server + path + "plus.img"
```

The Spark context has been created with the URL for the Spark instance, which now has a different port number--8077. The application name is ANN 1. This will appear on the Spark web UI when the application is run:

```
val sparkMaster = "spark://localhost:8077"
val appName = "ANN 1"
val conf = new SparkConf()

conf.setMaster(sparkMaster)
conf.setAppName(appName)

val sparkCxt = new SparkContext(conf)
```

The HDFS-based input training and test data files are loaded. The values on each line are split by space characters, and the numeric values have been converted into doubles. The variables that contain this data are then stored in an array called **inputs**. At the same time, an array called outputs is created, containing the labels from 0.1 to 0.6. These values will be used to classify the input patterns:

```
val rData1 = sparkCxt.textFile(data1).map(_.split("
")).map(_.toDouble)).collect
val rData2 = sparkCxt.textFile(data2).map(_.split("
")).map(_.toDouble)).collect
val rData3 = sparkCxt.textFile(data3).map(_.split("
")).map(_.toDouble)).collect
val rData4 = sparkCxt.textFile(data4).map(_.split("
")).map(_.toDouble)).collect
val rData5 = sparkCxt.textFile(data5).map(_.split("
")).map(_.toDouble)).collect
val rData6 = sparkCxt.textFile(data6).map(_.split("
")).map(_.toDouble)).collect
val inputs = Array[Array[Double]] (
    rData1(0), rData2(0), rData3(0), rData4(0), rData5(0), rData6(0) )
val outputs = Array[Double]( 0.1, 0.2, 0.3, 0.4, 0.5, 0.6 )
```

The input and output data, representing the input data features and labels, are then combined and converted into a LabeledPoint structure. Finally, the data is parallelised in order to partition it for optimal parallel processing:

```
val ioData = inputs.zip( outputs )
val lpData = ioData.map{ case(features, label) =>

  LabeledPoint( label, Vectors.dense(features) )
}
val rddData = sparkCxt.parallelize( lpData )
```

Variables are created to define the hidden layer topology of the ANN. In this case, we have chosen to have two hidden layers, each with 100 neurons. The maximum number of iterations is defined as well as a batch size (six patterns) and convergence tolerance. The tolerance refers to how big the training error can get before we can consider training to have worked. Then, an ANN model is created using these configuration parameters and the input data:

```
val hiddenTopology : Array[Int] = Array( 100, 100 )
val maxNumIterations = 1000
val convTolerance    = 1e-4
val batchSize        = 6
val annModel = ANNClassifier.train(rddData,
                                   batchSize,
                                   hiddenTopology,
                                   maxNumIterations,
                                   convTolerance)
```

In order to test the trained ANN model, the same input training data is used as testing data to obtain prediction labels. First, an input data variable is created called `rPredictData`. Then, the data is partitioned and, finally, the predictions are obtained using the trained ANN model. For this model to work, it must output the labels, `0.1` to `0.6`:

```
val rPredictData = inputs.map{ case(features) =>
  ( Vectors.dense(features) )
}
val rddPredictData = sparkCxt.parallelize( rPredictData )
val predictions = annModel.predict( rddPredictData )
```

The label predictions are printed and the script closes with a closing bracket:

```
predictions.toArray().foreach( value => println( "prediction > " + value )
)
} // end ann1
```

So, in order to run this code sample, it must first be compiled and packaged. By now, you must be familiar with the `sbt` command, executed from the `ann` subdirectory:

```
[hadoop@hc2nn ann]$ pwd
/home/hadoop/spark/ann
[hadoop@hc2nn ann]$ sbt package
```

The `spark-submit` command is then used from within the new `spark/spark` path using the new Spark-based URL at port `8077` to run the application, `testann1`:

```
/home/hadoop/spark/spark/bin/spark-submit \
  --class testann1 \
  --master spark://localhost:8077 \
```

```
--executor-memory 700M \
--total-executor-cores 100 \
/home/hadoop/spark/ann/target/scala-2.10/a-n-n_2.10-1.0.jar
```

By checking the Apache Spark web URL at `http://localhost:19080/`, it is now possible to see the application running. The following figure shows the `ANN 1` application running as well as the previously completed executions:

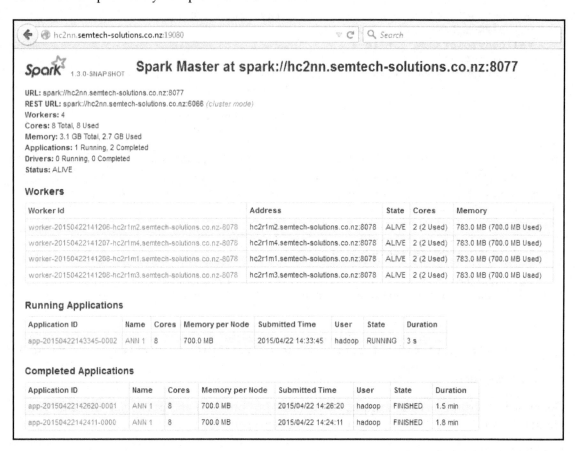

By selecting one of the cluster host worker instances, it is possible to see a list of executors that actually carry out cluster processing for that worker:

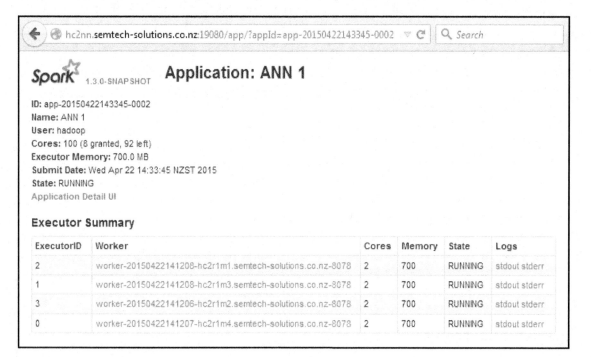

Finally, by selecting one of the executors, it is possible to see its history and configuration as well as links to the log file and error information. At this level, with the log information provided, debugging is possible. These log files can be checked to process error messages:

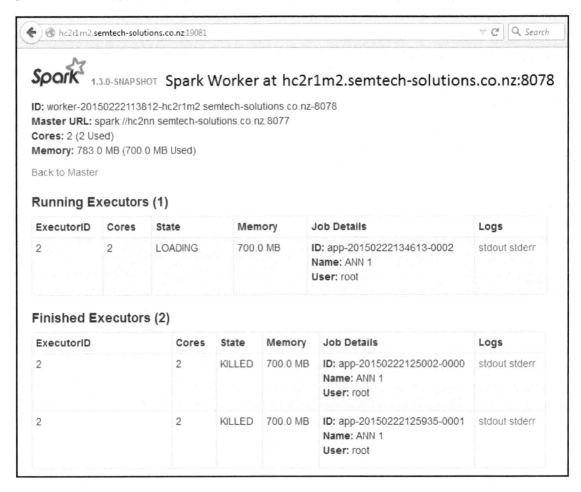

The ANN 1 application provides the following output to show that it has reclassified the same input data correctly. The reclassification has been successful as each of the input patterns has been given the same label that it was trained with:

```
prediction > 0.1
prediction > 0.2
prediction > 0.3
prediction > 0.4
prediction > 0.5
prediction > 0.6
```

So, this shows that ANN training and test prediction will work with the same data. Now, we will train with the same data, but test with distorted or noisy data, an example of which we already demonstrated. This example can be found in the file called `test_ann2.scala` in your software package. It is very similar to the first example, so we will just demonstrate the changed code. The application is now called `testann2`:

```
object testann2 extends App
```

An extra set of testing data is created, after the ANN model has been created using the training data. This testing data contains noise:

```
val tData1 = server + path + "close_square_test.img"
val tData2 = server + path + "close_triangle_test.img"
val tData3 = server + path + "lines_test.img"
val tData4 = server + path + "open_square_test.img"
val tData5 = server + path + "open_triangle_test.img"
val tData6 = server + path + "plus_test.img"
```

This data is processed into input arrays and partitioned for cluster processing:

```
val rtData1 = sparkCxt.textFile(tData1).map(_.split("
").map(_.toDouble)).collect
val rtData2 = sparkCxt.textFile(tData2).map(_.split("
").map(_.toDouble)).collect
val rtData3 = sparkCxt.textFile(tData3).map(_.split("
").map(_.toDouble)).collect
val rtData4 = sparkCxt.textFile(tData4).map(_.split("
").map(_.toDouble)).collect
val rtData5 = sparkCxt.textFile(tData5).map(_.split("
").map(_.toDouble)).collect
val rtData6 = sparkCxt.textFile(tData6).map(_.split("
").map(_.toDouble)).collect
val tInputs = Array[Array[Double]] (
    rtData1(0), rtData2(0), rtData3(0), rtData4(0), rtData5(0), rtData6(0)
)

val rTestPredictData = tInputs.map{ case(features) => (
Vectors.dense(features) ) }
val rddTestPredictData = sparkCxt.parallelize( rTestPredictData )
```

It is then used to generate label predictions in the same way as the first example. If the model classifies the data correctly, then the same label values should be printed from `0.1` to `0.6`:

```
val testPredictions = annModel.predict( rddTestPredictData )
testPredictions.toArray().foreach( value => println( "test prediction > "
+ value ) )
```

The code has already been compiled, so it can be run using the `spark-submit` command:

```
/home/hadoop/spark/spark/bin/spark-submit \
  --class testann2 \
  --master spark://localhost:8077 \
  --executor-memory 700M \
  --total-executor-cores 100 \
  /home/hadoop/spark/ann/target/scala-2.10/a-n-n_2.10-1.0.jar
```

Here is the cluster output from this script, which shows a successful classification using a trained ANN model and some noisy test data. The noisy data has been classified correctly. For instance, if the trained model had become confused, it might have given a value of 0.15 for the noisy `close_square_test.img` test image in position one, instead of returning `0.1` as it did:

```
test prediction > 0.1
test prediction > 0.2
test prediction > 0.3
test prediction > 0.4
test prediction > 0.5
test prediction > 0.6
```

Summary

This chapter has attempted to provide you with an overview of some of the functionality available within the Apache Spark MLlib module. It has also shown the functionality that will soon be available in terms of ANNs or artificial neural networks. You might have been impressed how well ANNs work, so there is a lot more on ANNs in a later Chapter covering DeepLearning. It is not possible to cover all the areas of MLlib due to the time and space allowed for this chapter. In addition, we now want to concentrate more on the SparkML library in the next chapter, which speeds up machine learning by supporting DataFrames and the underlying Catalyst and Tungsten optimizations.

We saw how to develop Scala-based examples for Naive Bayes classification, K-Means clustering, and ANNs. You learned how to prepare test data for these Spark MLlib routines. You also saw that they all accept the `LabeledPoint` structure, which contains features and labels.

Additionally, each approach takes a training and prediction step to training and testing a model using different datasets. Using the approach shown in this chapter, you can now investigate the remaining functionality in the MLlib library. You can refer to `http://spark.apache.org/` and ensure that you refer to the correct version when checking documentation.

Having examined the Apache Spark MLlib machine learning library in this chapter, it is now time to consider Apache Spark's SparkML. The next chapter will examine machine learning on top of DataFrames.

8
Apache SparkML

So now that you've learned a lot about MLlib, why another ML API? First of all, it is a common task in data science to work with multiple frameworks and ML libraries as there are always advantages and disadvantages; mostly, it is a trade-off between performance and functionality. R, for instance, is the king when it comes to functionality--there exist more than 6000 R add-on packages. However, R is also one of the slowest execution environments for data science. SparkML, on the other hand, currently has relatively limited functionality but is one of the fastest libraries. Why is this so? This brings us to the second reason why SparkML exists.

The duality between RDD on the one hand and DataFrames and Datasets on the other is like a red thread in this book and doesn't stop influencing the machine learning chapters. As MLlib is designed to work on top of RDDs, SparkML works on top of DataFrames and Datasets, therefore making use of all the new performance benefits that Catalyst and Tungsten bring.

We will cover the following topics in this chapter:

- Introduction to the SparkML API
- The concept of pipelines
- Transformers and estimators
- A working example

What does the new API look like?

When it comes to machine learning on Apache Spark, we are used to transforming data into an appropriate format and data types before we actually feed them to our algorithms. Machine learning practitioners around the globe discovered that the preprocessing tasks on a machine learning project usually follow the same pattern:

- Data preparation
- Training
- Evaluating
- Hyperparameter tuning

Therefore, the new ApacheSparkML API supports this process out of the box. It is called **pipelines** and is inspired by scikit-learn http://scikit-learn.org, a very popular machine learning library for the Python programming language. The central data structure is a DataFrame and all operations run on top of it.

The concept of pipelines

ApacheSparkML pipelines have the following components:

- **DataFrame**: This is the central data store where all the original data and intermediate results are stored in.
- **Transformer**: As the name suggests, a transformer transforms one DataFrame into another by adding additional (feature) columns in most of the cases. Transformers are stateless, which means that they don't have any internal memory and behave exactly the same each time they are used; this is a concept you might be familiar with when using the map function of RDDs.
- **Estimator**: In most of the cases, an estimator is some sort of machine learning model. In contrast to a transformer, an estimator contains an internal state representation and is highly dependent on the history of the data that it has already seen.
- **Pipeline**: This is the glue which is joining the preceding components, DataFrame, Transformer and Estimator, together.
- **Parameter**: Machine learning algorithms have many knobs to tweak. These are called **hyperparameters** and the values learned by a machine learning algorithm to fit data are called parameters. By standardizing how hyperparameters are expressed, ApacheSparkML opens doors to task automation, as we will see later.

Transformers

Let's start with something simple. One of the most common tasks in machine learning data preparation is string indexing and one-hot encoding of categorical values. Let's see how this can be done.

String indexer

Let's assume that we have a DataFrame `df` containing a column called color of categorical labels--red, green, and blue. We want to encode them as integer or float values. This is where `org.apache.spark.ml.feature.StringIndexer` kicks in. It automatically determines the cardinality of the category set and assigns each one a distinct value. So in our example, a list of categories such as red, red, green, red, blue, green should be transformed into 1, 1, 2, 1, 3, 2:

```
import org.apache.spark.ml.feature.StringIndexer
var indexer = new StringIndexer()
  .setInputCol("colors")
  .setOutputCol("colorsIndexed")

var indexed = indexer.fit(df).transform(df)
```

The result of this transformation is a DataFrame called indexed that, in addition to the colors column of the String type, now contains a column called `colorsIndexed` of type double.

OneHotEncoder

We are only halfway through. Although machine learning algorithms are capable of making use of the `colorsIndexed` column, they perform better if we one-hot encode it. This actually means that, instead of having a `colorsIndexed` column containing label indexes between one and three, it is better if we have three columns--one for each color--with the constraint that every row is allowed to set only one of these columns to one, otherwise zero. Let's do it:

```
var encoder = new OneHotEncoder()
  .setInputCol("colorIndexed")
  .setOutputCol("colorVec")

var encoded = encoder.transform(indexed)
```

Intuitively, we would expect that we get three additional columns in the encoded DataFrame, for example, `colorIndexedRed`, `colorIndexedGreen`, and `colorIndexedBlue`. However, this is not the case. In contrast, we just get one additional column in the DataFrame and its type is `org.apache.spark.ml.linalg.Vector`. It uses its internal representation and we basically don't have to care about it, as all ApacheSparkML transformers and estimators are compatible to that format.

VectorAssembler

Before we start with the actual machine learning algorithm, we need to apply one final transformation. We have to create one additional `feature` column containing all the information of the columns that we want the machine learning algorithm to consider. This is done by `org.apache.spark.ml.feature.VectorAssembler` as follows:

```
import org.apache.spark.ml.feature.VectorAssembler
vectorAssembler = new VectorAssembler()
        .setInputCols(Array("colorVec", "field2", "field3","field4"))
        .setOutputCol("features")
```

This transformer adds only one single column to the resulting DataFrame called **features**, which is of the `org.apache.spark.ml.linalg.Vector` type. In other words, this new column called features, created by the `VectorAssembler`, contains all the defined columns (in this case, `colorVec`, `field2`, `field3`, and `field4`) encoded in a single vector object for each row. This is the format the Apache SparkML algorithms are happy with.

Pipelines

Before we dive into estimators--we've already used one in `StringIndexer`--let's first understand the concept of pipelines. As you might have noticed, the transformers add only one single column to a DataFrame and basically omit all other columns not explicitly specified as input columns; they can only be used in conjunction with `org.apache.spark.ml.Pipeline`, which glues individual transformers (and estimators) together to form a complete data analysis process. So let's do this for our two `Pipeline` stages:

```
var transformers = indexer :: encoder :: vectorAssembler :: Nil
var pipeline = new Pipeline().setStages(transformers).fit(df)
var transformed = pipeline.transform(df)
```

The now obtained DataFrame called **transformed** contains all the original columns plus the columns added by the `indexer` and `encoder` stages. This is the way in which ApacheSparkML data processing jobs are defined.

Estimators

We've used estimators before in `StringIndexer`. We've already stated that estimators somehow contain state that changes while looking at data, whereas this is not the case for transformers. So why is `StringIndexer` an estimator? This is because it needs to remember all the previously seen strings and maintain a mapping table between strings and label indexes.

 In machine learning, it is common to use at least a training and testing subset of your available training data. It can happen that an estimator in the pipeline, such as `StringIndexer`, has not seen all the string labels while looking at the training dataset. Therefore, you'll get an exception when evaluating the model using the test dataset as the `StringIndexer` now encounters labels that it has not seen before. This is, in fact, a very rare case and basically could mean that the sample function you use to separate the training and testing datasets is not working; however, there is an option called `setHandleInvalid("skip")` and your problem is solved.

Another easy way to distinguish between an estimator and a transformer is the additional method called `fit` on the estimators. Fit actually populates the internal data management structure of the estimators based on a given dataset, which, in the case of `StringIndexer`, is the mapping table between label strings and label indexes. So now let's take a look at another estimator, an actual machine learning algorithm.

RandomForestClassifier

Let's assume that we are in a binary classification problem setting and want to use `RandomForestClassifier`. All SparkML algorithms have a compatible API, so they can be used interchangeably. So it really doesn't matter which one we use, but `RandomForestClassifier` has more (hyper)parameters than more simple models like logistic regression. At a later stage we'll use (hyper)parameter tuning which is also inbuilt in Apache SparkML. Therefore it makes sense to use an algorithm where more knobs can be tweaked. Adding such a binary classifier to our `Pipeline` is very simple:

```
import org.apache.spark.ml.classification.RandomForestClassifier
```

```
var rf = new RandomForestClassifier()
  .setLabelCol("label")
  .setFeaturesCol("features")

var model = new Pipeline().setStages(transformers :+ rf).fit(df)

var result = model.transform(df)
```

As you can see, RandomForestClassifier takes two parameters: the column name of the actual labels (remember that we are in a supervised learning setting) and the features that we've created before. All other parameters are default values and we'll take care of them later. We can just add this machine learning model as a final stage to the Pipeline: transformers :+ rf. Then, we call fit and transform--always passing our DataFrame as a parameter--and we obtain a final DataFrame called result, which basically contains everything from the df DataFrame plus an additional column called predictions. Done! We've created our first machine learning Pipeline with Apache SparkML. Now, we want to check how well we are doing against our test dataset. This is also built-in to Apache SparkML.

Model evaluation

As mentioned before, model evaluation is built-in to ApacheSparkML and you'll find all that you need in the org.apache.spark.ml.evaluation package. Let's continue with our binary classification. This means that we'll have to use org.apache.spark.ml.evaluation.BinaryClassificationEvaluator:

```
import org.apache.spark.ml.evaluation.BinaryClassificationEvaluator
val evaluator = new BinaryClassificationEvaluator()

import org.apache.spark.ml.param.ParamMap
var evaluatorParamMap = ParamMap(evaluator.metricName -> "areaUnderROC")
var aucTraining = evaluator.evaluate(result, evaluatorParamMap)
```

To code previous initialized a BinaryClassificationEvaluator function and tells it to calculate the areaUnderROC, one of the many possible metrics to assess the prediction performance of a machine learning algorithm.

As we have the actual label and the prediction present in a DataFrame called result, it is simple to calculate this score and is done using the following line of code:

```
var aucTraining = evaluator.evaluate(result, evaluatorParamMap)
```

CrossValidation and hyperparameter tuning

We will be looking at one example each of CrossValidation and hyperparameter tuning. Let's take a look at CrossValidation.

CrossValidation

As stated before, we've used the default parameters of the machine learning algorithm and we don't know if they are a good choice. In addition, instead of simply splitting your data into training and testing, or training, testing, and validation sets, CrossValidation might be a better choice because it makes sure that eventually all the data is seen by the machine learning algorithm.

CrossValidation basically splits your complete available training data into a number of **k** folds. This parameter **k** can be specified. Then, the whole Pipeline is run once for every fold and one machine learning model is trained for each fold. Finally, the different machine learning models obtained are joined. This is done by a voting scheme for classifiers or by averaging for regression.

The following figure illustrates ten-fold CrossValidation:

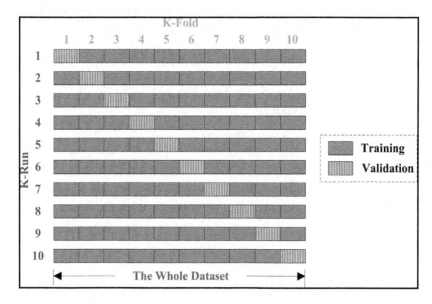

Hyperparameter tuning

`CrossValidation` is often used in conjunction with so-called (hyper)parameter tuning. What are hyperparameters? These are the various knobs that you can tweak on your machine learning algorithm. For example, these are some parameters of the Random Forest classifier:

- Number of trees
- Feature subset strategy
- Impurity
- Maximal number of bins
- Maximal tree depth

Setting these parameters can have a significant influence on the performance of the trained classifier. Often, there is no way of choosing them based on a clear recipe--of course, experience helps--but hyperparameter tuning is considered as black magic. Can't we just choose many different parameters and test the prediction performance? Of course we can. This feature is also inbuilt in Apache SparkML. The only thing to consider is that such a search can be quite exhaustive. So luckily, Apache Spark is a linearly scalable infrastructure and we can test multiple models very fast.

 Note that the hyperparameters form an n-dimensional space where n is the number of hyperparameters. Every point in this space is one particular hyperparameter configuration, which is a hyperparameter vector. Of course, we can't explore every point in this space, so what we basically do is a grid search over a (hopefully evenly distributed) subset in that space.

All of this is completely integrated and standardized in Apache SparkML; isn't that great? Let's take a look at the following code:

```
import org.apache.spark.ml.param.ParamMap
import org.apache.spark.ml.tuning.{CrossValidator, ParamGridBuilder}
var paramGrid = new ParamGridBuilder()
    .addGrid(rf.numTrees, 3 :: 5 :: 10 :: Nil)
    .addGrid(rf.featureSubsetStrategy, "auto" :: "all" :: Nil)
    .addGrid(rf.impurity, "gini" :: "entropy" :: Nil)
    .addGrid(rf.maxBins, 2 :: 5 :: Nil)
    .addGrid(rf.maxDepth, 3 :: 5 :: Nil)
    .build()
```

In order to perform such a grid search over the hyperparameter space, we need to define it first. Here, the functional programming properties of Scala are quite handy because we just add function pointers and the respective parameters to be evaluated to the parameter grid:

```
var crossValidator = new CrossValidator()
      .setEstimator(new Pipeline().setStages(transformers :+ rf))
      .setEstimatorParamMaps(paramGrid)
      .setNumFolds(5)
.setEvaluator(evaluator)
```

Then we create a `CrossValidator`. Note that in the `setEstimator` method of the `CrossValidator` object, we set our existing `Pipeline`. We are able to do so since the Pipeline by itself turns out to be an estimator as it extends from it. In the `setEstimatorParamMaps` method we set our parameter grid. Finally, we define the number of folds used for `CrossValidation`, pass an instance of our `BinaryClassificationEvaluator`, and we are done:

```
var crossValidatorModel = crossValidator.fit(df)
```

Although there is so much stuff going on behind the scenes, the interface to our `CrossValidator` object stays slim and well-known as `CrossValidator` also extends from `Estimator` and supports the `fit` method. This means that, after calling fit, the complete predefined `Pipeline`, including all feature preprocessing and the RandomForest classifier, is executed multiple times--each time with a different hyperparameter vector.

So let's do some math. How many RandomForest models are executed once this code has run? Basically, this is a number exponentially dependent on the number of parameters to be evaluated and the different parameter values for each parameter. In this case, we have five parameters with parameter values ranging between 2 and 3. So the math is as simple as this: $3 * 2 * 2 * 2 = 24$. 24 models have completed, and by just adding additional parameters or parameter values, this number always doubles. So here we are really happy to run on a linearly scalable infrastructure!

So let's evaluate the result:

```
var newPredictions = crossValidatorModel.transform(df)
```

As `CrossValidator` is an `Estimator` returning a model of the `CrossValidatorModel` type, we can use it as an ordinary Apache SparkML model by just calling transform on it in order to obtain predictions. The `CrossValidatorModel` automatically chooses the learned hyperparameters of the underlying model (in this case, `RandomForestClassifier`) to do the prediction. In order to check how well we are doing, we can run our `evaluator` again:

```
evaluator.evaluate(newPredictions, evaluatorParamMap)
```

In case we are curious and want to know the optimal parameters, we can pull the stages from the `Pipeline` and check on the parameters used:

```
var bestModel = crossValidatorModel.bestModel
var bestPipelineModel =
crossValidatorModel.bestModel.asInstanceOf[PipelineModel]
var stages = bestPipelineModel.stages
```

Then we pull `RandomForestClassificationModel` from the best stage and check on the parameters:

```
import org.apache.spark.ml.classification.RandomForestClassificationModel
val rfStage =
stages(stages.length-1).asInstanceOf[RandomForestClassificationModel]
rfStage.getNumTrees
rfStage.getFeatureSubsetStrategy
rfStage.getImpurity
rfStage.getMaxBins
rfStage.getMaxDepth
```

This is enough of theory and it is impossible to cover all transformers, estimators, and helper functions of Apache SparkML but we think this is a very good start. So let's conclude this chapter with a practical example.

The illustrated image is a good example of the pipeline we want to implement:

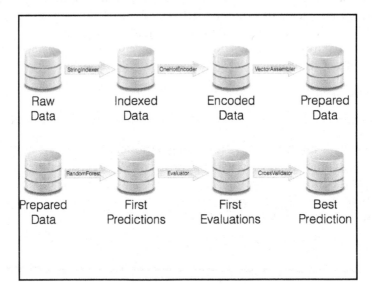

Winning a Kaggle competition with Apache SparkML

Winning a Kaggle competition is an art by itself, but we just want to show you how the Apache SparkML tooling can be used efficiently to do so.

We'll use an archived competition for this offered by BOSCH, a German multinational engineering and electronics company, on production line performance data. Details for the competition data can be found at `https://www.kaggle.com/c/bosch-production-line-performance/data`.

Data preparation

The challenge data comes in three ZIP packages but we only use two of them. One contains categorical data, one contains continuous data, and the last one contains timestamps of measurements, which we will ignore for now.

If you extract the data, you'll get three large CSV files. So the first thing that we want to do is re-encode them into parquet in order to be more space-efficient:

```
def convert(filePrefix : String) = {
   val basePath = "yourBasePath"
   var df = spark
              .read
              .option("header",true)
              .option("inferSchema", "true")
              .csv("basePath+filePrefix+".csv")
    df = df.repartition(1)
    df.write.parquet(basePath+filePrefix+".parquet")
}

convert("train_numeric")
convert("train_date")
convert("train_categorical")
```

First, we define a function convert that just reads the .csv file and rewrites it as a .parquet file. As you can see, this saves a lot of space:

train_date.csv	11 Aug 2016, 18:12	2.89 GB	comma-separated values
train_categorical.csv	11 Aug 2016, 17:50	2.68 GB	comma-separated values
train_numeric.csv	11 Aug 2016, 17:41	2.14 GB	comma-separated values
train_date.parquet	26 Apr 2017, 16:52	890.5 MB	Document
train_numeric.parquet	26 Apr 2017, 16:27	257.4 MB	Document
train_categorical.parquet	26 Apr 2017, 17:06	40.6 MB	Document

Now we read the files in again as DataFrames from the parquet files:

```
var df_numeric = spark.read.parquet(basePath+"train_numeric.parquet")

var df_categorical =
spark.read.parquet(basePath+"train_categorical.parquet")
```

Here is the output of the same:

```
scala> var df_numeric = spark.read.parquet(basePath+"train_numeric.parquet")
df_numeric: org.apache.spark.sql.DataFrame = [Id: int, L0_S0_F0: double ... 968 more fields]

scala>

scala> var df_date = spark.read.parquet(basePath+"train_date.parquet")
df_date: org.apache.spark.sql.DataFrame = [Id: int, L0_S0_D1: double ... 1155 more fields]

scala>

scala> var df_categorical = spark.read.parquet(basePath+"train_categorical.parquet")
df_categorical: org.apache.spark.sql.DataFrame = [Id: int, L0_S1_F25: string ... 2139 more fields]
```

This is very high-dimensional data; therefore, we will take only a subset of the columns for this illustration:

```
df_categorical.createOrReplaceTempView("dfcat")
var dfcat = spark.sql("select Id, L0_S22_F545 from dfcat")
```

In the following picture, you can see the unique categorical values of that column:

```
scala> dfcat.select("L0_S22_F545").distinct.show
+-----------+
|L0_S22_F545|
+-----------+
|        T16|
|   T12582912|
|       null|
|      T48576|
|   T16777232|
|        T512|
|     T589824|
|       T1372|
|          T8|
|   T16777557|
|         T32|
|       T6553|
|   T-18748192|
|         T96|
+-----------+
```

Now let's do the same with the numerical dataset:

```
df_numeric.createOrReplaceTempView("dfnum")
var dfnum = spark.sql("select Id,L0_S0_F0,L0_S0_F2,L0_S0_F4,Response from
dfnum")
```

Here is the output of the same:

```
scala> dfnum.show
+---+--------+--------+--------+--------+
| Id|L0_S0_F0|L0_S0_F2|L0_S0_F4|Response|
+---+--------+--------+--------+--------+
|  4|    0.03|  -0.034|  -0.197|       0|
|  6|    null|    null|    null|       0|
|  7|   0.088|   0.086|   0.003|       0|
|  9|  -0.036|  -0.064|   0.294|       0|
| 11|  -0.055|  -0.086|   0.294|       0|
| 13|   0.003|   0.019|   0.294|       0|
| 14|    null|    null|    null|       0|
| 16|    null|    null|    null|       0|
| 18|  -0.016|  -0.041|  -0.179|       0|
| 23|    null|    null|    null|       0|
| 26|   0.016|   0.093|  -0.015|       0|
| 27|  -0.062|  -0.153|  -0.197|       0|
| 28|  -0.075|  -0.093|   0.367|       0|
| 31|  -0.003|  -0.093|  -0.161|       0|
| 34|  -0.016|  -0.138|  -0.197|       0|
| 38|   0.252|    0.25|   0.003|       0|
| 41|    null|    null|    null|       0|
| 44|  -0.016|  -0.041|   0.003|       0|
| 47|    null|    null|    null|       0|
| 49|   0.088|   0.033|    0.33|       0|
+---+--------+--------+--------+--------+
only showing top 20 rows
```

Finally, we rejoin these two relations:

```
var df = dfcat.join(dfnum,"Id")
df.createOrReplaceTempView("df")
```

Then we have to do some NA treatment:

```
var df_notnull = spark.sql("""
select
    Response as label,
    case
        when L0_S22_F545 is null then 'NA'
        else L0_S22_F545 end as L0_S22_F545,
    case
        when L0_S0_F0 is null then 0.0
        else L0_S0_F0 end as L0_S0_F0,
    case
        when L0_S0_F2 is null then 0.0
        else L0_S0_F2 end as L0_S0_F2,
    case
        when L0_S0_F4 is null then 0.0
        else L0_S0_F4 end as L0_S0_F4
from df
""")
```

Feature engineering

Now it is time to run the first transformer (which is actually an estimator). It is `StringIndexer` and needs to keep track of an internal mapping table between strings and indexes. Therefore, it is not a transformer but an estimator:

```
import org.apache.spark.ml.feature.{OneHotEncoder, StringIndexer}

var indexer = new StringIndexer()
  .setHandleInvalid("skip")
  .setInputCol("L0_S22_F545")
  .setOutputCol("L0_S22_F545Index")

var indexed = indexer.fit(df_notnull).transform(df_notnull)
indexed.printSchema
```

As we can see clearly in the following image, an additional column called `L0_S22_F545Index` has been created:

```
root
 |-- label: integer (nullable = true)
 |-- L0_S22_F545: string (nullable = true)
 |-- L0_S0_F0: double (nullable = true)
 |-- L0_S0_F2: double (nullable = true)
 |-- L0_S0_F4: double (nullable = true)
 |-- L0_S22_F545Index: double (nullable = true)
```

Finally, let's examine some content of the newly created column and compare it with the source column.

We can clearly see how the category string gets transformed into a float index:

```
scala> indexed.select("L0_S22_F545","L0_S22_F545Index").distinct.show
+-----------+----------------+
|L0_S22_F545|L0_S22_F545Index|
+-----------+----------------+
|  T12582912|             6.0|
|      T1372|            10.0|
|        T16|             7.0|
|        T32|             9.0|
|     T48576|             2.0|
| T-18748192|             8.0|
|         NA|             0.0|
|  T16777557|             1.0|
|  T16777232|            11.0|
|         T8|             4.0|
|       T512|             3.0|
|    T589824|            13.0|
|      T6553|            12.0|
|        T96|             5.0|
+-----------+----------------+
```

Now we want to apply OneHotEncoder, which is a transformer, in order to generate better features for our machine learning model:

```
var encoder = new OneHotEncoder()
  .setInputCol("L0_S22_F545Index")
  .setOutputCol("L0_S22_F545Vec")

var encoded = encoder.transform(indexed)
```

As you can see in the following figure, the newly created column `L0_S22_F545Vec` contains `org.apache.spark.ml.linalg.SparseVector` objects, which is a compressed representation of a sparse vector:

```
scala> encoded.select("L0_S22_F545Index","L0_S22_F545Vec").distinct.show
+----------------+---------------+
|L0_S22_F545Index| L0_S22_F545Vec|
+----------------+---------------+
|            11.0|(13,[11],[1.0])|
|             2.0| (13,[2],[1.0])|
|             8.0| (13,[8],[1.0])|
|             3.0| (13,[3],[1.0])|
|            10.0|(13,[10],[1.0])|
|             6.0| (13,[6],[1.0])|
|             7.0| (13,[7],[1.0])|
|            12.0|(13,[12],[1.0])|
|             9.0| (13,[9],[1.0])|
|             4.0| (13,[4],[1.0])|
|             5.0| (13,[5],[1.0])|
|             0.0| (13,[0],[1.0])|
|             1.0| (13,[1],[1.0])|
|            13.0|     (13,[],[])|
+----------------+---------------+
```

Sparse vector representations: The `OneHotEncoder`, as many other algorithms, returns a sparse vector of the `org.apache.spark.ml.linalg.SparseVector` type as, according to the definition, only one element of the vector can be one, the rest has to remain zero. This gives a lot of opportunity for compression as only the position of the elements that are non-zero has to be known. Apache Spark uses a sparse vector representation in the following format: *(l,[p],[v])*, where *l* stands for length of the vector, *p* for position (this can also be an array of positions), and *v* for the actual values (this can be an array of values). So if we get (13,[10],[1.0]), as in our earlier example, the actual sparse vector looks like this: (0.0,0.0,0.0,0.0,0.0,0.0,0.0,0.0,0.0,0.0,1.0,0.0,0.0,0.0).

So now that we are done with our feature engineering, we want to create one overall sparse vector containing all the necessary columns for our machine learner. This is done using `VectorAssembler`:

```
import org.apache.spark.ml.feature.VectorAssembler
import org.apache.spark.ml.linalg.Vectors

var vectorAssembler = new VectorAssembler()
        .setInputCols(Array("L0_S22_F545Vec", "L0_S0_F0",
"L0_S0_F2","L0_S0_F4"))
```

```
    .setOutputCol("features")

var assembled = vectorAssembler.transform(encoded)
```

We basically just define a list of column names and a target column, and the rest is done for us:

```
scala> assembled.show
+-----+----------+--------+--------+--------+---------------+-------------+--------------------+
|label|L0_S22_F545|L0_S0_F0|L0_S0_F2|L0_S0_F4|L0_S22_F545Index|L0_S22_F545Vec|          features|
+-----+----------+--------+--------+--------+---------------+-------------+--------------------+
|    0|        NA|    0.03| -0.034| -0.197|            0.0|(13,[0],[1.0])|(16,[0,13,14,15],...|
|    0|        NA|     0.0|    0.0|    0.0|            0.0|(13,[0],[1.0])|   (16,[0],[1.0])|
|    0|        NA|   0.088|  0.086|  0.003|            0.0|(13,[0],[1.0])|(16,[0,13,14,15],...|
|    0|        NA|  -0.036| -0.064|  0.294|            0.0|(13,[0],[1.0])|(16,[0,13,14,15],...|
|    0|        NA|  -0.055| -0.086|  0.294|            0.0|(13,[0],[1.0])|(16,[0,13,14,15],...|
|    0|        NA|   0.003|  0.019|  0.294|            0.0|(13,[0],[1.0])|(16,[0,13,14,15],...|
|    0|        NA|     0.0|    0.0|    0.0|            0.0|(13,[0],[1.0])|   (16,[0],[1.0])|
|    0|        NA|     0.0|    0.0|    0.0|            0.0|(13,[0],[1.0])|   (16,[0],[1.0])|
|    0|        NA|  -0.016| -0.041| -0.179|            0.0|(13,[0],[1.0])|(16,[0,13,14,15],...|
|    0|        NA|     0.0|    0.0|    0.0|            0.0|(13,[0],[1.0])|   (16,[0],[1.0])|
|    0|        NA|   0.016|  0.093| -0.015|            0.0|(13,[0],[1.0])|(16,[0,13,14,15],...|
|    0|        NA|  -0.062| -0.153| -0.197|            0.0|(13,[0],[1.0])|(16,[0,13,14,15],...|
|    0|        NA|  -0.075| -0.093|  0.367|            0.0|(13,[0],[1.0])|(16,[0,13,14,15],...|
|    0|        NA|  -0.003| -0.093| -0.161|            0.0|(13,[0],[1.0])|(16,[0,13,14,15],...|
|    0|        NA|  -0.016| -0.138| -0.197|            0.0|(13,[0],[1.0])|(16,[0,13,14,15],...|
|    0|        NA|   0.252|   0.25|  0.003|            0.0|(13,[0],[1.0])|(16,[0,13,14,15],...|
|    0|        NA|     0.0|    0.0|    0.0|            0.0|(13,[0],[1.0])|   (16,[0],[1.0])|
|    0|        NA|  -0.016| -0.041|  0.003|            0.0|(13,[0],[1.0])|(16,[0,13,14,15],...|
|    0|        NA|     0.0|    0.0|    0.0|            0.0|(13,[0],[1.0])|   (16,[0],[1.0])|
|    0|        NA|   0.088|  0.033|   0.33|            0.0|(13,[0],[1.0])|(16,[0,13,14,15],...|
+-----+----------+--------+--------+--------+---------------+-------------+--------------------+
only showing top 20 rows
```

As the view of the features column got a bit squashed, let's inspect one instance of the feature field in more detail:

```
[scala> assembled.select("features").first.get(0)
res27: Any = (16,[0,13,14,15],[1.0,0.03,-0.034,-0.197])
```

We can clearly see that we are dealing with a sparse vector of length 16 where positions **0, 13, 14,** and **15** are non-zero and contain the following values: 1.0, 0.03, -0.034, and -0.197. Done! Let's create a Pipeline out of these components.

Testing the feature engineering pipeline

Let's create a `Pipeline` out of our transformers and estimators:

```
import org.apache.spark.ml.Pipeline
import org.apache.spark.ml.PipelineModel

//Create an array out of individual pipeline stages
var transformers = Array(indexer,encoder,assembled)


var pipeline = new Pipeline().setStages(transformers).fit(df_notnull)

var transformed = pipeline.transform(df_notnull)
```

Note that the `setStages` method of `Pipeline` just expects an array of `transformers` and `estimators`, which we had created earlier. As parts of the `Pipeline` contain estimators, we have to run `fit` on our `DataFrame` first. The obtained `Pipeline` object takes a `DataFrame` in the `transform` method and returns the results of the transformations:

```
scala> transformed.show
+-----+----------+-------+-------+-------+---------------+-----------------+--------------------+
|label|L0_S22_F545|L0_S0_F0|L0_S0_F2|L0_S0_F4|L0_S22_F545Index|L0_S22_F545Vec|            features|
+-----+----------+-------+-------+-------+---------------+-----------------+--------------------+
|    0|        NA|   0.03| -0.034| -0.197|            0.0|(13,[0],[1.0])|(16,[0,13,14,15],...|
|    0|        NA|    0.0|    0.0|    0.0|            0.0|(13,[0],[1.0])|    (16,[0],[1.0])|
|    0|        NA|  0.088|  0.086|  0.003|            0.0|(13,[0],[1.0])|(16,[0,13,14,15],...|
|    0|        NA| -0.036| -0.064|  0.294|            0.0|(13,[0],[1.0])|(16,[0,13,14,15],...|
|    0|        NA| -0.055| -0.086|  0.294|            0.0|(13,[0],[1.0])|(16,[0,13,14,15],...|
|    0|        NA|  0.003|  0.019|  0.294|            0.0|(13,[0],[1.0])|(16,[0,13,14,15],...|
|    0|        NA|    0.0|    0.0|    0.0|            0.0|(13,[0],[1.0])|    (16,[0],[1.0])|
|    0|        NA|    0.0|    0.0|    0.0|            0.0|(13,[0],[1.0])|    (16,[0],[1.0])|
|    0|        NA| -0.016| -0.041| -0.179|            0.0|(13,[0],[1.0])|(16,[0,13,14,15],...|
|    0|        NA|    0.0|    0.0|    0.0|            0.0|(13,[0],[1.0])|    (16,[0],[1.0])|
|    0|        NA|  0.016|  0.093| -0.015|            0.0|(13,[0],[1.0])|(16,[0,13,14,15],...|
|    0|        NA| -0.062| -0.153| -0.197|            0.0|(13,[0],[1.0])|(16,[0,13,14,15],...|
|    0|        NA| -0.075| -0.093|  0.367|            0.0|(13,[0],[1.0])|(16,[0,13,14,15],...|
|    0|        NA| -0.003| -0.093| -0.161|            0.0|(13,[0],[1.0])|(16,[0,13,14,15],...|
|    0|        NA| -0.016| -0.138| -0.197|            0.0|(13,[0],[1.0])|(16,[0,13,14,15],...|
|    0|        NA|  0.252|   0.25|  0.003|            0.0|(13,[0],[1.0])|(16,[0,13,14,15],...|
|    0|        NA|    0.0|    0.0|    0.0|            0.0|(13,[0],[1.0])|    (16,[0],[1.0])|
|    0|        NA| -0.016| -0.041|  0.003|            0.0|(13,[0],[1.0])|(16,[0,13,14,15],...|
|    0|        NA|    0.0|    0.0|    0.0|            0.0|(13,[0],[1.0])|    (16,[0],[1.0])|
|    0|        NA|  0.088|  0.033|   0.33|            0.0|(13,[0],[1.0])|(16,[0,13,14,15],...|
+-----+----------+-------+-------+-------+---------------+-----------------+--------------------+
only showing top 20 rows
```

As expected, we obtain the very same DataFrame as we had while running the stages individually in a sequence.

Training the machine learning model

Now it's time to add another component to the `Pipeline`: the actual machine learning algorithm--RandomForest:

```
import org.apache.spark.ml.classification.RandomForestClassifier
var rf = new RandomForestClassifier()
   .setLabelCol("label")
   .setFeaturesCol("features")

var model = new Pipeline().setStages(transformers :+ rf).fit(df_notnull)

var result = model.transform(df_notnull)
```

This code is very straightforward. First, we have to instantiate our algorithm and obtain it as a reference in `rf`. We could have set additional parameters to the model but we'll do this later in an automated fashion in the `CrossValidation` step. Then, we just add the stage to our `Pipeline`, fit it, and finally transform. The `fit` method, apart from running all upstream stages, also calls fit on the `RandomForestClassifier` in order to train it. The trained model is now contained within the `Pipeline` and the `transform` method actually creates our predictions column:

```
scala> result.show
+-----+----------+--------+--------+--------+---------------+------------+--------------------+--------------------+--------------------+----------+
|label|L0_S22_F545|L0_S0_F0|L0_S0_F2|L0_S0_F4|L0_S22_F545Index|L0_S22_F545Vec|            features|       rawPrediction|         probability|prediction|
+-----+----------+--------+--------+--------+---------------+------------+--------------------+--------------------+--------------------+----------+
|    0|        NA|    0.03|  -0.034|  -0.197|            0.0|(13,[0],[1.0])|(16,[0,13,14,15],...|[19.8764711847913...|[0.99382355923956...|       0.0|
|    0|        NA|     0.0|     0.0|     0.0|            0.0|(13,[0],[1.0])|       (16,[0],[1.0])|[19.8734515671497...|[0.99367257835748...|       0.0|
|    0|        NA|   0.088|   0.086|   0.003|            0.0|(13,[0],[1.0])|(16,[0,13,14,15],...|[19.8936982048582...|[0.99468491024291...|       0.0|
|    0|        NA|  -0.036|  -0.064|   0.294|            0.0|(13,[0],[1.0])|(16,[0,13,14,15],...|[19.9103667119433...|[0.99551833559716...|       0.0|
|    0|        NA|  -0.055|  -0.086|   0.294|            0.0|(13,[0],[1.0])|(16,[0,13,14,15],...|[19.9128187397603...|[0.99564093698801...|       0.0|
|    0|        NA|   0.003|   0.019|   0.294|            0.0|(13,[0],[1.0])|(16,[0,13,14,15],...|[19.9021809064659...|[0.99510904532329...|       0.0|
|    0|        NA|     0.0|     0.0|     0.0|            0.0|(13,[0],[1.0])|       (16,[0],[1.0])|[19.8734515671497...|[0.99367257835748...|       0.0|
|    0|        NA|  -0.016|  -0.041|  -0.179|            0.0|(13,[0],[1.0])|(16,[0,13,14,15],...|[19.8762685936784...|[0.99381342968392...|       0.0|
|    0|        NA|     0.0|     0.0|     0.0|            0.0|(13,[0],[1.0])|       (16,[0],[1.0])|[19.8734515671497...|[0.99367257835748...|       0.0|
|    0|        NA|   0.016|   0.093|  -0.015|            0.0|(13,[0],[1.0])|(16,[0,13,14,15],...|[19.8839359144095...|[0.99419679572047...|       0.0|
|    0|        NA|  -0.062|  -0.153|  -0.197|            0.0|(13,[0],[1.0])|(16,[0,13,14,15],...|[19.8900653890112...|[0.99450326945056...|       0.0|
|    0|        NA|  -0.075|  -0.093|   0.367|            0.0|(13,[0],[1.0])|(16,[0,13,14,15],...|[19.9155130528803...|[0.99577565264401...|       0.0|
|    0|        NA|  -0.003|  -0.093|  -0.161|            0.0|(13,[0],[1.0])|(16,[0,13,14,15],...|[19.8830065488786...|[0.99415032744393...|       0.0|
|    0|        NA|  -0.016|  -0.138|  -0.197|            0.0|(13,[0],[1.0])|(16,[0,13,14,15],...|[19.8787059668007...|[0.99393529834003...|       0.0|
|    0|        NA|   0.252|    0.25|   0.003|            0.0|(13,[0],[1.0])|(16,[0,13,14,15],...|[19.8899480526405...|[0.99449740263202...|       0.0|
|    0|        NA|  -0.016|  -0.041|   0.003|            0.0|(13,[0],[1.0])|(16,[0,13,14,15],...|[19.8929538865276...|[0.99464769432638...|       0.0|
|    0|        NA|     0.0|     0.0|     0.0|            0.0|(13,[0],[1.0])|       (16,[0],[1.0])|[19.8734515671497...|[0.99367257835748...|       0.0|
|    0|        NA|   0.088|   0.033|    0.33|            0.0|(13,[0],[1.0])|(16,[0,13,14,15],...|[19.9092368840784...|[0.99546184420392...|       0.0|
+-----+----------+--------+--------+--------+---------------+------------+--------------------+--------------------+--------------------+----------+
only showing top 20 rows
```

As we can see, we've now obtained an additional column called prediction, which contains the output of the `RandomForestClassifier` model. Of course, we've only used a very limited subset of available features/columns and have also not yet tuned the model, so we don't expect to do very well; however, let's take a look at how we can evaluate our model easily with Apache SparkML.

Model evaluation

Without evaluation, a model is worth nothing as we don't know how accurately it performs. Therefore, we will now use the built-in `BinaryClassificationEvaluator` in order to assess prediction performance and a widely used measure called `areaUnderROC` (going into detail here is beyond the scope of this book):

```
import org.apache.spark.ml.evaluation.BinaryClassificationEvaluator
val evaluator = new BinaryClassificationEvaluator()

import org.apache.spark.ml.param.ParamMap
var evaluatorParamMap = ParamMap(evaluator.metricName -> "areaUnderROC")
var aucTraining = evaluator.evaluate(result, evaluatorParamMap)
```

As we can see, there is a built-in class called `org.apache.spark.ml.evaluation.BinaryClassificationEvaluator` and there are some other classes for other prediction use cases such as `RegressionEvaluator` or `MuliclassClassificationEvaluator`. The `evaluator` takes a parameter map--in this case, we are telling it to use the `areaUnderROC` metric--and finally, the evaluate method evaluates the result:

```
scala> var aucTraining = evaluator.evaluate(result, evaluatorParamMap)
aucTraining: Double = 0.5424418446501833
```

As we can see, `areaUnderROC` is `0.5424418446501833`. An ideal classifier would return a score of one. So we are only doing a bit better than random guesses but, as already stated, the number of features that we are looking at is fairly limited.

> In the previous example we are using the `areaUnderROC` metric which is used for evaluation of binary classifiers. There exist an abundance of other metrics used for different disciplines of machine learning such as accuracy, precision, recall and F1 score. The following provides a good overview `http://www.cs.cornell.edu/courses/cs578/2003fa/perform ance_measures.pdf`

This `areaUnderROC` is in fact a very bad value. Let's see if choosing better parameters for our `RandomForest` model increases this a bit in the next section.

CrossValidation and hyperparameter tuning

As explained before, a common step in machine learning is cross-validating your model using testing data against training data and also tweaking the knobs of your machine learning algorithms. Let's use Apache SparkML in order to do this for us, fully automated!

First, we have to configure the parameter map and CrossValidator:

```
import org.apache.spark.ml.tuning.{CrossValidator, ParamGridBuilder}
var paramGrid = new ParamGridBuilder()
    .addGrid(rf.numTrees, 3 :: 5 :: 10 :: 30 :: 50 :: 70 :: 100 :: 150 ::
Nil)
    .addGrid(rf.featureSubsetStrategy, "auto" :: "all" :: "sqrt" :: "log2"
:: "onethird" :: Nil)
    .addGrid(rf.impurity, "gini" :: "entropy" :: Nil)
    .addGrid(rf.maxBins, 2 :: 5 :: 10 :: 15 :: 20 :: 25 :: 30 :: Nil)
    .addGrid(rf.maxDepth, 3 :: 5 :: 10 :: 15 :: 20 :: 25 :: 30 :: Nil)
    .build()

var crossValidator = new CrossValidator()
      .setEstimator(new Pipeline().setStages(transformers :+ rf))
      .setEstimatorParamMaps(paramGrid)
      .setNumFolds(5)
.setEvaluator(evaluator)
var crossValidatorModel = crossValidator.fit(df_notnull)
var newPredictions = crossValidatorModel.transform(df_notnull)
```

The org.apache.spark.ml.tuning.ParamGridBuilder is used in order to define the hyperparameter space where the CrossValidator has to search and finally, the org.apache.spark.ml.tuning.CrossValidator takes our Pipeline, the hyperparameter space of our RandomForest classifier, and the number of folds for the CrossValidation as parameters. Now, as usual, we just need to call fit and transform on the CrossValidator and it will basically run our Pipeline multiple times and return a model that performs the best. Do you know how many different models are trained? Well, we have five folds on CrossValidation and five-dimensional hyperparameter space cardinalities between two and eight, so let's do the math: 5 * 8 * 5 * 2 * 7 * 7 = 19600 times!

Using the evaluator to assess the quality of the cross-validated and tuned model

Now that we've optimized our `Pipeline` in a fully automatic fashion, let's see how our best model can be obtained:

```
var bestPipelineModel =
crossValidatorModel.bestModel.asInstanceOf[PipelineModel]
    var stages = bestPipelineModel.stages
import org.apache.spark.ml.classification.RandomForestClassificationModel
    val rfStage =
stages(stages.length-1).asInstanceOf[RandomForestClassificationModel]
rfStage.getNumTrees
rfStage.getFeatureSubsetStrategy
rfStage.getImpurity
rfStage.getMaxBins
rfStage.getMaxDepth
```

The `crossValidatorModel.bestModel` code basically returns the best `Pipeline`. Now we use `bestPipelineModel.stages` to obtain the individual stages and obtain the tuned `RandomForestClassificationModel` using `stages(stages.length-1).asInstanceOf[RandomForestClassificationModel]`. Note that `stages.length-1` addresses the last stage in the `Pipeline`, which is our `RandomForestClassifier`.

So now, we can basically run `evaluator` using the best model and see how it performs:

```
[scala> evaluator.evaluate(newPredictions, evaluatorParamMap)
res6: Double = 0.5362224872557545
```

You might have noticed that `0.5362224872557545` is less than `0.5424418446501833`, as we've obtained before. So why is this the case? Actually, this time we used cross-validation, which means that the model is less likely to over fit and therefore the score is a bit lower.

So let's take a look at the parameters of the best model:

```
scala> rfStage.getNumTrees
res1: Int = 5

scala> rfStage.getFeatureSubsetStrategy
res2: String = auto

scala> rfStage.getImpurity
res3: String = entropy

scala> rfStage.getMaxBins
res4: Int = 5

[scala> rfStage.getMaxDepth
res5: Int = 5
```

Note that we've limited the hyperparameter space, so numTrees, maxBins, and maxDepth have been limited to five, and bigger trees will most likely perform better. So feel free to play around with this code and add features, and also use a bigger hyperparameter space, say, bigger trees.

Summary

You've learned that, as in many other places, the introduction of DataFrames leads to the development of complementary frameworks that are not using RDDs directly anymore. This is also the case for machine learning but there is much more to it. Pipeline actually takes machine learning in Apache Spark to the next level as it improves the productivity of the data scientist dramatically.

The compatibility between all intermediate objects and well-thought-out concepts is just awesome. This framework makes it very easy to build your own stacked and bagged model with the full support of the underlying performance optimizations with **Tungsten** and **Catalyst**.

Great! Finally, we've applied the concepts that we discussed on a real dataset from a Kaggle competition, which is a very nice starting point for your own machine learning project with Apache SparkML. The next Chapter covers Apache SystemML, which is a 3rd party machine learning library for Apache Spark. Let's see why it is useful and what the differences are to SparkML.

9
Apache SystemML

So far, we have only covered components that came along with the standard distribution of Apache Spark (except HDFS, Kafka and Flume, of course). However, Apache Spark can also serve as runtime for third-party components, making it as some sort of operating system for big data applications. In this chapter, we want to introduce Apache SystemML, an amazing piece of technology initially developed by the *IBM Almaden Research Lab* in California. Apache SystemML went through many transformation stages and has now become an Apache top level project.

In this chapter, we will cover the following topics to get a greater insight into the subject:

- Using SystemML for your own machine learning applications on top of Apache Spark
- Learning the fundamental differences between SystemML and other machine learning libraries for Apache Spark
- Discovering the reason why another machine library exists for Apache Spark

Why do we need just another library?

In order to answer this question, we have to know something about SystemML's history, which began ten years ago in 2007 as a research project in the *IBM Almaden Research Lab* in California. The project was driven by the intention to improve the workflow of data scientists, especially those who want to improve and add functionality to existing machine learning algorithms.

So, **SystemML** is a declarative markup language that can transparently distribute work on Apache Spark. It supports Scale-up using multithreading and SIMD instructions on CPUs as well as GPUs and also Scale-out using a cluster, and of course, both together.

Finally, there is a cost-based optimizer in place to generate low-level execution plans taking statistics about the Dataset sizes into account. In other words, **Apache SystemML** is for machine learning, what Catalyst and Tungsten are for DataFrames.

Why on Apache Spark?

Apache Spark solves a lot of common issues in data processing and machine learning, so Apache SystemML can make use of these features. For example, Apache Spark supports the unification of SQL, Graph, Stream, and machine learning data processing on top of a common RDD structure.

In other words, it is a general **DAG** (**directed acyclic graph**) execution engine supporting lazy evaluation and distributed in-memory caching.

The history of Apache SystemML

Apache SystemML is already ten years old. Of course, it went through multiple refactorings and is now a state-of-the-art, and one of the fastest, machine learning libraries in the world. Recently, DeepLearning has also been added, which we will cover briefly in the following chapter on DeepLearning:

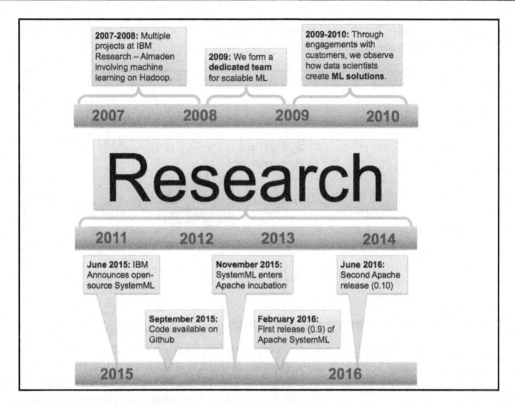

As you can see in the preceding figure, a lot of research has been done for Apache SystemML. It is two years older than Apache Spark and in 2017 it has been turned into a top level Apache project, leaving **incubator** status. Even during the time SystemML was started, the researchers at *IBM Research Almaden* realized that, very often, out-of-the box machine learning algorithms perform very poorly on large Datasets.

So, the data analysis pipeline had to be tuned after a small-scale version of it had been prototyped. The following figure illustrates this:

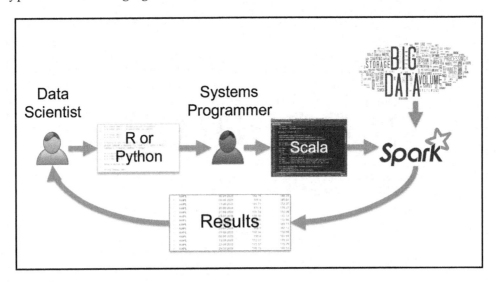

This means that the data scientist will prototype his application in a programming language of his choice, most likely Matlab, R or python and, finally, a systems programmer will pick this up and re-implement this in a JVM language like Java or Scala, which usually turns out to provide better performance and also linearly scales on data parallel framework like Apache Spark.

The scaled version of the prototype will return results on the whole Dataset and the data scientist again is in charge of modifying the prototype and the whole cycle begins again. Not only the IBM Almaden Research staff members have experienced this, but even our team has seen it. So let's make the systems programmer redundant (or at least require him only to take care of our Apache Spark jobs) using Apache SystemML.

A cost-based optimizer for machine learning algorithms

Let's start with an example to exemplify how Apache SystemML works internally. Consider a recommender system.

An example - alternating least squares

A recommender system tries to predict the potential items that a user might be interested in, based on a history from other users.

So let's consider a so-called item-user or product-customer matrix, as illustrated here:

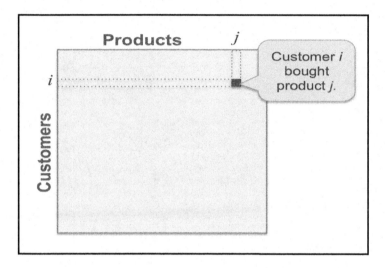

This is a so-called **sparse** matrix because only a couple of cells are populated with non-zero values indicating a match between a customer i and a product j. Either by just putting a **one** in the cell or any other numerical value, for example, indicating the number of products bought or a rating for that particular product j from customer i. Let's call this matrix r_{ui}, where u stands for user and i for item.

Those of you familiar with linear algebra might know that any matrix can be factorized by two smaller matrices. This means that you have to find two matrices p_u and q_i that, when multiplied with each other, reconstruct the original matrix r_{ui}; let's call the reconstruction r_{ui}'. The goal is to find p_u and q_i to reconstruct r_{ui}' such that it doesn't differ too much from r_{ui}. This is done using a sum of squared errors objective.

The following figure illustrates this and the sparsity property of the matrix:

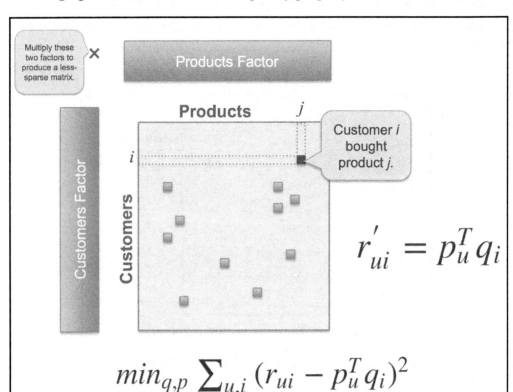

Once we've found good factors p_u and q_i, we can construct r_{ui}' and, finally, new non-zero cells will be present, which become the new predicted product suggestions. In case you haven't understood all the details, don't worry, as we don't need too much of this example to understand the rest of this chapter.

A common algorithm to find p_u and q_i is called **alternating least squares (ALS)**--alternating because in each iteration the optimization objective switches from p_u to q_i and vice versa. Don't get bothered with it too much, but this is how it actually works, and, in Apache Spark MLlib, this is just a single line of Scala code:

```
val model = ALS.train(ratings, rank, numIterations, 0.01)
```

So what's wrong with this? Before we explain this, let's take a look at how ALS is implemented in a statistical programming language such as R:

```
U = rand(nrow(X), r, min = -1.0, max = 1.0);
V = rand(r, ncol(X), min = -1.0, max = 1.0);
while(i < mi) {
    i = i + 1; ii = 1;
    if (is_U)
       G = (W * (U %*% V - X)) %*% t(V) + lambda * U;
    else
       G = t(U) %*% (W * (U %*% V - X)) + lambda * V;
    norm_G2 = sum(G ^ 2); norm_R2 = norm_G2;
    R = -G; S = R;
    while(norm_R2 > 10E-9 * norm_G2 & ii <= mii) {
      if (is_U) {
        HS = (W * (S %*% V)) %*% t(V) + lambda * S;
        alpha = norm_R2 / sum (S * HS);
        U = U + alpha * S;
      } else {
        HS = t(U) %*% (W * (U %*% S)) + lambda * S;
        alpha = norm_R2 / sum (S * HS);
        V = V + alpha * S;
      }
      R = R - alpha * HS;
      old_norm_R2 = norm_R2; norm_R2 = sum(R ^ 2);
      S = R + (norm_R2 / old_norm_R2) * S;
      ii = ii + 1;
    }
    is_U = ! is_U;
}
```

Again, don't worry if you don't understand each line, but the purpose of this figure is to show you that in R, this algorithm needs only 27 lines of code to be expressed. If we now take a look at the ALS implementation in MLlib, we'll see that it has more than 800 lines. You can find this implementation at `https://github.com/apache/spark/tree/master/ml lib/src/main/scala/org/apache/spark/mllib/recommendation`.

So why do we need more than 800 lines in Scala on Spark and only 27 in R? This is because of performance optimizations. The ALS implementation in MLlib consists of more than 50% of performance optimization code. So what if we could perform the following?

- Get rid of all performance optimizations in our algorithm implementation
- Port our R code 1:1 to some parallel framework
- In case of changes, just change our R implementation

This is where Apache SystemML kicks in, it supports all this. Apache SystemML's **DSL** (**domain specific language**) is a subset of R syntax, so you can just take the previous example and run it 1:1 without any modification on top of Apache SystemML. In addition, a cost-based performance optimizer generates a physical execution plan on top of Apache Spark in order to minimize execution time based on size properties of your data. So let's find out how this works.

ApacheSystemML architecture

So the key thing on Apache SystemML is the optimizer. This component turns a high-level description of an algorithm in a domain-specific language into a highly optimized physical execution on Apache Spark, as shown in the following figure:

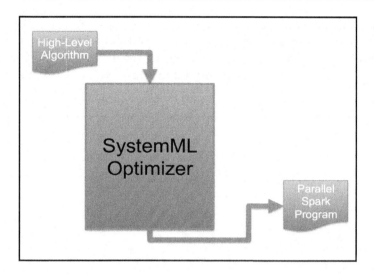

Language parsing

Let's open this black box a bit in order to understand what exactly is going on in the Apache SystemML optimizer. The first thing that the engine does is a compile step on the DSL. So first, syntax checking, then live variable analysis in order to determine which intermediate results are still needed, and finally a semantic check.

High-level operators are generated

Once the previous step is passed, the execution plan using so-called **high-level operators** (**HOPs**) is generated. These are constructed from the **abstract syntax tree** (**AST**) of the DSL. The following important optimization steps are taking place during this phase:

- **Static rewrites**: The DSL offers a rich set of syntactical and semantic features that makes an implementation easy to understand but may result in a non-optimal execution. Apache SystemML detects these branches of the AST and statically rewrites them to a better version, maintaining the semantic equivalency.
- **Dynamic rewrites**: Dynamic rewrites are very similar to static rewrites but are driven by cost-based statistics considering the size of the Datasets to be processed.

The following figure illustrates a static rewrite where a branch of the AST performing a matrix multiplication, is actually rewritten to use a HOP called **wdivmm (weighted divide matrix multiplication)**, which is a way of computing results of matrix multiplication of that particular form, without materializing a very large intermediate dense matrix in order to save memory:

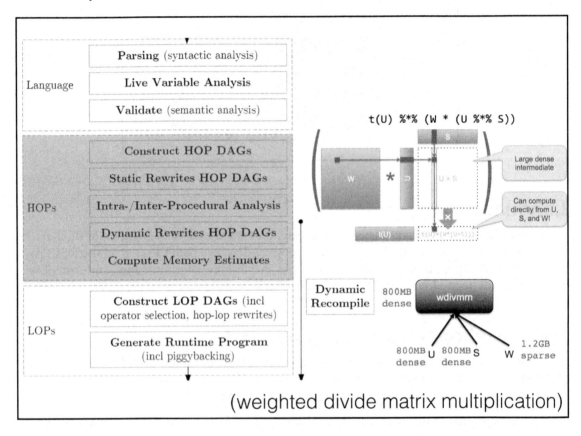

(weighted divide matrix multiplication)

How low-level operators are optimized on

Let's have a look on how low-level operators are selected and optimized on. We'll stick to the weighted divide matrix multiplication example--a HOP that has been selected before the HOP optimizations process over an ordinary sequence of matrix multiplications. So now the question arises, for example, if it makes sense to use a parallel version of a LOP running parallel on the Apache Spark workers, or whether a local execution is preferable. In this example, Apache SystemML determines that all intermediate results fit into the main memory of the driver node and chooses the local operator, **WDivMM**, over the parallel operator, **MapWDivMM**. The following figure illustrates this process:

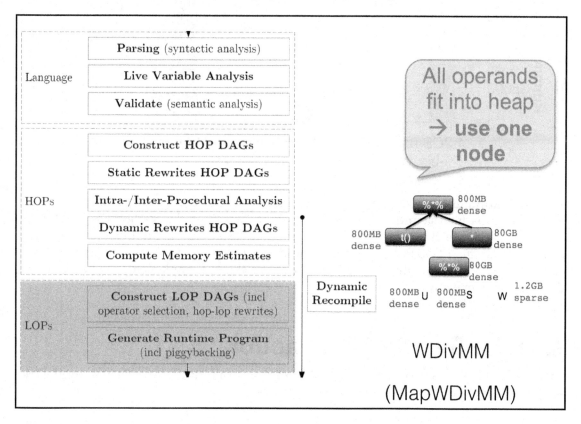

Performance measurements

So is all this effort worth it? Let's take a look at some performance comparisons between a local R script, MLlib, and Apache SystemML:

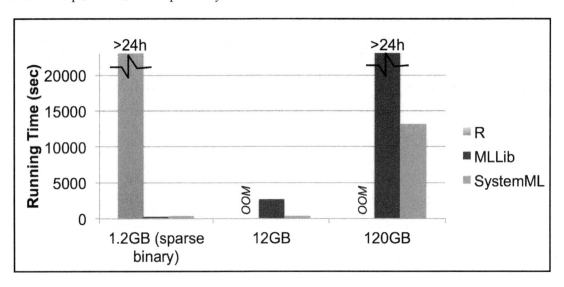

The ALS algorithm has been run on different Datasets with 1.2, 12, and 120 GB size using R, MLlib, and ApacheSystemML. We can clearly see that, even on the smallest Dataset, R is not a feasible solution as it took more than 24 hours, and we are not sure if it would have ever completed. On the 12 GB Dataset, we've noticed that ApacheSystemML runs significantly faster than MLlib, and finally, on the 120 GB Dataset, the ALS implementation of MLlib didn't finish in one day and we gave up.

Apache SystemML in action

So let's take a look at a very simple example. Let's create a script in Apache SystemML DSL--an R-like syntax--in order to multiply two matrices:

```
import org.apache.sysml.api.MLOutput
import org.apache.spark.sql.SQLContext
import org.apache.spark.mllib.util.LinearDataGenerator
import org.apache.sysml.api.MLContext
import
org.apache.sysml.runtime.instructions.spark.utils.{RDDConverterUtilsExt =>
RDDConverterUtils}
import org.apache.sysml.runtime.matrix.MatrixCharacteristics;
```

```
val sqlContext = new SQLContext(sc)

val simpleScript -
"""
fileX = "";
fileY = "";
fileZ = "";

X = read (fileX);
Y = read (fileY);

Z = X %*% Y

write (Z,fileZ);
"""
```

Then, we generate some test data:

```
// Generate data
val rawDataX =
sqlContext.createDataFrame(LinearDataGenerator.generateLinearRDD(sc, 100,
10, 1))
val rawDataY =
sqlContext.createDataFrame(LinearDataGenerator.generateLinearRDD(sc, 10,
100, 1))

// Repartition into a more parallelism-friendly number of partitions
val dataX = rawDataX.repartition(64).cache()
val dataY = rawDataY.repartition(64).cache()
```

In order to use Apache SystemML, we have to create an `MLContext` object:

```
// Create SystemML context
val ml = new MLContext(sc)
```

Now we have to convert our data to a format that Apache SystemML understands:

```
// Convert data to proper format
val mcX = new MatrixCharacteristics()
val mcY = new MatrixCharacteristics()
val X = RDDConverterUtils.vectorDataFrameToBinaryBlock(sc, dataX, mcX,
false, "features")
val Y = RDDConverterUtils.vectorDataFrameToBinaryBlock(sc, dataY, mcY,
false, "features")
```

Now, we pass the data X and Y to the Apache SystemML runtime and also preregister a variable called Z in order to obtain the result from the runtime:

```
// Register inputs & outputs
ml.reset()
ml.registerInput("X", X, mcX)
ml.registerInput("Y", Y, mcY)
ml.registerOutput("Z")
```

Finally, we actually execute the script stored in `simpleScript` with the `executeScript` method and obtain the result from the runtime:

```
val outputs = ml.executeScript(simpleScript)

// Get outputs
val Z = outputs.getDF(sqlContext, "Z")
```

Now Z contains `DataFrame` with the result of the matrix multiplication. Done!

Summary

You've learned that there is room for additional machine learning frameworks and libraries on top of Apache Spark and that a cost-based optimizer similar to what we are already using in Catalyst can speed things up tremendously. In addition, separation from performance optimizations code and code for the algorithm facilitates further improvements on the algorithm side without having to care about performance at all.

Additionally, these execution plans are highly adaptable to the size of the data and also to the available hardware configuration based on main memory size and potential accelerators such as GPUs. Apache SystemML dramatically improves on the life cycle of machine learning applications, especially if machine learning algorithms are not used out of the box, but an experienced data scientists works on low level details on it in a mathematical or statistical programming language.

In Apache SystemML, this low level, mathematical code can be used out of the box, without any manual transformation or translation to other programming languages . It can be executed on top of Apache Spark.

In the next chapter we'll cover DeepLearning and how it can be used on top of Apache Spark. This is one of the hottest topics in 2017, so stay tuned!

10

Deep Learning on Apache Spark with DeepLearning4j and H2O

This chapter will give you an introduction to Deep Learning and how you can use third-party machine learning libraries on top of Apache Spark in order to do so. Deep Learning is outperforming a variety of state-of-the-art machine learning algorithms, and it is a very active area of research, so there is more to come soon. Therefore, it is important to know how Deep Learning works and how it can be applied in a parallel data processing environment such as Apache Spark.

This chapter will cover the following topics in detail:

- Introduction to the installation and usage of the H2O framework
- Introduction to Deeplearning4j with an IoT anomaly detection example

H2O

H2O is an open source system developed in Java by `http://h2o.ai/` for machine learning. It offers a rich set of machine learning algorithms and a web-based data processing user interface. It offers the ability to develop in a range of languages: Java, Scala, Python, and R.

It also has the ability to interface with Spark, HDFS, SQL, and NoSQL databases. This chapter will concentrate on H2O's integration with Apache Spark using the Sparkling Water component of H2O. A simple example developed in Scala will be used based on real data to create a deep-learning model.

The next step will be to provide an overview of the H2O functionality and the Sparkling Water architecture that will be used in this chapter.

Overview

Since it is only possible to examine and use a small amount of H2O's functionality in this chapter, we thought that it would be useful to provide a list of all of the functional areas that it covers. This list is taken from the `http://h2o.ai/` website at `http://h2o.ai/produc t/algorithms/` and is based upon wrangling data, modeling using the data, and scoring the resulting models:

- Process
- Model
- The score tool
- Data profiling
- Generalized linear models (GLM)
- Predict
- Summary statistics
- Decision trees
- Confusion matrix
- Aggregate, filter, bin, and derive columns
- Gradient boosting machine (GBM)
- AUC
- Slice, log transform, and anonymize
- K-means
- Hit ratio
- Variable creation
- Anomaly detection
- PCA/PCA score
- Deep learning
- Multimodel scoring
- Training and validation sampling plan
- Naive Bayes
- Gild search

The following section will explain the environment used for the Spark and H2O examples in this chapter and some of the problems encountered.

For completeness, we will show you how we downloaded, installed, and used H2O. Although we finally settled on version 0.2.12-95, we first downloaded and used 0.2.12-92. This section is based on the earlier install, but the approach used to source the software is the same. The download link changes over time, so follow the Sparkling Water download option at `http://h2o.ai/download/`.

This will source the zipped Sparkling Water release, as shown in the file listing here:

```
[hadoop@hc2r1m2 h2o]$ pwd ; ls -l
/home/hadoop/h2o
total 15892
-rw-r--r-- 1 hadoop hadoop 16272364 Apr 11 12:37 sparkling-
water-0.2.12-92.zip
```

This zipped release file is unpacked using the Linux `unzip` command, and it results in a Sparkling Water release file tree:

```
[hadoop@hc2r1m2 h2o]$ unzip sparkling-water-0.2.12-92.zip

[hadoop@hc2r1m2 h2o]$ ls -d sparkling-water*
sparkling-water-0.2.12-92   sparkling-water-0.2.12-92.zip
```

We have moved the release tree to the `/usr/local/` area using the root account and created a simple symbolic link to the release called H2O. This means that our H2O-based build can refer to this link, and it doesn't need to change as new versions of Sparkling Water are sourced. We have also made sure, using the Linux `chmod` command, that our development account, Hadoop, has access to the release:

```
[hadoop@hc2r1m2 h2o]$ su -
[root@hc2r1m2 ~]# cd /home/hadoop/h2o
[root@hc2r1m2 h2o]# mv sparkling-water-0.2.12-92 /usr/local
[root@hc2r1m2 h2o]# cd /usr/local

[root@hc2r1m2 local]# chown -R hadoop:hadoop sparkling-water-0.2.12-92
[root@hc2r1m2 local]#  ln -s sparkling-water-0.2.12-92 h2o

[root@hc2r1m2 local]# ls -lrt  | grep sparkling
total 52
drwxr-xr-x   6 hadoop hadoop 4096 Mar 28 02:27 sparkling-water-0.2.12-92
lrwxrwxrwx   1 root   root     25 Apr 11 12:43 h2o -> sparkling-
water-0.2.12-92
```

The release has been installed on all the nodes of our Hadoop clusters.

The build environment

From past examples, you know that we favor **sbt** as a build tool for developing Scala source examples.

We have created a development environment on the Linux server called `hc2r1m2` using the Hadoop development account. The development directory is called `h2o_spark_1_2`:

```
[hadoop@hc2r1m2 h2o_spark_1_2]$ pwd
/home/hadoop/spark/h2o_spark_1_2
```

Our SBT build configuration file named `h2o.sbt` is located here; it contains the following:

```
[hadoop@hc2r1m2 h2o_spark_1_2]$ more h2o.sbt

name := "H 2 O"

version := "1.0"

scalaVersion := "2.10.4"

libraryDependencies += "org.apache.hadoop" % "hadoop-client" % "2.3.0"

libraryDependencies += "org.apache.spark" % "spark-core"  % "1.2.0" from
"file:///usr/hdp/2.6.0.3-8/spark/lib/spark-assembly-1.6.3.2.6.0.3-8-
hadoop2.7.3.2.6.0.3-8.jar"

libraryDependencies += "org.apache.spark" % "mllib"  % "1.2.0" from
"file:///usr/hdp/2.6.0.3-8/spark/lib/spark-assembly-1.6.3.2.6.0.3-8-
hadoop2.7.3.2.6.0.3-8.jar"

libraryDependencies += "org.apache.spark" % "sql"  % "1.2.0" from
"file:///usr/hdp/2.6.0.3-8/spark/lib/spark-assembly-1.6.3.2.6.0.3-8-
hadoop2.7.3.2.6.0.3-8.jar"

libraryDependencies += "org.apache.spark" % "h2o"  % "0.2.12-95" from
"file:///usr/local/h2o/assembly/build/libs/sparkling-water-
assembly-0.2.12-95-all.jar"

libraryDependencies += "hex.deeplearning" % "DeepLearningModel"  %
"0.2.12-95" from "file:///usr/local/h2o/assembly/build/libs/sparkling-
water-assembly-0.2.12-95-all.jar"

libraryDependencies += "hex" % "ModelMetricsBinomial"  % "0.2.12-95" from
"file:///usr/local/h2o/assembly/build/libs/sparkling-water-
assembly-0.2.12-95-all.jar"

libraryDependencies += "water" % "Key"  % "0.2.12-95" from
```

```
"file:///usr/local/h2o/assembly/build/libs/sparkling-water-
assembly-0.2.12-95-all.jar"

 libraryDependencies += "water" % "fvec"  % "0.2.12-95" from
 "file:///usr/local/h2o/assembly/build/libs/sparkling-water-
 assembly-0.2.12-95-all.jar"
```

We provided sbt configuration examples in the previous chapters, so we won't go into line-by line-detail here. We have used the file-based URLs to define the library dependencies and sourced the Hadoop JAR files from Hadoop home.

The Sparkling Water JAR path is defined as /usr/local/h2o/ that was just created. We use a Bash script called run_h2o.bash within this development directory to execute our H2O-based example code. It takes the application class name as a parameter and is shown as follows:

```
[hadoop@hc2r1m2 h2o_spark_1_2]$ more run_h2o.bash

#!/bin/bash

SPARK_HOME=/usr/hdp/current/spark-client
SPARK_LIB=$SPARK_HOME/lib
SPARK_BIN=$SPARK_HOME/bin
SPARK_SBIN=$SPARK_HOME/sbin
SPARK_JAR=$SPARK_LIB/spark-assembly-1.6.3.2.6.0.3-8-
hadoop2.7.3.2.6.0.3-8.jar

H2O_PATH=/usr/local/h2o/assembly/build/libs
H2O_JAR=$H2O_PATH/sparkling-water-assembly-0.2.12-95-all.jar

PATH=$SPARK_BIN:$PATH
PATH=$SPARK_SBIN:$PATH
export PATH

cd $SPARK_BIN

./spark-submit \
  --class $1 \
  --master spark://hc2nn.semtech-solutions.co.nz:7077  \
  --executor-memory 512m \
  --total-executor-cores 50 \
  --jars $H2O_JAR \
  /home/hadoop/spark/h2o_spark_1_2/target/scala-2.10/h-2-o_2.10-1.0.jar
```

This example of Spark application submission has already been covered, so again, we won't go into detail. Setting the executor memory at a correct value was critical to avoiding out-of-memory issues and performance problems. This is examined in the *Performance tuning* section.
As in the previous examples, the application Scala code is located in the `src/main/scala` subdirectory under the development directory level. The next section will examine the Apache Spark and the H2O architectures.

Architecture

The diagrams in this section have been sourced from the `http://h2o.ai/` website at `http://h2o.ai/blog/2014/09/how-sparkling-water-brings-h2o-to-spark/` to provide a clear method of describing the way in which H2O Sparkling Water can be used to extend the functionality of Apache Spark. Both H2O and Spark are open source systems. Spark MLlib contains a great deal of functionality, while H2O extends this with a wide range of extra functionality, including Deep Learning. It offers tools to munge (transform), model, and score the data, as we can find in Apache SparkML. It also offers a web-based user interface to interact with.

The next diagram, borrowed from `http://h2o.ai/`, shows how H2O integrates with Spark. As we already know, Spark has master and worker servers; the workers create executors to do the actual work.

The following steps occur to run a Sparkling Water-based application:

- Spark's submit command sends the Sparkling Water JAR to the Spark master
- The Spark master starts the workers and distributes the JAR file
- The Spark workers start the executor JVMs to carry out the work
- The Spark executor starts an H2O instance

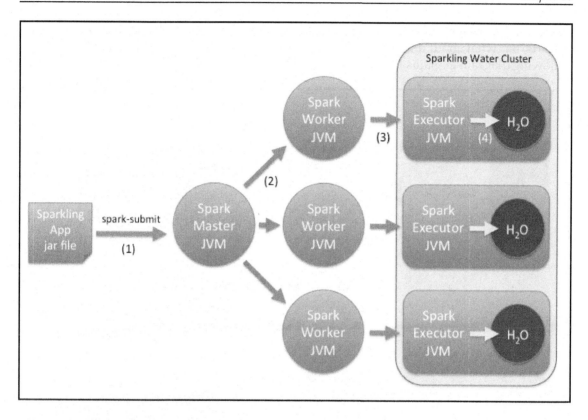

The H2O instance is embedded with the Executor JVM, and so it shares the JVM heap space with Spark. When all of the H2O instances have started, H2O forms a cluster, and then the H2O flow web interface is made available.

The preceding diagram explains how H2O fits into the Apache Spark architecture and how it starts, but what about data sharing? How does data pass between Spark and H2O? The following diagram explains this:

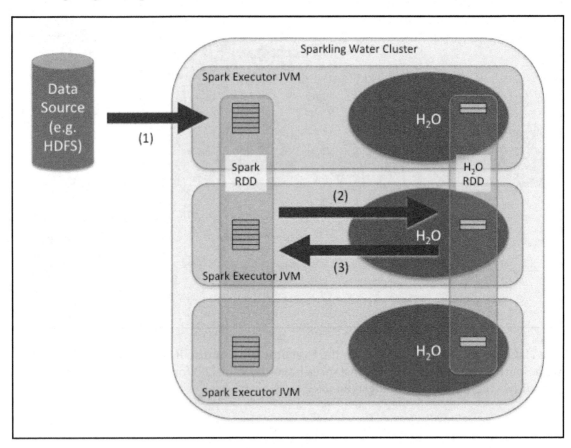

A new H2O RDD data structure has been created for H2O and Sparkling Water. It is a layer based at the top of an H2O frame, each column of which represents a data item and is independently compressed to provide the best compression ratio.

In the Deep Learning example Scala code presented later in this chapter, you will see that a data frame has been created implicitly from a Spark schema RDD, and a columnar data item income has been enumerated.

We won't dwell on this now, as it will be explained later, but this is a practical example of the architecture explained earlier:

```
val testFrame:DataFrame = schemaRddTest
testFrame.replace( testFrame.find("income"),
                   testFrame.vec("income").toEnum)
```

In the Scala-based example that will be tackled in this chapter, the following actions will take place:

- Data will be sourced from HDFS and stored in a Spark RDD
- Spark SQL will be used to filter data
- The Spark schema RDD will be converted into an H2O RDD
- The H2O-based processing and modeling will occur
- The results will be passed back to Spark for accuracy checking

At this point, the general architecture of H2O has been examined, and the product has been sourced for use. The development environment has been explained, and the process by which H2O and Spark integrate has been considered. Now it is time to delve into a practical example of the use of H2O. First though, some real-world data must be sourced for modeling purposes.

Sourcing the data

Since we have already used the **Artificial Neural Net** (**ANN**) functionality, in the chapter on Apache Spark MLlib to classify images, it seems only fitting that we use H2O deep learning to classify data in this chapter. In order to do this, we need to source Datasets that are suitable for classification. We need either image data with associated image labels or data containing vectors and a label that we can enumerate so that we can force H2O to use its classification algorithm.

The MNIST test and training image data was sourced from `ann.lecun.com/exdb/mnist/`. It contains 50,000 training rows and 10,000 rows for testing. It contains digital images of the numbers 0 to 9 and associated labels.
We were not able to use this data, as, at the time of writing, there was a bug in H2O Sparkling Water which limited the record size to 128 elements. The MNIST data has a record size of 28 x 28 + 1 elements for the image plus the label, since one image is 28 pixels wide, 28 pixels high and has one label assigned to it:

```
15/05/14 14:05:27 WARN TaskSetManager: Lost task 0.0 in stage 9.0 (TID 256,
hc2r1m4.semtech-solutions.co.nz): java.lang.ArrayIndexOutOfBoundsException:
-128
```

This issue should have been fixed and released by the time you read this, but in the short term, we sourced another Dataset called income from `http://www.cs.toronto.edu/~delv e/data/datasets.html`, which contains Canadian employee income data. The following information shows the attributes and the data volume. It also shows the list of columns in the data and a sample row of the data:

```
Number of attributes: 16
Number of cases: 45,225

age workclass fnlwgt education educational-num marital-status occupation
relationship race gender capital-gain capital-loss hours-per-week native-
country income

39, State-gov, 77516, Bachelors, 13, Never-married, Adm-clerical, Not-in-
family, White, Male, 2174, 0, 40, United-States, <=50K
```

We will enumerate the last column in the data, the income bracket, so `<=50K` will enumerate to 0. This will allow us to force the H2O deep learning algorithm to carry out classification rather than regression. We will also use Spark SQL to limit the data columns and filter the data.

As in all machine learning applications, data quality is absolutely critical when creating an H2O-based example as described in this chapter. The next section examines the steps that can be taken to improve the data quality and, hence, save time.

Data quality

When importing CSV data files from HDFS to the Spark Scala H2O example code, we can filter the incoming data. The following example code contains two filter lines--the first checks that a data line is not empty, while the second checks that the final column in each data row (income), which will be enumerated, is not empty:

```
val testRDD  = rawTestData
    .filter(!_.isEmpty)
    .map(_.split(","))
    .filter( rawRow => ! rawRow(14).trim.isEmpty )
```

We also needed to clean our raw data. There are two Datasets, one for training and another for testing. It is important that the training and testing data have the following:

- The same number of columns
- The same data types
- The enumerated type values must match, especially for the labels

So, we think that time and effort should be spent safeguarding the data quality as a pre-step to training and testing machine learning functionality, so that time is not lost and no extra labor cost incurres.

Performance tuning

It is important to monitor the Spark application errors and the standard output logs in the Spark web user interface if you see errors such as the following:

```
05-15 13:55:38.176 192.168.1.105:54321   6375   Thread-10 ERRR: Out of
Memory and no swap space left from hc2r1m1.semtech-
solutions.co.nz/192.168.1.105:54321
```

If you encounter instances where application executors seem to hang without response, you may need to tune your executor memory. You need to do so if you see an error such as the following in your executor log:

```
05-19 13:46:57.300 192.168.1.105:54321   10044   Thread-11 WARN: Unblock
allocations; cache emptied but memory is low:  OOM but cache is emptied:
MEM_MAX = 89.5 MB, DESIRED_CACHE = 96.4 MB, CACHE = N/A, POJO = N/A, this
request bytes = 36.4 MB
```

This can cause a loop, as the application requests more memory than is available and, hence, waits until the next iteration retries.

The application can seem to hang until the executors are killed, and the tasks are re-executed on alternate nodes. A short task's runtime can extend considerably due to such problems.

Monitor the Spark logs for these types of errors. In the previous example, changing the executor memory setting in the spark-submit command removes the error and reduces the runtime substantially.

The memory value requested has been reduced to a number below that which is available.

Deep Learning

Neural networks were introduced in the chapter on Apache Spark MLlib. This chapter builds upon this understanding by introducing Deep Learning, which uses deep neural networks. These are neural networks that are feature-rich and contain extra hidden layers so that their ability to extract data features is increased.

These networks are generally feed-forward networks, where the feature characteristics are inputs to the input layer neurons. These neurons then fire and spread the activation through the hidden layer neurons to an output layer, which should present the feature label values.

Errors in the output are then propagated back through the network (at least in back propagation), adjusting the neuron connection weight matrices so that classification errors are reduced during training.

The following diagram is a good illustration:

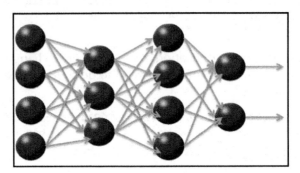

The previous example diagram, described in the H2O booklet at https://leanpub.com/dee plearning, shows a deep learning network with four input neurons to the left, two hidden layers in the middle, and two output neurons. The arrows show both the connections between neurons and the direction that activation takes through the network.

These networks are feature-rich because they provide the following options:

- Multiple training algorithms
- Automated network configuration
- The ability to configure many options
- Structure
- Hidden layer structure
- Training
- Learning rate, annealing, and momentum

So, after giving this brief introduction to deep learning, it is now time to look at some of the sample Scala-based code. H2O provides a great deal of functionality; the classes that are needed to build and run the network have been developed for you. You just need to do the following:

- Prepare the data and parameters
- Create and train the model
- Validate the model with a second Dataset
- Score the validation Dataset output

When scoring your model, you must hope for a high value in percentage terms. Your model must be able to accurately predict and classify your data.

Example code – income

This section examines the Scala-based H2O Sparkling Water Deep Learning example using the previous Canadian income data source. First, the Spark (Context, Conf, MLlib, and RDD) and H2O (h2o, deeplearning, and water) classes are imported:

```
import org.apache.spark.SparkContext
import org.apache.spark.SparkContext._
import org.apache.spark.SparkConf

import hex.deeplearning.{DeepLearningModel, DeepLearning}
import hex.deeplearning.DeepLearningModel.DeepLearningParameters
import org.apache.spark.h2o._
import org.apache.spark.mllib
import org.apache.spark.mllib.feature.{IDFModel, IDF, HashingTF}
import org.apache.spark.rdd.RDD
import water.Key
```

Next, an application class called h2o_spark_dl2 is defined, the master URL is created, and then a configuration object is created based on this URL and the application name.

The Spark context is then created using the configuration object:

```
object h2o_spark_dl2  extends App
  {
    val sparkMaster = "spark://localhost:7077"
    val appName = "Spark h2o ex1"
    val conf = new SparkConf()

    conf.setMaster(sparkMaster)
    conf.setAppName(appName)

    val sparkCxt = new SparkContext(conf)
```

An H2O context is created from the Spark context, and also an SQL context:

```
import org.apache.spark.h2o._
implicit val h2oContext = new
```

```
org.apache.spark.h2o.H2OContext(sparkCxt).start()

    import h2oContext._
    import org.apache.spark.sql._

    implicit val sqlContext = new SQLContext(sparkCxt)
```

The H2O Flow user interface is started with the `openFlow` command:

```
    import sqlContext._
    openFlow
```

The training and testing of the data files are now defined (on HDFS) using the server URL, path, and the filenames:

```
val server    = "hdfs://localhost:8020"
val path      = "/data/spark/h2o/"

val train_csv =  server + path + "adult.train.data" // 32,562 rows
val test_csv  =  server + path + "adult.test.data"  // 16,283 rows
```

The CSV-based training and testing data is loaded using the Spark SQL context's `textFile` method:

```
val rawTrainData = sparkCxt.textFile(train_csv)
val rawTestData  = sparkCxt.textFile(test_csv)
```

Now the schema is defined in terms of a string of attributes. Then, a schema variable is created by splitting the string using a series of `StructField`, based on each column. The data types are left as String, and the true value allows for the null values in the data:

```
val schemaString = "age workclass fnlwgt education " +
"educationalnum maritalstatus " + "occupation relationship race
gender " + "capitalgain capitalloss " + hoursperweek nativecountry income"
val schema = StructType( schemaString.split(" ")
    .map(fieldName => StructField(fieldName, StringType, true)))
```

The raw CSV line training and testing data is now split by commas into columns. The data is filtered on empty lines to ensure that the last column (income) is not empty. The actual data rows are created from the fifteen (0-14) trimmed elements in the raw CSV data. Both the training and the test Datasets are processed:

```
val trainRDD  = rawTrainData
        .filter(!_.isEmpty)
        .map(_.split(","))
        .filter( rawRow => ! rawRow(14).trim.isEmpty )
        .map(rawRow => Row(
            rawRow(0).toString.trim,  rawRow(1).toString.trim,
```

```
                rawRow(2).toString.trim,   rawRow(3).toString.trim,
                rawRow(4).toString.trim,   rawRow(5).toString.trim,
                rawRow(6).toString.trim,   rawRow(7).toString.trim,
                rawRow(8).toString.trim,   rawRow(9).toString.trim,
                rawRow(10).toString.trim,  rawRow(11).toString.trim,
                rawRow(12).toString.trim,  rawRow(13).toString.trim,
                rawRow(14).toString.trim
                            )
        )

val testRDD   = rawTestData
        .filter(!_.isEmpty)
        .map(_.split(","))
        .filter( rawRow => ! rawRow(14).trim.isEmpty )
        .map(rawRow => Row(
                rawRow(0).toString.trim,   rawRow(1).toString.trim,
                rawRow(2).toString.trim,   rawRow(3).toString.trim,
                rawRow(4).toString.trim,   rawRow(5).toString.trim,
                rawRow(6).toString.trim,   rawRow(7).toString.trim,
                rawRow(8).toString.trim,   rawRow(9).toString.trim,
                rawRow(10).toString.trim,  rawRow(11).toString.trim,
                rawRow(12).toString.trim,  rawRow(13).toString.trim,
                rawRow(14).toString.trim
                            )
        )
```

Spark Schema RDD variables are now created for the training and test Datasets by applying the schema variable created previously for the data using the Spark context's `applySchema` method:

```
val trainSchemaRDD = sqlContext.applySchema(trainRDD, schema)
val testSchemaRDD  = sqlContext.applySchema(testRDD,  schema)
```

Temporary tables are created for the training and testing data:

```
trainSchemaRDD.registerTempTable("trainingTable")
testSchemaRDD.registerTempTable("testingTable")
```

Now, SQL is run against these temporary tables, both to filter the number of columns and to potentially limit the data. We could have added a WHERE or LIMIT clause. This is a useful approach that enables us to manipulate both the column and row-based data:

```
val schemaRddTrain = sqlContext.sql(
    """SELECT
        |age,workclass,education,maritalstatus,
        |occupation,relationship,race,
        |gender,hoursperweek,nativecountry,income
        |FROM trainingTable """.stripMargin)
```

```
val schemaRddTest = sqlContext.sql(
   """SELECT
        |age,workclass,education,maritalstatus,
        |occupation,relationship,race,
        |gender,hoursperweek,nativecountry,income
        |FROM testingTable """.stripMargin)
```

The H2O data frames are now created from the data. The final column in each Dataset (income) is enumerated because this is the column that will form the Deep Learning label for the data. Also, enumerating this column forces the Deep Learning model to carry out classification rather than regression:

```
val trainFrame:DataFrame = schemaRddTrain
   trainFrame.replace( trainFrame.find("income"),
trainFrame.vec("income").toEnum)
   trainFrame.update(null)

   val testFrame:DataFrame = schemaRddTest
   testFrame.replace( testFrame.find("income"),
testFrame.vec("income").toEnum)
   testFrame.update(null)
```

The enumerated results data income column is now saved so that the values in this column can be used to score the tested model prediction values:

```
val testResArray = schemaRddTest.collect()
val sizeResults  = testResArray.length
var resArray     = new Array[Double](sizeResults)

for ( i <- 0 to ( resArray.length - 1)) {
    resArray(i) = testFrame.vec("income").at(i)
}
```

The Deep Learning model parameters are now set up in terms of the number of epochs or iterations--the Datasets for training and validation and the label column income, which will be used to classify the data.

Also, we chose to use variable importance to determine which data columns are the most important in the data. This parameter tells the model to calculate the effect of each feature to the target variable. This way, after the training, a table with that data can be plotted. The Deep Learning model is then created:

```
val dlParams = new DeepLearningParameters()

dlParams._epochs                = 100
dlParams._train                 = trainFrame
dlParams._valid                 = testFrame
```

```
dlParams._response_column    = 'income'
dlParams._variable_importances = true
val dl = new DeepLearning(dlParams)
val dlModel = dl.trainModel.get
```

The model is then scored against the test Dataset for predictions, and these income predictions are compared to the previously stored enumerated test data income values. Finally, an accuracy percentage is output from the test data:

```
val testH2oPredict  = dlModel.score(schemaRddTest )('predict)
val testPredictions  = toRDD[DoubleHolder](testH2oPredict)
        .collect.map(_.result.getOrElse(Double.NaN))
var resAccuracy = 0
for ( i <- 0 to ( resArray.length - 1)) {
  if (  resArray(i) == testPredictions(i) )
    resAccuracy = resAccuracy + 1
}

println()
println( ">>>>>>>>>>>>>>>>>>>>>>>>>>>>>>>>>>>>>>" )
println( ">>>>>> Model Test Accuracy = "
      + 100*resAccuracy / resArray.length  + " % " )
println( ">>>>>>>>>>>>>>>>>>>>>>>>>>>>>>>>>>>>>>" )
println()
```

In the last step, the application is stopped, the H2O functionality is terminated via a `shutdown` call, and then the Spark context is stopped:

```
water.H2O.shutdown()
sparkCxt.stop()

 println( " >>>>> Script Finished <<<<< " )

} // end application
```

Based upon a training Dataset of 32,000 and a test Dataset of 16,000 income records, this Deep Learning model is quite accurate. It reaches an accuracy level of 83 percent, which is impressive for a few lines of code, small Datasets, and just 100 epochs, as the run output shows:

```
>>>>>>>>>>>>>>>>>>>>>>>>>>>>>>>>>>>>>>>>>
>>>>>> Model Test Accuracy = 83 %
>>>>>>>>>>>>>>>>>>>>>>>>>>>>>>>>>>>>>>>>>
```

This is of course not a very impressive number. The next steps to improve this number would include hyper-parameter tuning in order to find a better parametrization of the neural network, but in order to really outperform this number, a different neural network type has to be used, which is called a **convolutional neural network (CNN)**. Unfortunately, H2O lacks direct support for CNNs and needs to make use of third-party integration to frameworks such as TensorFlow, Caffe, and MXNet. But Deeplearning4j, which is also covered in this chapter, supports CNNs out-of-the-box.

In the next section, we will examine some of the coding needed to process the MNIST data, even though that example could not be completed due to an H2O limitation at the time of coding.

The example code – MNIST

Since the MNIST image data record is so big, it presents problems while creating a Spark SQL schema and processing a data record. The records in this data are in CSV format and are formed from a 28 x 28 digit image.

Each line is then terminated by a label value for the image. We have created our schema by defining a function to create the schema string to represent the record and then calling it:

```
def getSchema(): String = {

    var schema = ""
    val limit = 28*28

    for (i <- 1 to limit){
      schema += "P" + i.toString + " "
    }
    schema += "Label"

    schema // return value
}

val schemaString = getSchema()
val schema = StructType( schemaString.split(" ")
    .map(fieldName => StructField(fieldName, IntegerType, false)))
```

The same general approach to Deep Learning can be taken to data processing as the previous example, apart from the actual processing of the raw CSV data. There are too many columns to process individually, and they all need to be converted into integers to represent their data type. This can be done in two ways.

In the first example, var args can be used to process all the elements in the row:

```
val trainRDD  = rawTrainData.map( rawRow => Row(
rawRow.split(",").map(_.toInt): _* ))
```

The second example uses the `fromSeq` method to process the row elements:

```
val trainRDD  = rawTrainData.map(rawRow => Row.fromSeq(rawRow.split(",")
.map(_.toInt)))
```

In the next section, the H2O Flow user interface will be examined to see how it can be used to both monitor H2O and process the data.

H2O Flow

H2O Flow is a web-based open source user interface for H2O and, given that it is being used with Spark, Sparkling Water. It is a fully functional H2O web interface for monitoring the H2O Sparkling Water cluster jobs, and also for manipulating data and training models.

We have created some simple example code to start the H2O interface. As in the previous Scala-based code samples, all we need to do is create a Spark, an H2O context, and then call the `openFlow` command, which will start the Flow interface.

The following Scala code example just imports classes for Spark context, configuration, and H2O. It then defines the configuration in terms of the application name and the Spark cluster URL.

A Spark context is then created using the configuration object:

```
import org.apache.spark.SparkContext
import org.apache.spark.SparkContext._
import org.apache.spark.SparkConf
import org.apache.spark.h2o._

object h2o_spark_ex2  extends App {
   val sparkMaster = "spark://localhost:7077"
   val appName = "Spark h2o ex2"
   val conf = new SparkConf()

   conf.setMaster(sparkMaster)
   conf.setAppName(appName)

   val sparkCxt = new SparkContext(conf)
```

An H2O context is then created and started using the Spark context. The H2O context classes are imported, and the Flow user interface is started with the `openFlow` command:

```
implicit val h2oContext = new
org.apache.spark.h2o.H2OContext(sparkCxt).start()

import h2oContext._

// Open H2O UI

openFlow
```

Note that, for the purposes of this example and to enable us to use the Flow application, we have commented out the H2O shutdown and the Spark context stop options. We would not normally do this, but we wanted to make this application long-running so that it gives us plenty of time to use the interface:

```
// shutdown h20

//   water.H2O.shutdown()
//   sparkCxt.stop()

println( " >>>>> Script Finished <<<<< " )

} // end application
```

We use our Bash script `run_h2o.bash` with the application class name called `h2o_spark_ex2` as a parameter. This script contains a call to the `spark-submit` command, which will execute the compiled application:

```
[hadoop@hc2r1m2 h2o_spark_1_2]$ ./run_h2o.bash h2o_spark_ex2
```

When the application runs, it lists the state of the H2O cluster and provides a URL by which the H2O Flow browser can be accessed:

```
15/05/20 13:00:21 INFO H2OContext: Sparkling Water started, status of
context:
 Sparkling Water Context:
  * number of executors: 4
  * list of used executors:
   (executorId, host, port)
   ------------------------
   (1,hc2r1m4,54321)
   (3,hc2r1m2,54321)
   (0,hc2r1m3,54321)
   (2,hc2r1m1,54321)
   ------------------------
```

Open H2O Flow in browser: `http://192.168.1.108:54323` (CMD + click in macOS). The previous example shows that we can access the H2O interface using the port number `54323` on the host IP address `192.168.1.108`.

So, we can access the interface using the `hc2r1m2:54323` URL. The following screenshot shows the Flow interface with no data loaded.

There are data processing and administration menu options, and buttons at the top of the page. To the right, there are help options to enable you to learn more about H2O:

The following screenshot shows the menu options and buttons in greater detail. In the following sections, we will use a practical example to explain some of these options, but there will not be enough space in this chapter to cover all the functionality. Check the `http://h2o.ai/` website to learn about the Flow application in detail, available at `http://h2o.ai/product/flow/`:

In greater definition, you can see that the previous menu options and buttons allow you to both administer your H2O Spark cluster and also manipulate the data that you wish to process.

The following screenshot shows a reformatted list of the help options available, so that if you get stuck, you can investigate solving your problem from the same interface:

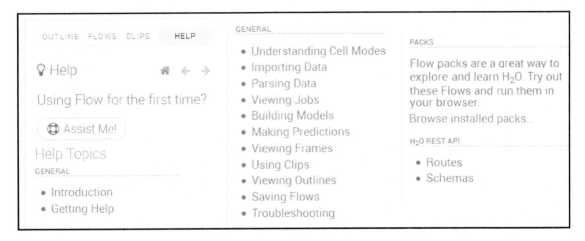

If we go to **Menu | Admin | Cluster Status**, we will obtain the following screenshot, which shows us the status of each cluster server in terms of memory, disk, load, and cores.

It's a useful snapshot that provides us with a color-coded indication of the status:

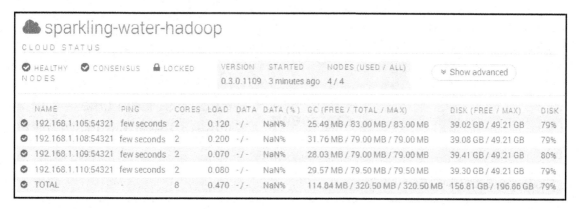

The menu option, **Admin | Jobs**, provides details of the current cluster jobs in terms of the start, end, runtimes, and status. Clicking on the job name provides further details, as shown next, including data processing details and an estimated runtime, which is useful. Also, if you select the **Refresh** button, the display will continuously refresh until it is deselected:

The **Admin | Water Meter** option provides a visual display of the CPU usage on each node in the cluster.

As you can see in the following screenshot, our meter shows that my cluster was idle:

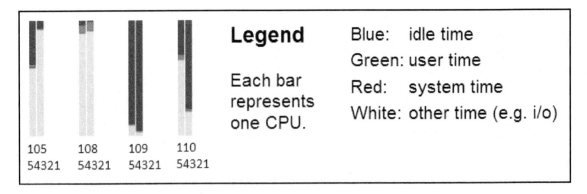

Using the menu option, **Flow | Upload File**, we have uploaded some of the training data used in the previous Deep Learning Scala-based example.

The data has been loaded into a data preview pane; we can see a sample of the data that has been organized into cells. Also, an accurate guess has been made of the data types so that we can see which columns can be enumerated. This is useful if we want to consider classification:

DATA PREVIEW

Numeric ▾	Enum ▾	Numeric ▾	Enum ▾	Numeric ▾	Enum ▾	Enum ▾
39	State-gov	77516	Bachelors	13	Never-married	Adm-clerical
50	Self-emp-not-inc	83311	Bachelors	13	Married-civ-spouse	Exec-managerial
38	Private	215646	HS-grad	9	Divorced	Handlers-cleaners
53	Private	234721	11th	7	Married-civ-spouse	Handlers-cleaners

Having loaded the data, we are now presented with a Frame display, which offers us the ability to view, inspect, build a model, create a prediction, or download the data. The data display shows information such as min, max, and mean.

It shows data types, labels, and a zero data count, as shown in the following screenshot:

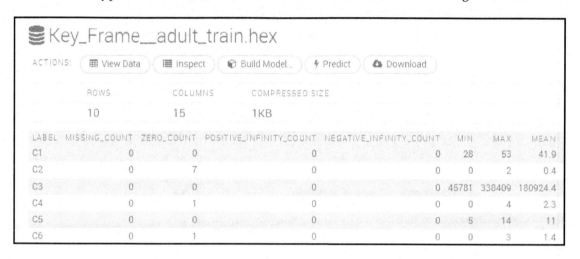

LABEL	MISSING_COUNT	ZERO_COUNT	POSITIVE_INFINITY_COUNT	NEGATIVE_INFINITY_COUNT	MIN	MAX	MEAN
C1	0	0	0		0	28	53	41.9
C2	0	7	0		0	0	2	0.4
C3	0	0	0		0	45781	338409	180924.4
C4	0	1	0		0	0	4	2.3
C5	0	0	0		0	5	14	11
C6	0	1	0		0	0	3	1.4

We thought that it would be useful to create a Deep Learning classification model based on this data to compare the Scala-based approach to this H2O user interface. Using the **view** and **inspect** options, it is possible to visually and interactively check the data, as well as create plots relating to the data. For instance, using the previous inspect option followed by the **plot columns** option, we were able to create a plot of data labels versus zero counts in the column data. The following screenshot shows the result:

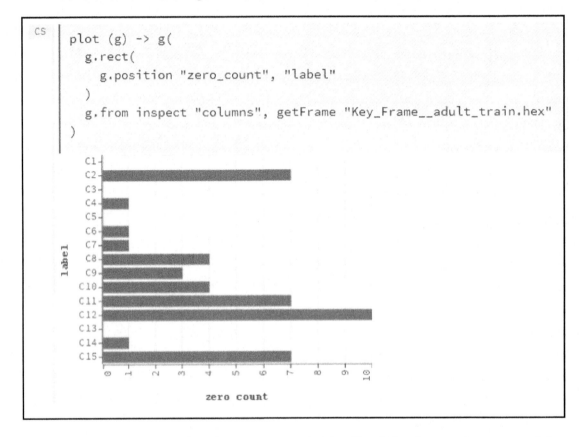

By selecting the Build Model option, a menu option is offered that lets us choose a model type. We will select **deeplearning**, as we already know that this data is suited to this classification approach.

The previous Scala-based model resulted in an accuracy level of 83 percent:

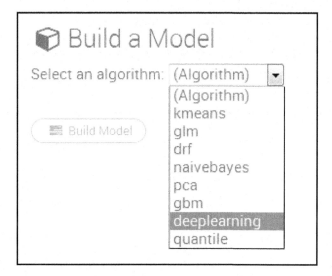

We have selected the **deeplearning** option. Having chosen this option, we are able to set model parameters such as training and validation Datasets, as well as choose the data columns that our model should use (obviously, the two Datasets should contain the same columns).

The following screenshot displays the Datasets and the model columns being selected:

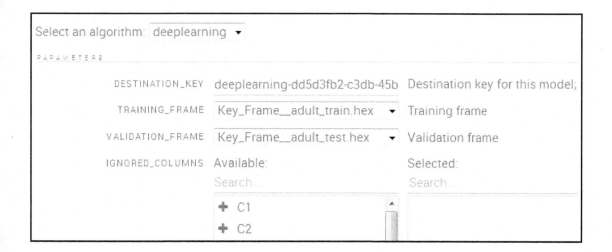

There is a large range of basic and advanced model options available. A selection of them is shown in the following screenshot.

We have set the response column to 15 as the income column. We have also set the **VARIABLE_IMPORTANCES** option. Note that we don't need to enumerate the response column, as it has been done automatically:

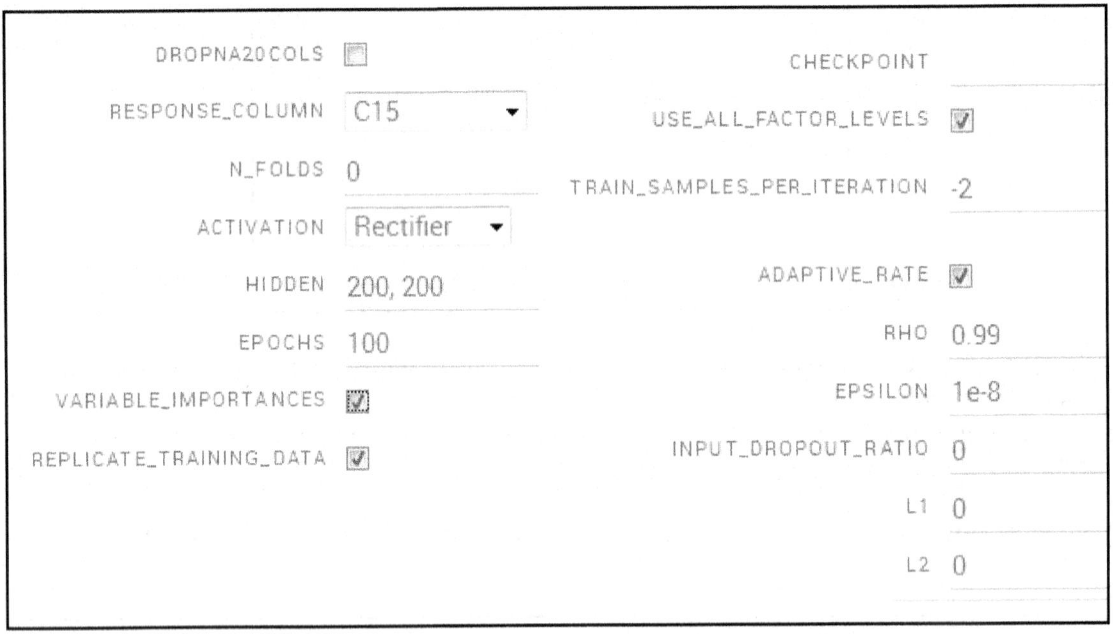

DROPNA20COLS	☐		CHECKPOINT	
RESPONSE_COLUMN	C15 ▼		USE_ALL_FACTOR_LEVELS	☑
N_FOLDS	0		TRAIN_SAMPLES_PER_ITERATION	-2
ACTIVATION	Rectifier ▼			
HIDDEN	200, 200		ADAPTIVE_RATE	☑
EPOCHS	100		RHO	0.99
VARIABLE_IMPORTANCES	☑		EPSILON	1e-8
REPLICATE_TRAINING_DATA	☑		INPUT_DROPOUT_RATIO	0
			L1	0
			L2	0

Note also that the epochs or iterations option is set to `100`, as before. Also, the figure `200`, `200` for the hidden layers indicates that the network has two hidden layers, each with 200 neurons. Selecting the **Build Model** option causes the model to be created with these parameters.

The following screenshot shows the model being trained, including an estimation of training time and an indication of the data processed so far:

Viewing the model, once trained, shows training and validation metrics, as well as a list of the important training parameters:

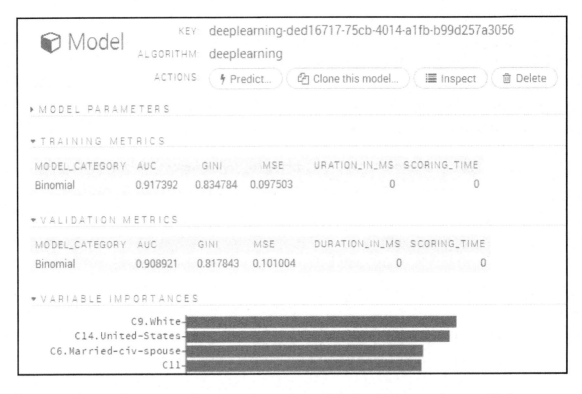

Selecting the **Predict** option allows an alternative validation Dataset to be specified. Choosing the **Predict** option using the new Dataset causes the already trained model to be validated against a new test Dataset:

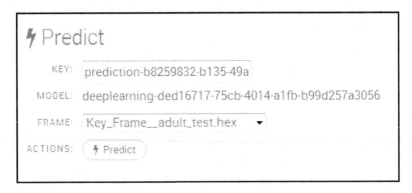

Selecting the **Predict** option causes the prediction details for the DeepLearning model and the Dataset to be displayed, as shown in the following screenshot:

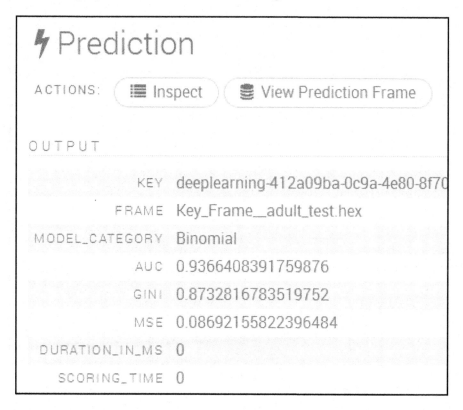

The preceding screenshot shows the test data frame and the model category, as well as the validation statistics in terms of AUC, GINI, and MSE.

The AUC value, or area under the curve, relates to the ROC, or the receiver operator characteristics curve, which is also shown in the following screenshot.

TPR means **True Positive Rate**, and **FPR** means **False Positive Rate**.

AUC is a measure of accuracy, with a value of one being perfect. So, the blue line shows greater accuracy than that of the red line, which is basically random guessing:

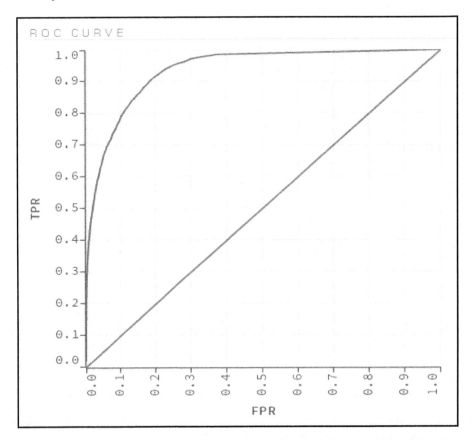

There is a great deal of functionality available within this interface that we have not explained, but we hope that we have given you a feel for its power and potential. You can use this interface to inspect your data and create reports before attempting to develop code, or as an application in its own right to delve into your data.

Deeplearning4j

Deeplearning4j is developed by a Silicon Valley startup called **Skymind** and can be found at `www.deeplearning4j.org`. It is open source and runs in many different environments, including Apache Spark.

The most important components of the framework are as follows:

- **Deeplearning4j runtime**: This is the core module that allows you to define and execute all sorts of neural networks on top of Apache Spark, but it does not use Apache Spark directly; it uses a a tensor library similar to NumPy for Python.
- **ND4J/ND4S**: This tensor library is really the heart of Deeplearning4j. It can also be used standalone and provides accelerated linear algebra on top of CPUs and GPUs. For porting code to a GPU, no code changes are required, since a JVM property configures the underlying execution engine, which can also be a CUDA backend for nVidia GPU cards.

In contrast to H2O, Deeplearning4j doesn't necessarily need any additional components to be installed, since it is a native Apache Spark application using the interfaces that Apache Spark provides.

ND4J - high performance linear algebra for the JVM

Let's have a look at ND4J first. As already mentioned, **ND4J** is a tensor and linear algebra library. This means multidimensional arrays (also called tensors) and operations on them are the main purpose. Operations are simple but fast, for example, like in NumPy for Python, if you are familiar with it.

So what's the advantage of using ND4J over NumPy?

- First of all, when using Apache Spark, we stay in the same JVM process and don't have to pay the overhead of **IPC** (**inter process communication**) at all.
- Then, ND4J is capable of using SIMD instruction sets on modern CPUs, which doubles the performance of ND4J over NumPy. This is achieved by using OpenBLAS.
- Finally, ND4J can take advantage of the GPUs present on your machine by just setting a system property on the JVM, provided a recent version of the CUDA drivers and framework is installed on your system.

So, let's have a taste of what this looks like, syntax wise, in Scala:

```
import org.nd4j.linalg.factory.Nd4j
import org.nd4j.linalg.api.ndarray.INDArray
var v: INDArray = Nd4j.create(Array(Array(1d, 2d, 3d), Array(4d, 5d, 6d)))
var w: INDArray = Nd4j.create(Array(Array(1d, 2d), Array(3d, 4d), Array(5d,
6d)))
print(v.mul(w))
```

As you can see, we are creating two matrices v and w of type INDArray using the
Nd4j.create method. In order to do so, we have to provide a nested Scala array of type
double, which we can create inline like this:

```
Array(Array(1d, 2d, 3d), Array(4d, 5d, 6d))
```

Finally, the v.mul(w) code actually triggers the matrix multiplication, again, either on a
CPU or GPU, but this is totally transparent to us.

Deeplearning4j

So, now that we've covered ND4J, we want to actually create our neural network. So let's
start with the famous XOR example, which actually trains a neural network for learning
XOR.

Let's first generate some training data inline:

```
/*
     * list off input values, 4 training samples with data for 2 input-
neurons each
     */
    var input: INDArray = Nd4j.zeros(4, 2)

    /*
     * correspondending list with expected output values, 4 training
samples with
     * data for 2 output-neurons each
     */
    var labels: INDArray = Nd4j.zeros(4, 2);

    /*
     * create first dataset when first input=0 and second input=0
     */
    input.putScalar(Array(0, 0), 0);
    input.putScalar(Array(0, 1), 0);

    /*
```

```
     *   then the first output fires for false, and the second is 0 (see
class comment)
     */
    labels.putScalar(Array(0, 0), 1);
    labels.putScalar(Array(0, 1), 0);

    /*
     * when first input=1 and second input=0
     */
    input.putScalar(Array(1, 0), 1);
    input.putScalar(Array(1, 1), 0);

    /*
     *   then xor is true, therefore the second output neuron fires
     */
    labels.putScalar(Array(1, 0), 0);
    labels.putScalar(Array(1, 1), 1);

    /*
     *   same as above
     */
    input.putScalar(Array(2, 0), 0);
    input.putScalar(Array(2, 1), 1);
    labels.putScalar(Array(2, 0), 0);
    labels.putScalar(Array(2, 1), 1);

    /*
     *   when both inputs fire, xor is false again - the first output
should fire
     */
    input.putScalar(Array(3, 0), 1);
    input.putScalar(Array(3, 1), 1);
    labels.putScalar(Array(3, 0), 1);
    labels.putScalar(Array(3, 1), 0);
```

Now we have created two ND4J arrays, one called `input` containing the features, and one called `labels` containing the expected outcome.

Just as a reminder, the XOR function table looks like this:

Input 1	Input 2	Output
0	0	0
0	1	1
1	0	1
1	1	0

Please note that the output is one if only, and exactly, one of the two inputs is one. This is the function table of the XOR function.

Now let's use the data we created in the preceding section in order to prepare it for neural network training:

```
var ds: DataSet = new DataSet(input, labels)
print(ds)
```

A Dataset, not to be confused with the one from Apache SparkSQL, is a Deeplearning4j data structure containing ND4J arrays for training.

Here, you can see what this looks like internally:

```
===========INPUT===================
[[0.00, 0.00],
 [1.00, 0.00],
 [0.00, 1.00],
 [1.00, 1.00]]
================OUTPUT==================
[[1.00, 0.00],
 [0.00, 1.00],
 [0.00, 1.00],
 [1.00, 0.00]]
```

This reflects the structure of the XOR function table with two differences:

- ND4J uses `float` as internal data type representation
- The output is in binary form, for example, a two-dimensional array, a fact very handy for training binary classifiers with neural networks where we have two output neurons

Now it's time to create a `NeuralNetConfiguration Builder`--this is the way to define and create neural networks in Deeplearning4j:

```
/*
     * Set up network configuration
     */
    var builder: NeuralNetConfiguration.Builder = new
NeuralNetConfiguration.Builder();

    /*
     *   how often should the training set be run, we need something above
     *   1000, or a higher learning-rate - found this values just by trial
and error
     */
    builder.iterations(10000);

    /*
     * learning rate
     */
    builder.learningRate(0.1);

    /*
     * fixed seed for the random generator, so any run of this program
     * brings the same results - may not work if you do something like
ds.shuffle()
     */
    builder.seed(123);

    /*
     *   not applicable, this network is to small - but for bigger networks
it
     *   can help that the network will not only recite the training data
     */
    builder.useDropConnect(false);

    /*
     *   a standard algorithm for moving on the error-plane, this one works
     *   best for me, LINE_GRADIENT_DESCENT or CONJUGATE_GRADIENT can do
the
     *   job, too - it's an empirical value which one matches best to
     *   your problem
     */
builder.optimizationAlgo(OptimizationAlgorithm.STOCHASTIC_GRADIENT_DESCENT)
;

    /*
     *   init the bias with 0 - empirical value, too
     */
```

```
        builder.biasInit(0);

        /*
         *  from "http://deeplearning4j.org/architecture": The networks can
         *  process the input more quickly and more accurately by ingesting
         *  minibatches 5-10 elements at a time in parallel.
         *  this example runs better without, because the dataset is smaller
than
         *  the mini batch size
         */
        builder.miniBatch(false);

        /*
         * create a multilayer network with 2 layers (including the output
layer, excluding the input payer)
         */
        var listBuilder: ListBuilder = builder.list();
        var hiddenLayerBuilder: DenseLayer.Builder = new DenseLayer.Builder();

        /*
         * two input connections - simultaneously defines the number of input
         * neurons, because it's the first non-input-layer
         */
        hiddenLayerBuilder.nIn(2);

        /*
         * number of outgooing connections, nOut simultaneously defines the
         * number of neurons in this layer
         */
        hiddenLayerBuilder.nOut(4);

        /*
         * put the output through the sigmoid function, to cap the output
         * valuebetween 0 and 1
         */
        hiddenLayerBuilder.activation(Activation.SIGMOID);

        /*
         * random initialize weights with values between 0 and 1
         */
        hiddenLayerBuilder.weightInit(WeightInit.DISTRIBUTION);
        hiddenLayerBuilder.dist(new UniformDistribution(0, 1));
```

The preceding code basically just sets parameters global to the neural network. Digging into each of those is beyond the scope of this book. Now let's add individual neural network layers in order to form a deep neural network:

```
    /*
```

```
    * build and set as layer 0
    */
   listBuilder.layer(0, hiddenLayerBuilder.build());

   /*
    * MCXENT or NEGATIVELOGLIKELIHOOD (both are mathematically
equivalent) work ok for this example - this
    * function calculates the error-value (aka 'cost' or 'loss function
value'), and quantifies the goodness
    * or badness of a prediction, in a differentiable way
    * For classification (with mutually exclusive classes, like here),
use multiclass cross entropy, in conjunction
    * with softmax activation function
    */
   var outputLayerBuilder: Builder = new
OutputLayer.Builder(LossFunctions.LossFunction.NEGATIVELOGLIKELIHOOD);

   /*
    *  must be the same amout as neurons in the layer before
    */
   outputLayerBuilder.nIn(4);

   /*
    *  two neurons in this layer
    */
   outputLayerBuilder.nOut(2);
   outputLayerBuilder.activation(Activation.SOFTMAX);
   outputLayerBuilder.weightInit(WeightInit.DISTRIBUTION);
   outputLayerBuilder.dist(new UniformDistribution(0, 1));
   listBuilder.layer(1, outputLayerBuilder.build());
```

This code basically adds two layers to the neural network: an input layer with two neurons (each one for one column of the XOR function table) and an output layer with two neurons, one for each class (as we have outcomes zero and one in the XOR function table). Again, you see that we can specify an abundance of layer-specific parameters (also beyond the scope of this book). Now let's actually create the neural network:

```
   /*
    * no pretrain phase for this network
    */
   listBuilder.pretrain(false);

   /*
    * seems to be mandatory
    * according to agibsoncccc: You typically only use that with
    * pretrain(true) when you want to do pretrain/finetune without
changing
```

```
      * the previous layers finetuned weights that's for autoencoders and
rbms
      */
    listBuilder.backprop(true);

    /*
     * build and init the network, will check if everything is configured
correct
     */
    var conf: MultiLayerConfiguration = listBuilder.build();
    var net: MultiLayerNetwork = new MultiLayerNetwork(conf);
    net.init();
```

Now the `net` variable contains our ready-made neural network, and the only thing we have to do in order to train it with our XOR function table is run the following code:

```
net.fit(ds)
```

If we now look at the output (`sysout`), we see a debug message on how the learning progresses:

```
08:52:56.714 [main] INFO  o.d.o.l.ScoreIterationListener - Score at
iteration 400 is 0.6919901371002197
08:52:56.905 [main] INFO  o.d.o.l.ScoreIterationListener - Score at
iteration 500 is 0.6902942657470703
 08:52:57.085 [main] INFO  o.d.o.l.ScoreIterationListener - Score at
iteration 600 is 0.6845208406448364
....
08:53:11.720 [main] INFO  o.d.o.l.ScoreIterationListener - Score at
iteration 9700 is 0.0012604787480086088
 08:53:11.847 [main] INFO  o.d.o.l.ScoreIterationListener - Score at
iteration 9800 is 0.0012446331093087792
 08:53:11.994 [main] INFO  o.d.o.l.ScoreIterationListener - Score at
iteration 9900 is 0.00122913101222223661
```

As you can see, there are `9900` iterations where the neural network is trained (so basically, the very same Dataset is shown to the neural network multiple times), and for every 100 iterations, a measure called score is printed.

This is the so-called **Root Mean Square Error (RMSE)**--a measure of how well the neural network fits to the data; the lower the better. As you can observe, after 10,000 iterations, the RMSE went down to `0.00122913101222223661`, which is a very good value in this case. So, let's check on how well we are actually doing. As in Apache SparkML, Deeplearning4j has a built-in component for the evaluation:

```
    /*
     * let Evaluation prints stats how often the right output had the
```

```
 */
var eval: Evaluation = new Evaluation(2);
eval.eval(ds.getLabels(), output);
println(eval.stats());
```

The code produces an output of the following measures on the prediction (classification) performance:

```
===========================Scores===========================
  Accuracy:         1
  Precision:        1
  Recall:           1
  F1 Score:         1
============================================================
```

This actually means that we have 100 percent on all the measures, so we've built a perfect classifier to compute XOR. Well done!

> In reality, things such as perfect classifiers don't exist. It is trivial to train a neural network in order to do zero errors on the set of only four possible inputs on XOR. But in reality, as soon as you at least have one continuous feature as opposed to categorical ones, you'll end up with infinite input possibilities. So you can only approximate a perfect classifier. This is known as the bias-variance trade-off. Let's consider spam classification as an example. This means either you build a classifier that is capable of recognizing all spam, but then will also mark real emails as spam (false positives), or it won't mark real emails as spam but will miss marking all spam emails as spam (false negatives).

Example: an IoT real-time anomaly detector

Now let's get started with building something useful on Apache Spark with Deeplearning4j. We're using an IoT use case again as we did in Chapter 6, *Structured Streaming*.

Again, we need an IBM Cloud account for the test data generator. The test data generator is Node-RED based, but this time, it generates a different type of data.

Mastering chaos: the Lorenz attractor model

In order to get good simulated test data, we are using the so-called Lorenz attractor model.

Let's start with a little sample use case. Consider the task of detecting anomalies in vibration (accelerometer) sensor data measuring a bearing. In order to obtain such a data stream, we simply attach such a sensor to or near the bearing:

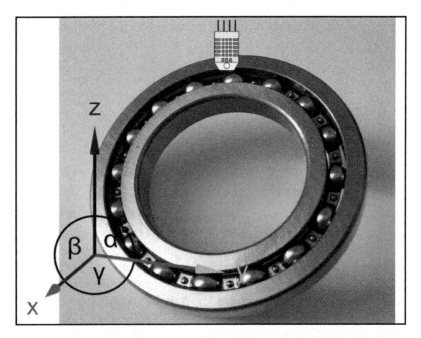

The **Lorenz attractor** model is a physical model capable of generating a three-dimensional data stream, which we will use in place of a real accelerometer sensor stream. By the way, Lorenz was one of the founders of the chaos theory.

Now our task is to detect anomalies using a neural network, basically predicting when a bearing is about to break.

Therefore, we can switch the test data generator between two states, healthy and broken. This is a phase plot showing the three vibration dimensions on a time series:

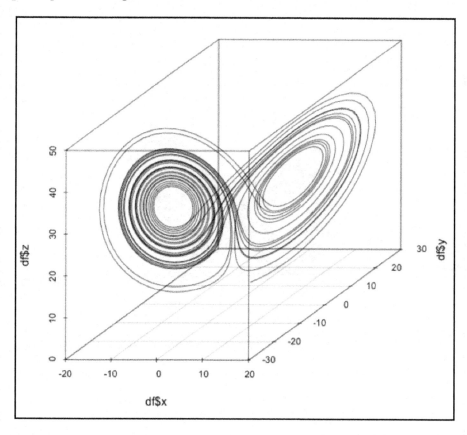

We can observe the same when changing the parameters of the physical model slightly in order to get a faulty state:

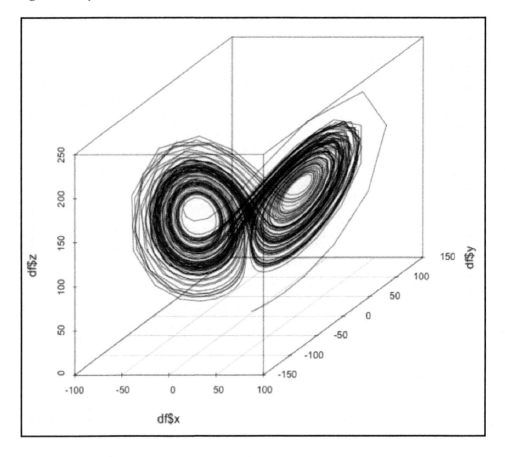

For those not familiar with phase plots, let's use a run chart for the three time series, again in the healthy state:

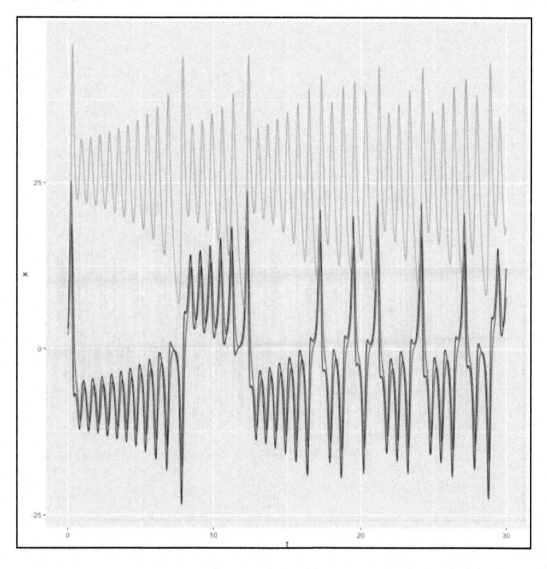

This is in the faulty state:

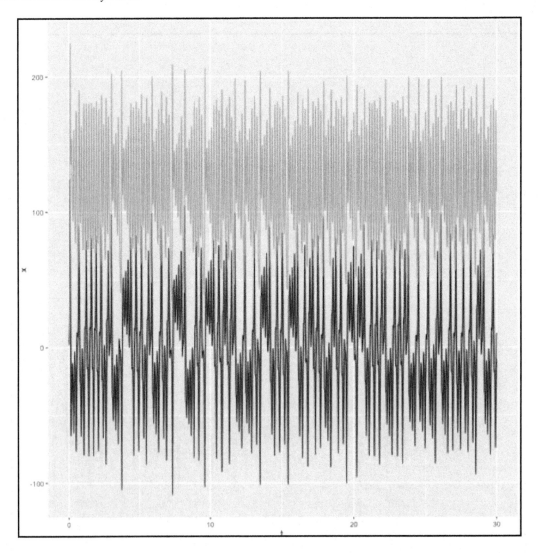

One common technique is to transform these data from the time to the frequency domain using **discrete Fourier transformation (DFT)** or wavelets.

Again, the FFT for the healthy state is shown here:

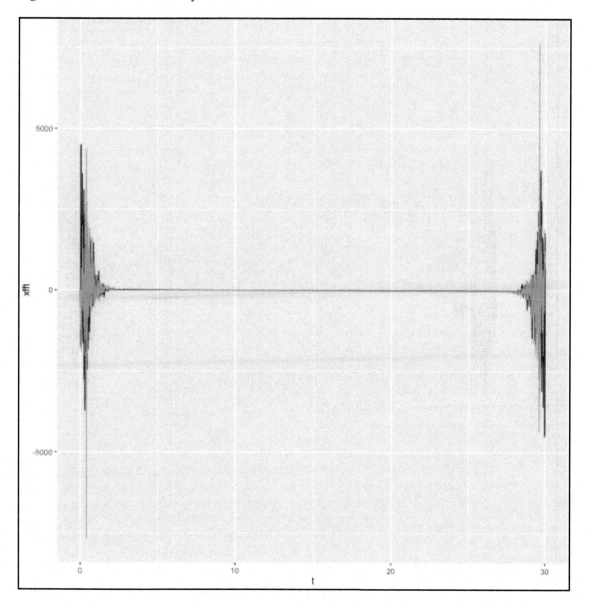

And this is for the faulty state:

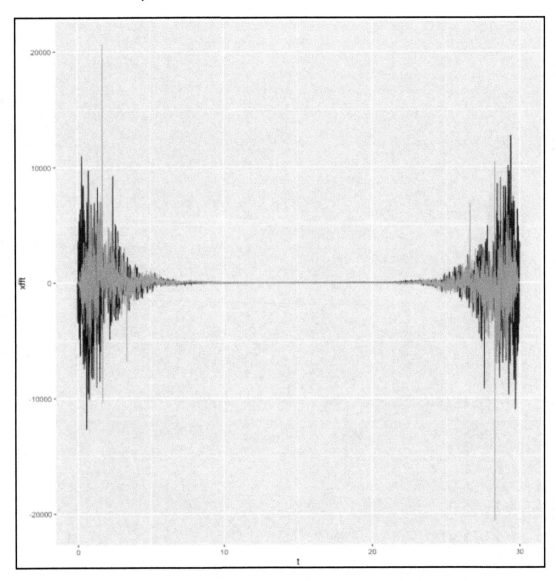

We can clearly observe that the faulty state has more energy and additional frequencies present. So, this would be sufficient to train a classifier, as we learned before, but we can do better. Let's construct a system capable of learning normal behavior from data, and once it sees data (or sequential patterns) it hasn't seen before, have it raise an alert.

Such a system is an LSTM-based auto-encoder as shown in the following figure:

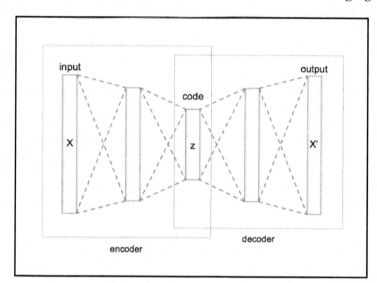

This basically compresses the vast amount of data through a neural bottleneck in order to try to reconstruct the very same data it has seen but, of course, via a bottleneck losing vast amounts of irrelevant information.

Therefore, such a neural network will learn how a system normally behaves, and as soon as new patterns are seen, it will have a hard time reconstructing the data, and therefore, we can raise an alert.

The LSTM layers keep track of the inherent state, basically making the neural network aware of the time domain by adding memory to the neurons. We will now implement this system end-to-end from the sensor to the insight, so stay tuned!

Deploying the test data generator

In order to have a simple framework for creating data, we started writing a test data creator, which will be part of a bigger time series and machine learning toolkit. This tool is running on the open source data flow platform called Node-RED--a graphical flow editor on top of Node.js. This is quite handy since Node.js is very lightweight and can, therefore, run on nearly any device, even IoT gateways such as the Raspberry Pi or BeagleBone.

We covered Node-RED and how to use it for generating test data in `Chapter 6`, *Structured Streaming*. So, in this case, we'll use it in order to implement the Lorenz attractor model, as explained previously.

The final idea is that this becomes part of the time series toolkit as well, with the capability of generating data by sampling various physical models, and you can decide on the degree of noise and also switch between different states of the physical model for anomaly detection and classification tasks.

But, for now, we've implemented the Lorenz attractor model only. This is a very simple but interesting physical model. Lorenz was one of the pioneers of the chaos theory, and he was able to show that a very simple model consisting only of three equations and four model parameters can create chaotic behaviour, a system highly sensitive to initial conditions and also oscillating between multiple semi-stable states, where state transitions are very hard to predict.

As the simulator is completely implemented as a Node-RED flow, we can just create a Node-RED IoT Starter Boilerplate on the IBM Cloud (of course, it runs on any Node-RED instance, even on a Raspberry Pi, where it can be used to simulate sensor data on the edge) or on your local machine.

The steps to get the simulator up and running are as follows:

1. Deploy the Node-RED IoT Starter Boilerplate to the IBM Cloud.
2. Deploy the test data generator flow.
3. Test the test data generator.
4. Get the IBM Watson IoT platform credentials in order to consume the data via MQTT from any place in the world.

Deploy the Node-RED IoT Starter Boilerplate to the IBM Cloud

You'll need an IBM Bluemix Cloud account. Most likely, you already have one, since examples of other chapters are dependent on it as well. If not, you can get one for free here: `https://ibm.biz/CloudFreemium`. Once done, here are the steps to get Node-RED deployed to your cloud account:

1. Open the following link: `https://console-regional.ng.bluemix.net/catalog/starters/internet-of-things-platform-starter?env_id=ibm:yp:us-south`.

2. Name your application (note that the hostname gets updated as well), and click on **Create**.

3. Once done, click on **Connections.**

4. On the **Internet of Things Platform** tile, click on **View credentials**.

5. Write down the values of the following properties, as you will need them later:
   - `org`
   - `apiKey`
   - `apiToken`

6. Close this view.

7. Wait until your application starts, and then click on **Visit App URL**.

8. When asked, set a `username` and `password` for your application, and note it down.

9. Click on **Go to our Node-RED flow editor**.

Congratulations, you should see something like this:

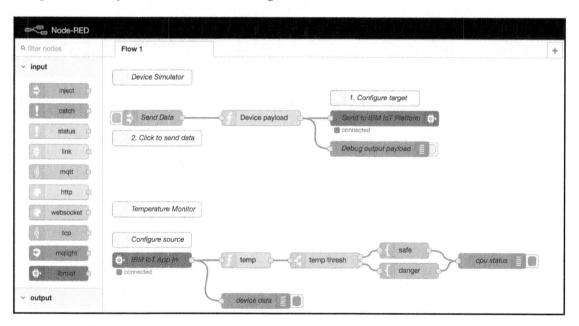

This is the Node-RED flow pane where you can design real-time data processing workflows. But we have already created the Lorenz attractor flow for you, so let's deploy it.

Deploying the test data generator flow

Now it's time to deploy our test data generator Node-RED flow. In order to do so, we create an empty panel by clicking on the plus sign, as illustrated in the following screenshot:

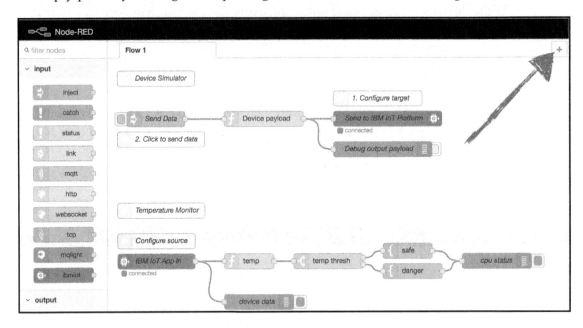

Now it's time to click on the upper-right menu, as illustrated in the following screenshot:

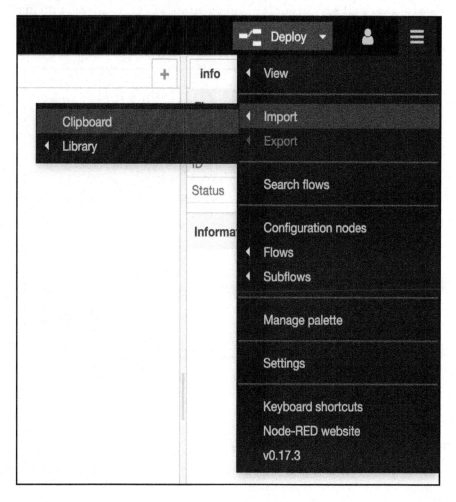

We now paste the contents of the URL `https://raw.githubusercontent.com/romeokienz ler/developerWorks/master/lorenzattractor/simulatorflow.json`, into the text area by opening the URL and copy-pasting the JSON contents into the text area, as illustrated here:

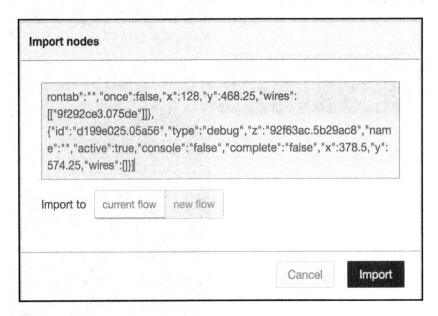

We click on **Import**, drag the flow to the panel, and click on it in order to fix it. Now we hit deploy at the top right, and we are done!

Testing the test data generator

This is an easy step. Just click on the reset button once, and the generator will generate 3,000 data points in order for us to analyze them.

If you click on the **debug** tab on the right-hand side, you'll see the data points being generated:

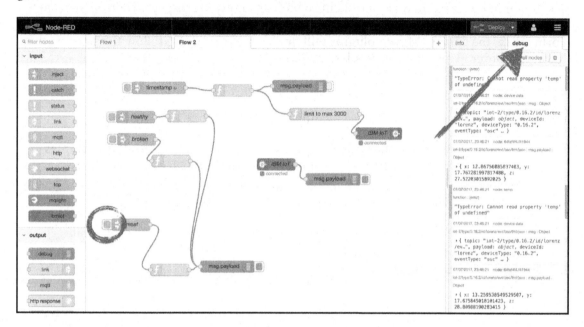

In the **debug** pane, you'll see some error messages:

`TypeError: Cannot read property 'temp' of undefined`

These are due to the flow running in tab one, and these can be ignored.

Install the Deeplearning4j example within Eclipse

The first thing we need to do is start Eclipse with an empty workspace. Then we have to grab the whole Deeplearning4j examples tree from **Git** and install it through **Maven**. Fortunately, the Git and Maven plugins will do this for you. Please follow the steps on this tutorial in order to install the examples: `https://github.com/romeokienzler/deeplearning4j/blob/gh-pages/gettingstarted.md#using-dl4j-examples-in-eclipse-with-direct-checkout-from-git-via-the-maven-plugin`.

Once we've run the XOR example successfully, we can finalize the installation:

1. First, we switch to the Scala perspective. We right-click on the **dl4j-examples-spark project**, and then go to **Configure | Add Scala Nature**.
2. Then, we right-click on the **dl4j-examples-spark project** again, and then click on **Maven | Update Project...** and wait until the rebuild takes place.

 Please ignore the Maven errors so far. As long as `Run.scala` compiles without error, you are fine!

3. Then we update `src/resources/ibm_watson_iot_mqtt.properties` with the credentials of the IBM Watson IoT platform by setting the `org`, `apiKey`, and `apiToken` we discovered previously during the installation of the test data generator.

Running the examples in Eclipse

Now, as everything is set up, let's run the examples. We can simply run the `Run.scala` class as the Scala application, as illustrated in the following screenshot:

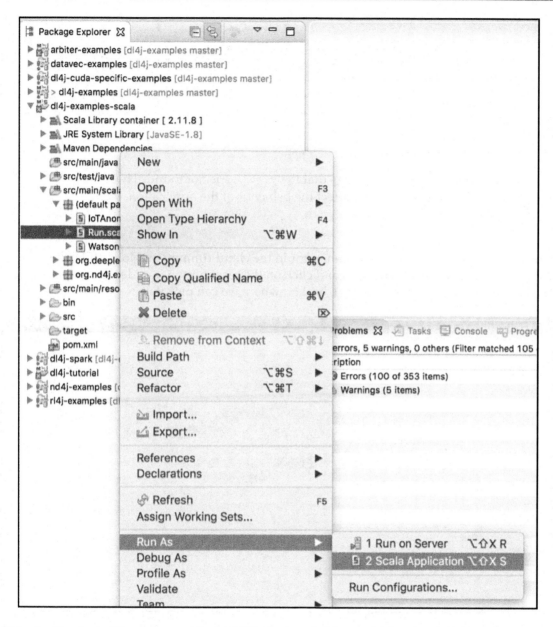

This application will connect to the MQTT message broker, which is part of the IBM Watson IoT Platform running in the cloud. That's the message hub where the test data generator published data to, and we'll just subscribe to this data:

```
Markers    Properties    Servers    Data Source Explorer    Snippets    Console    Progress
Run$ [Scala Application] /Library/Java/JavaVirtualMachines/jdk1.8.0_65.jdk/Contents/Home/bin/java (23 Jun 2017, 07:34:54)
jar:file:/Users/romeokienzler/.m2/repository/org/nd4j/nd4j-common/0.8.0/nd4j-common-0.8.0.jar!/
jar:file:/Users/romeokienzler/.m2/repository/org/nd4j/nd4j-native/0.8.0/nd4j-native-0.8.0-windows-x86_64.jar!/
07:34:59.589 [main] INFO org.reflections.Reflections - Reflections took 91 ms to scan 14 urls, producing 373 keys and 1449 values
Jun 23, 2017 7:34:59 AM com.ibm.iotf.client.AbstractClient createClient
INFO: main: Org ID     = rwyrty
        Client ID  = a:rwyrty:o2g6k39sl6r5
Jun 23, 2017 7:34:59 AM com.ibm.iotf.client.AbstractClient connect
INFO: main: Connecting client a:rwyrty:o2g6k39sl6r5 to ssl://rwyrty.messaging.internetofthings.ibmcloud.com:8883 (attempt #1)...
Jun 23, 2017 7:35:09 AM com.ibm.iotf.client.AbstractClient connect
INFO: main: Successfully connected to the IBM Watson IoT Platform
Mainthread blocking...
```

Please ignore warnings that the `Vfs.Dir` is not found. Those are only warnings and don't affect the behavior of the application.

Now it's time to start the test data generator in the cloud running on Node-RED, therefore, we will open up the browser again, and click on the **reset** button in order to send another 30 seconds worth of data to the message broker, where we can pick it up:

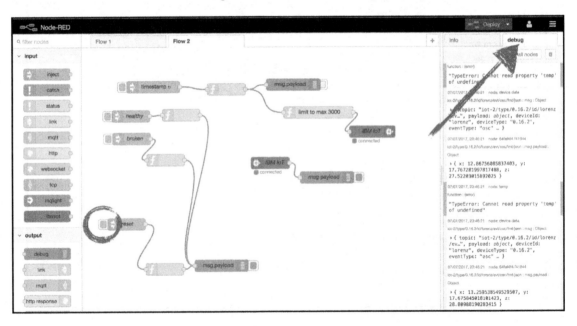

Now the application will receive the subscribed data from the message hub and fill a tumbling, count-based window. We covered sliding, tumbling, count and time-based windows in Chapter 6, *Structured Streaming*.

```
Markers    Properties    Servers    Data Source Explorer    Snippets    Console ☒    Progress
Run$ [Scala Application] /Library/Java/JavaVirtualMachines/jdk1.8.0_65.jdk/Contents/Home/bin/java (21 Jun 2017, 07:55:32)
Mainthread blocking...
Mainthread blocking...
Mainthread blocking...
Mainthread blocking...
Waiting for tumbling window to fill: 0
Waiting for tumbling window to fill: 100
Waiting for tumbling window to fill: 200
Waiting for tumbling window to fill: 300
Waiting for tumbling window to fill: 400
Waiting for tumbling window to fill: 500
Waiting for tumbling window to fill: 600
```

Once this window is full, the data is sent to the neural network, where it gets analyzed:

```
o.d.o.l.ScoreIterationListener - Score at iteration 0 is 392314.67211754626
o.d.o.l.ScoreIterationListener - Score at iteration 1 is 392312.42505880696
o.d.o.l.ScoreIterationListener - Score at iteration 2 is 392304.37555201456
o.d.o.l.ScoreIterationListener - Score at iteration 3 is 392282.8154061016
o.d.o.l.ScoreIterationListener - Score at iteration 4 is 392234.12018756795
o.d.o.l.ScoreIterationListener - Score at iteration 5 is 392139.0617437172
o.d.o.l.ScoreIterationListener - Score at iteration 6 is 391977.5299519522
o.d.o.l.ScoreIterationListener - Score at iteration 7 is 391732.0313246322
o.d.o.l.ScoreIterationListener - Score at iteration 8 is 391390.9885874034
o.d.o.l.ScoreIterationListener - Score at iteration 9 is 390949.9068585132
o.d.o.l.ScoreIterationListener - Score at iteration 10 is 390407.2208170733
o.d.o.l.ScoreIterationListener - Score at iteration 11 is 389766.7980037157
o.d.o.l.ScoreIterationListener - Score at iteration 12 is 389026.07803709887
o.d.o.l.ScoreIterationListener - Score at iteration 13 is 388180.6244370007
o.d.o.l.ScoreIterationListener - Score at iteration 14 is 387225.1191501263
o.d.o.l.ScoreIterationListener - Score at iteration 15 is 386161.5252982354
o.d.o.l.ScoreIterationListener - Score at iteration 16 is 384991.52117921936
o.d.o.l.ScoreIterationListener - Score at iteration 17 is 383719.54410875245
o.d.o.l.ScoreIterationListener - Score at iteration 18 is 382351.4820195209
o.d.o.l.ScoreIterationListener - Score at iteration 19 is 380891.5161926356
o.d.o.l.ScoreIterationListener - Score at iteration 20 is 379344.3968079217
o.d.o.l.ScoreIterationListener - Score at iteration 21 is 377715.15848935687
o.d.o.l.ScoreIterationListener - Score at iteration 22 is 376010.77007275063
o.d.o.l.ScoreIterationListener - Score at iteration 23 is 374238.82619509666
o.d.o.l.ScoreIterationListener - Score at iteration 24 is 372405.6130678293
o.d.o.l.ScoreIterationListener - Score at iteration 25 is 370520.31821126794
o.d.o.l.ScoreIterationListener - Score at iteration 26 is 368582.4865625592
o.d.o.l.ScoreIterationListener - Score at iteration 27 is 366603.3535501402
o.d.o.l.ScoreIterationListener - Score at iteration 28 is 364589.54680638906
o.d.o.l.ScoreIterationListener - Score at iteration 29 is 362548.2627484569
o.d.o.l.ScoreIterationListener - Score at iteration 30 is 360485.1333794203
```

We see that we have started at iteration 0 with an initial reconstruction error of `392314.67211754626`. This is due to random initialization of the neural network weight parameters and will, therefore, change on each subsequent run.

 An autoencoder provides two things. First, through a neural bottleneck, it provides a non-linear lower dimensional representation of your data. Second, it tries to reconstruct the input signal at the output, running though the bottleneck. Therefore it doesn't learn noise and irrelevant data. Since an autoencoder measures the reconstruction error on the signal trained on, we can use it as anomaly detector. Data which has been seen before will yield to a lower reconstruction error. More on the topic can be found here: `http://deeplearning.net/tutorial/dA.html#da` and `http://dl.acm.org/citation.cfm?id=2689747`.

This is demonstrated as follows:

```
o.d.o.l.ScoreIterationListener - Score at iteration 969 is 425.6250059539804
o.d.o.l.ScoreIterationListener - Score at iteration 970 is 423.3333805602828
o.d.o.l.ScoreIterationListener - Score at iteration 971 is 421.4624281317155
o.d.o.l.ScoreIterationListener - Score at iteration 972 is 419.2211628537399
o.d.o.l.ScoreIterationListener - Score at iteration 973 is 417.4023765884213
o.d.o.l.ScoreIterationListener - Score at iteration 974 is 415.2149420317019
o.d.o.l.ScoreIterationListener - Score at iteration 975 is 413.440681888014
o.d.o.l.ScoreIterationListener - Score at iteration 976 is 411.2982748331003
o.d.o.l.ScoreIterationListener - Score at iteration 977 is 409.574493015976763
o.d.o.l.ScoreIterationListener - Score at iteration 978 is 407.4829112362655
o.d.o.l.ScoreIterationListener - Score at iteration 979 is 405.80495495344996
o.d.o.l.ScoreIterationListener - Score at iteration 980 is 403.7537126010534
o.d.o.l.ScoreIterationListener - Score at iteration 981 is 402.1170321945724
o.d.o.l.ScoreIterationListener - Score at iteration 982 is 400.1184546085061
o.d.o.l.ScoreIterationListener - Score at iteration 983 is 398.51955195517445
o.d.o.l.ScoreIterationListener - Score at iteration 984 is 396.5621405109357
o.d.o.l.ScoreIterationListener - Score at iteration 985 is 395.0127922092593
o.d.o.l.ScoreIterationListener - Score at iteration 986 is 393.09832353721544
o.d.o.l.ScoreIterationListener - Score at iteration 987 is 391.5845006616595
o.d.o.l.ScoreIterationListener - Score at iteration 988 is 389.7125865777661
o.d.o.l.ScoreIterationListener - Score at iteration 989 is 388.2405412156419
o.d.o.l.ScoreIterationListener - Score at iteration 990 is 386.410098613004
o.d.o.l.ScoreIterationListener - Score at iteration 991 is 384.97496987874547
o.d.o.l.ScoreIterationListener - Score at iteration 992 is 383.1866651763012
o.d.o.l.ScoreIterationListener - Score at iteration 993 is 381.78825748540373
o.d.o.l.ScoreIterationListener - Score at iteration 994 is 380.0387015850865
o.d.o.l.ScoreIterationListener - Score at iteration 995 is 378.67470982690736
o.d.o.l.ScoreIterationListener - Score at iteration 996 is 378.50384785501404
o.d.o.l.ScoreIterationListener - Score at iteration 997 is 375.642910710587
o.d.o.l.ScoreIterationListener - Score at iteration 998 is 373.96674036087035
o.d.o.l.ScoreIterationListener - Score at iteration 999 is 372.6741075529085
```

So, we end up with `372.6741075529085` as the reconstruction error, since the neural network got used to the inherit hidden patterns in this signal. Let's run it again by again clicking on the **reset** button of the test data generator:

```
o.d.o.l.ScoreIterationListener - Score at iteration 1969 is 44.70903950884105
o.d.o.l.ScoreIterationListener - Score at iteration 1970 is 45.2380225365112
o.d.o.l.ScoreIterationListener - Score at iteration 1971 is 45.8889230951459
o.d.o.l.ScoreIterationListener - Score at iteration 1972 is 46.46854959043279
o.d.o.l.ScoreIterationListener - Score at iteration 1973 is 47.17536573123725
o.d.o.l.ScoreIterationListener - Score at iteration 1974 is 47.81004132107224
o.d.o.l.ScoreIterationListener - Score at iteration 1975 is 48.57575742663159
o.d.o.l.ScoreIterationListener - Score at iteration 1976 is 49.27007691834137
o.d.o.l.ScoreIterationListener - Score at iteration 1977 is 50.101039358040985
o.d.o.l.ScoreIterationListener - Score at iteration 1978 is 50.85791943489326
o.d.o.l.ScoreIterationListener - Score at iteration 1979 is 51.757361700603106
o.d.o.l.ScoreIterationListener - Score at iteration 1980 is 52.58158597894784
o.d.o.l.ScoreIterationListener - Score at iteration 1981 is 53.556149354377496
o.d.o.l.ScoreIterationListener - Score at iteration 1982 is 54.453351759736925
o.d.o.l.ScoreIterationListener - Score at iteration 1983 is 55.506758667805
o.d.o.l.ScoreIterationListener - Score at iteration 1984 is 56.4806440514167
o.d.o.l.ScoreIterationListener - Score at iteration 1985 is 57.61902297956854
o.d.o.l.ScoreIterationListener - Score at iteration 1986 is 58.67646590078081
o.d.o.l.ScoreIterationListener - Score at iteration 1987 is 59.90408701956823
o.d.o.l.ScoreIterationListener - Score at iteration 1988 is 61.05119425005335
o.d.o.l.ScoreIterationListener - Score at iteration 1989 is 62.37603870187002
o.d.o.l.ScoreIterationListener - Score at iteration 1990 is 63.61836167255973
o.d.o.l.ScoreIterationListener - Score at iteration 1991 is 65.04312191353905
o.d.o.l.ScoreIterationListener - Score at iteration 1992 is 66.38540283674381
o.d.o.l.ScoreIterationListener - Score at iteration 1993 is 67.91764984573355
o.d.o.l.ScoreIterationListener - Score at iteration 1994 is 69.36393101040994
o.d.o.l.ScoreIterationListener - Score at iteration 1995 is 71.01005259072566
o.d.o.l.ScoreIterationListener - Score at iteration 1996 is 72.5647220289928
o.d.o.l.ScoreIterationListener - Score at iteration 1997 is 74.3255814684223
o.d.o.l.ScoreIterationListener - Score at iteration 1998 is 75.99247402491774
o.d.o.l.ScoreIterationListener - Score at iteration 1999 is 77.8737141122287
```

Now we end up with a value of `77.8737141122287`. This value will further decrease as long as we show the normal signal to the neural network over and over again, but will also converge to a minimal value.

So, now, let's change the nature of the signal by clicking on **broken** in the test data generator:

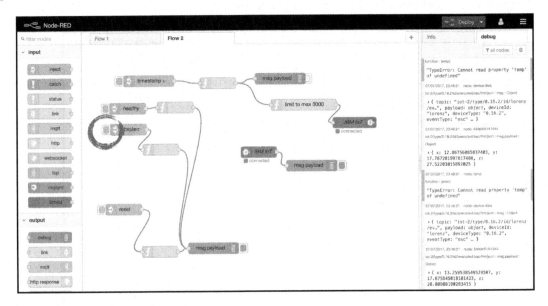

Then, again, we click on **reset** in order to send the next 30 seconds worth of data to the neural network:

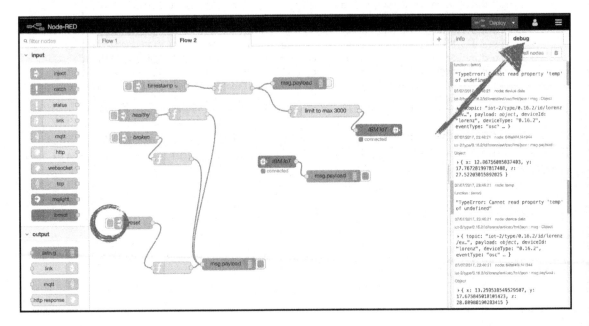

If we now check on the reconstruction error, we'll see something interesting:

```
o.d.o.l.ScoreIterationListener - Score at iteration 2969 is 10891.930373337565
o.d.o.l.ScoreIterationListener - Score at iteration 2970 is 10897.650306476724
o.d.o.l.ScoreIterationListener - Score at iteration 2971 is 10903.295572131516
o.d.o.l.ScoreIterationListener - Score at iteration 2972 is 10909.297284415812
o.d.o.l.ScoreIterationListener - Score at iteration 2973 is 10915.302549022963
o.d.o.l.ScoreIterationListener - Score at iteration 2974 is 10921.546926582616
o.d.o.l.ScoreIterationListener - Score at iteration 2975 is 10927.696193981876
o.d.o.l.ScoreIterationListener - Score at iteration 2976 is 10934.121015271206
o.d.o.l.ScoreIterationListener - Score at iteration 2977 is 10940.642727116407
o.d.o.l.ScoreIterationListener - Score at iteration 2978 is 10947.279991840644
o.d.o.l.ScoreIterationListener - Score at iteration 2979 is 10953.833701577507
o.d.o.l.ScoreIterationListener - Score at iteration 2980 is 10960.651412106614
o.d.o.l.ScoreIterationListener - Score at iteration 2981 is 10967.415789221683
o.d.o.l.ScoreIterationListener - Score at iteration 2982 is 10974.417499744583
o.d.o.l.ScoreIterationListener - Score at iteration 2983 is 10981.178323042242
o.d.o.l.ScoreIterationListener - Score at iteration 2984 is 10988.440476587411
o.d.o.l.ScoreIterationListener - Score at iteration 2985 is 10995.3844071995
o.d.o.l.ScoreIterationListener - Score at iteration 2986 is 11002.536337484873
o.d.o.l.ScoreIterationListener - Score at iteration 2987 is 11009.585159062908
o.d.o.l.ScoreIterationListener - Score at iteration 2988 is 11016.66864489814
o.d.o.l.ScoreIterationListener - Score at iteration 2989 is 11023.745910911426
o.d.o.l.ScoreIterationListener - Score at iteration 2990 is 11030.880953683412
o.d.o.l.ScoreIterationListener - Score at iteration 2991 is 11037.787551632187
o.d.o.l.ScoreIterationListener - Score at iteration 2992 is 11044.859483622726
o.d.o.l.ScoreIterationListener - Score at iteration 2993 is 11051.695858331497
o.d.o.l.ScoreIterationListener - Score at iteration 2994 is 11058.648678534704
o.d.o.l.ScoreIterationListener - Score at iteration 2995 is 11065.278833431727
o.d.o.l.ScoreIterationListener - Score at iteration 2996 is 11072.15876470129
o.d.o.l.ScoreIterationListener - Score at iteration 2997 is 11078.420031398582
o.d.o.l.ScoreIterationListener - Score at iteration 2998 is 11085.078628689993
o.d.o.l.ScoreIterationListener - Score at iteration 2999 is 11091.125671441947
```

Now we end up with a reconstruction error of `11091.125671441947`, which is significantly higher than `77.8737141122287` and clearly shows us how anomalies can be detected on any time series signal without further knowledge of the underlying domain.

So, the only remaining thing is pushing this application to Apache Spark, because you might have noticed that this example only runs locally on your machine. But, at least it supports OpenBLAS, so it makes use of the SIMD instructions on your CPU, which speeds things up a bit. So let's push to Apache Spark!

Run the examples in Apache Spark

In order to run on Apache Spark, we'll use the Hortonworks HDP Sandbox. In contrast to other chapters, where we just used the `spark-shell` and pasted some lines of Scala code, in this case, this is not possible anymore. So we need to create a self-contained JAR file that contains the Deeplearning4j application plus all dependencies in a single JAR file.

Sound tedious? Luckily, Maven is our best friend. So, first, using the command line we just `cd` into the root folder within the workspace of the `dl4j-examples-scala` folder, and run `mvn package`:

```
Romeos-MacBook-Pro:dl4j-examples-scala romeokienzler$ mvn package
[INFO] Scanning for projects...
[INFO]
[INFO]
[INFO] ------------------------------------------------------------------------
[INFO] Building DeepLearning4j Examples 0.8-SNAPSHOT
[INFO] ------------------------------------------------------------------------
[INFO]
```

It takes quite some time, but after a while, the command ends with the following output:

```
[INFO] Attaching shaded artifact.
[INFO]
[INFO] --- maven-assembly-plugin:2.4:single (make-jar-with-dependencies) @ dl4j-examples-scala ---
[INFO] Building jar: /Users/romeokienzler/Documents/tmp/deleteme6/deeplearning4j-examples-parent/dl4j-examples-scala/target/dl4j-examples-scala-0.8-SNAPSHOT-jar-with-dependencies.jar
[INFO] ------------------------------------------------------------------------
[INFO] BUILD SUCCESS
[INFO] ------------------------------------------------------------------------
[INFO] Total time: 02:25 min
[INFO] Finished at: 2017-07-07T16:25:13+02:00
[INFO] Final Memory: 85M/1571M
[INFO] ------------------------------------------------------------------------
```

Now we need to copy this JAR to the Apache Spark cluster using `scp` (SSH Secure Copy). On a Mac, we are using the following command line for doing so:

```
Romeos-MacBook-Pro:dl4j-examples-scala romeokienzler$ cd target/
Romeos-MacBook-Pro:target romeokienzler$ scp -P 2222 dl4j-examples-scala-0.8-SNAPSHOT-jar-with-dependencies.jar root@localhost:/root/
root@localhost's password:
dl4j-examples-scala-0.8-SNAPSHOT-jar-with-dependencies.jar                              100%  396MB  93.5MB/s   00:04
```

Then we SSH to the cluster, and run the following command:

```
[root@sandbox ~]# export SPARK_MAJOR_VERSION=2
[root@sandbox ~]# spark-submit --master yarn --num-executors 1 --driver-memory 1000m --executor-memory 1250m --executor-cores 1 --class Run  dl4j-examples-scala-0.8-SNAPSHOT-jar-with-dependencies.jar true
SPARK_MAJOR_VERSION is set to 2, using Spark2
17/07/07 17:57:33 INFO Nd4jBackend: Loaded [CpuBackend] backend
17/07/07 17:57:33 INFO NativeOpsHolder: Number of threads used for NativeOps: 4
17/07/07 17:57:34 INFO Reflections: Reflections took 349 ms to scan 1 urls, producing 29 keys and 109 values
17/07/07 17:57:34 INFO Nd4jBlas: Number of threads used for BLAS: 4
17/07/07 17:57:34 INFO DefaultOpExecutioner: Backend used: [CPU]; OS: [Linux]
17/07/07 17:57:34 INFO DefaultOpExecutioner: Cores: [4]; Memory: [0.9GB];
17/07/07 17:57:34 INFO DefaultOpExecutioner: Blas vendor: [OPENBLAS]
```

We see that the system is waiting for data. Therefore, we just click on the **reset** button of the test data generator again, and the tumbling window waits to be filled:

```
17/07/07 14:52:08 INFO LoggerUtility: main: Org ID       = rwyrty
        Client ID     = a:rwyrty:a2g6k39sl6r5
17/07/07 14:52:09 INFO LoggerUtility: main: Connecting client a:rwyrty:a2g6k39sl6r5 to ssl://rwyrty.messaging.internetofthings.ibmcloud.com:8883 (attempt #1)...
17/07/07 14:52:10 INFO LoggerUtility: main: Successfully connected to the IBM Watson IoT Platform
Mainthread blocking...
Mainthread blocking...
Mainthread blocking...
Waiting for tumbling window to fill: 0
Waiting for tumbling window to fill: 100
Waiting for tumbling window to fill: 200
Waiting for tumbling window to fill: 300
Mainthread blocking...
Waiting for tumbling window to fill: 400
Waiting for tumbling window to fill: 500
```

The Hortonworks HDP Sandbox V2.6.0 currently supports Apache Spark V1.6.1 and V2.1. Support for Apache Spark V2.2 will available shortly. In order to use V2.1, we need to always run this command in advance:

```
export SPARK_MAJOR_VERSION=2
```

In order to prevent this, just issue the following command once, and after the next login, you always will use Apache Spark V2.1:

```
echo "export SPARK_MAJOR_VERSION=2" >> /root/.bashrc
```

Finally, after this has happened, we see data arriving and the same neural networks that we've run within Eclipse now run in parallel on an Apache Spark cluster. Isn't that awesome?

Summary

Our continuing theme when examining both Apache Hadoop and Spark is that none of these systems stand alone. They need to be integrated to form ETL-based processing systems. Data needs to be sourced and processed in Spark and then passed to the next link in the ETL chain or stored. We hope that this chapter showed you that Spark functionality can be extended with extra libraries and systems such as H2O, DeepLearning4j. Even Apache SystemML supports DeepLearning now and TensorFlow can be run within Apache Spark using TensorFrames and TensorSpark.

Although Apache Spark MLlib and SparkML has a lot of functionality, the combination of H2O Sparkling Water and the Flow web interface provides an extra wealth of data analysis modeling options. Using Flow, you can also visually and interactively process your data. We hope that this chapter shows you, even though it cannot cover all that all these libraries offer, that the combination of Spark and third-party libraries widens your data processing possibilities.

We hope that you found this chapter useful. In the next two chapters we will cover Graph Processing, so stay tuned.

11
Apache Spark GraphX

In this chapter, we want to examine the Apache Spark GraphX module and graph processing, in general. So, this chapter will cover the topic of implementing graph analysis workflows on top of GraphX.

The *GraphX coding* section, written in Scala, will provide a series of graph coding examples.

Before writing code in Scala to use the Spark GraphX module, we think it will be useful to provide an overview of what a graph actually is in terms of graph processing. The following section provides a brief introduction using a couple of simple graphs as examples.

In this chapter we will cover:

- Creating a graph from raw data
- Counting
- Filtering
- PageRank
- Triangle count
- Connected components

Overview

A graph can be considered to be a data structure that consists of a group of vertices and edges connecting them. The vertices or nodes in the graph can be anything as long it is an object (so people for example), and the edges are the relationships between them. The edges can be un-directional or directional, meaning that the relationship operates from one node to another. For instance, node **A** is the parent of node **B**.

In the following diagram, the circles represent the vertices or nodes (**A** to **D**), while the thick lines represent the edges or relationships between them (**E1** to **E6**). Each node or edge may have properties, and these values are represented by the associated gray squares (**P1** to **P7**):

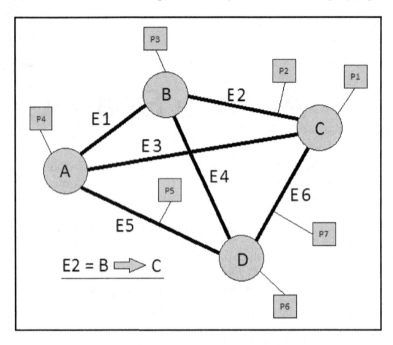

So, if a graph represents a physical route map, the edges might represent minor roads or motorways. The nodes would be motorway junctions or road intersections. Node and edge properties might be road types, speed limits, distance, cost, and grid location.

There are many types of graph implementation, but some examples might be fraud modeling, financial currency transaction modeling, and social modeling as in friend-to-friend connections on Facebook, map processing, web processing, and page ranking.

The preceding diagram shows a generic example of a graph with associated properties. It also shows that edge relationships can be directional, namely edge **E2** acts from node **B** to node **C**.

However, the following example uses family members and the relationships between them to create a graph:

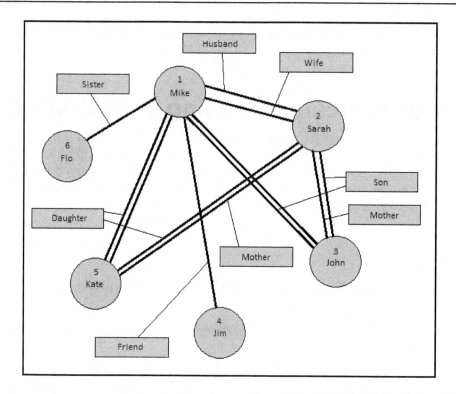

 Note that there can be multiple edges between two nodes or vertices, for instance, the husband and wife relationships between `Mike` and `Sarah`. Also, it is possible that there could be multiple properties on a node or edge.

So, in the preceding example, the `Sister` property acts from node 6 `Flo` to node 1 `Mike`. These are simple graphs to explain the structure of the graph and the element's nature. Real graph applications can reach extreme sizes and require both distributed processing and storage to enable them to be manipulated.

Facebook is able to process graphs containing over 1 trillion edges using Apache Giraph (source Avery Ching Facebook). **Giraph** (`http://giraph.apache.org/`) is an Apache Hadoop ecosystem tool for graph processing, which historically based its processing on MapReduce but now uses TinkerPop (`http://www.tinkerpop.incubator.apache.org/`).

 Although this book concentrates on Apache Spark, that number of the Facebook graph provides a very impressive indicator of the size that a graph can reach.

In the next section, we will examine the use of the Apache Spark GraphX module using Scala.

Graph analytics/processing with GraphX

This section will examine Apache Spark GraphX programming in Scala using the family relationship graph data sample shown in the last section. This data will be accessed as a list of vertices and edges. Although this data set is small, the graphs that you build in this way could be very large. For example we've been able to analyze 30 TB of financial transaction data of a large bank using only four Apache Spark workers.

The raw data

We are working with two data files. They contain the data that will be used for this section in terms of the vertices and edges that make up a graph:

```
graph1_edges.csv
graph1_vertex.csv
```

The `vertex` file contains just six lines representing the graph used in the last section. Each `vertex` represents a person and has a vertex ID number, a name, and an age value:

```
1,Mike,48
2,Sarah,45
3,John,25
4,Jim,53
5,Kate,22
6,Flo,52
```

The `edge` file contains a set of directed `edge` values in the form source vertex ID, destination vertex ID, and relationship. So, record 1 forms a `Sister` relationship between `Flo` and `Mike`:

```
6,1,Sister
1,2,Husband
2,1,Wife
5,1,Daughter
5,2,Daughter
3,1,Son
3,2,Son
4,1,Friend
1,5,Father
1,3,Father
```

```
2,5,Mother
2,3,Mother
```

Lets, examine some GraphX code samples.

Creating a graph

This section will explain generic Scala code up to the point of creating a GraphX graph from data. This will save time as the same code is reused in each example. Once this is explained, we will concentrate on the actual graph-based manipulation in each code example.

1. The generic code starts by importing Spark context, GraphX, and RDD functionality for use in the Scala code:

   ```
   import org.apache.spark.SparkContext
   import org.apache.spark.SparkContext._
   import org.apache.spark.SparkConf
   import org.apache.spark.graphx._
   import org.apache.spark.rdd.RDD
   ```

2. Then an application is defined, which `extends` the App class. The application name changes for each example from `graph1` to `graph5`. This application name will be used when running the application using `spark-submit`:

   ```
   object graph1 extends App {
   ```

3. As already mentioned, there are two data files that contain `vertex` and `edge` information:

   ```
   val vertexFile = "graph1_vertex.csv"
   val edgeFile   = "graph1_edges.csv"
   ```

4. The **Spark Master URL** is defined as the application name, which will appear in the Spark user interface when the application runs. A new Spark configuration object is created, and the URL and name are assigned to it:

   ```
   val sparkMaster = "spark://localhost:7077"
   val appName = "Graph 1"
   val conf = new SparkConf()
   conf.setMaster(sparkMaster)
   conf.setAppName(appName)
   ```

5. A new Spark context is created using the configuration that was just defined:

```
val sparkCxt = new SparkContext(conf)
```

6. The `vertex` information from the file is then loaded into an RDD-based structure called vertices using the `sparkCxt.textFile` method. The data is stored as a Long `VertexId` and strings to represent the person's name and age. The data lines are split by commas as this is CSV-based data:

```
val vertices: RDD[(VertexId, (String, String))] =
    sparkCxt.textFile(vertexFile).map { line =>
      val fields = line.split(",")
      ( fields(0).toLong, ( fields(1), fields(2) ) )
}
```

7. Similarly, the `edge` data is loaded into an RDD-based data structure called edges. The CSV-based data is again split by comma values. The first two data values are converted to long values as they represent the source and destination vertex IDs. The final value representing the relationship of the edge is left as `String`. Note that each record in the RDD structure edges is actually now an `Edge` record:

```
val edges: RDD[Edge[String]] =
    sparkCxt.textFile(edgeFile).map { line =>
      val fields = line.split(",")
      Edge(fields(0).toLong, fields(1).toLong, fields(2))
}
```

8. A default value is defined in case a connection or `vertex` is missing; the graph is then constructed from the RDD-based structures vertices and edges and the `default` record:

```
val default = ("Unknown", "Missing")
val graph = Graph(vertices, edges, default)
```

9. This creates a GraphX-based structure called `graph`, which can now be used for each of the examples. Remember that, although these data samples might be small, you could create extremely large graphs using this approach.

Many of these algorithms are iterative applications, for instance, PageRank and triangle count. As a result, the programs will generate many iterative Spark jobs.

Example 1 – counting

The graph has been loaded, and we know the data volumes in the data files. But what about the data content in terms of vertices and edges in the actual graph itself? It is very simple to extract this information using the vertices and edges `count` function shown as follows:

```
println( "vertices : " + graph.vertices.count )
println( "edges    : " + graph.edges.count )
```

Running the `graph1` example using the example name and the `.jar` file created earlier will provide the `count` information. The master URL is supplied to connect to the Spark cluster, and some default parameters are supplied for the executor memory and total executor cores:

```
spark-submit \
--class graph1 \
--master spark://localhost:7077 \
--executor-memory 700M \
--total-executor-cores 100 \
/home/hadoop/spark/graphx/target/scala-2.10/graph-x_2.10-1.0.jar
```

The Spark cluster job `graph1` provides the following output, which is what would be expected and matches the data files:

```
vertices : 6
edges    : 12
```

Example 2 – filtering

What happens if we need to create a sub graph from the main graph and filter on person age or relationships? The example code from the second example Scala file `graph2` shows how this can be done:

```
val c1 = graph.vertices.filter { case (id, (name, age)) => age.toLong > 40
}.count
val c2 = graph.edges.filter { case Edge(from, to, property)
    => property == "Father" | property == "Mother" }.count
println( "Vertices count : " + c1 )
println( "Edges    count : " + c2 )
```

Two example counts have been created from the main graph: the first filters person-based vertices on age only, taking those people who are greater than forty years old. Notice that the `age` value, which was stored as a string, has been converted to a long for the comparison.

The second example filters the edges on the relationship property of `Mother` or `Father`. Two count values `c1` and `c2` are created and printed as the Spark run output, shown as follows:

```
Vertices count : 4
Edges    count : 4
```

Example 3 – PageRank

The PageRank algorithm provides a ranking value for each of the vertices in a graph. It makes the assumption that the vertices that are connected to the most edges are the most important.

Search engines use PageRank to provide ordering for page display during a web search as can be seen from the following code:

```
val tolerance = 0.0001
val ranking = graph.pageRank(tolerance).vertices
val rankByPerson = vertices.join(ranking).map {
    case (id, ( (person,age) , rank )) => (rank, id, person)
}
```

The example code creates a tolerance value and calls the graph `pageRank` method using it. The vertices are then ranked into a new value ranking. In order to make the ranking more meaningful, the ranking values are joined with the original vertices RDD. The `rankByPerson` value then contains the rank, id, and person name.

The PageRank result held in `rankByPerson` is then printed record by record using a `case` statement to identify the record contents and a format statement to print the contents. We did this because we wanted to define the format of the rank value, which can vary:

```
rankByPerson.collect().foreach {
    case (rank, id, person) =>
        println ( f"Rank $rank%1.2f id $id person $person")
}
```

The output from the application is then shown as follows; as expected, `Mike` and `Sarah` have the highest rank as they have the most relationships:

```
Rank 0.15 id 4 person Jim
Rank 0.15 id 6 person Flo
Rank 1.62 id 2 person Sarah
Rank 1.82 id 1 person Mike
Rank 1.13 id 3 person John
Rank 1.13 id 5 person Kate
```

Example 4 – triangle counting

The triangle count algorithm provides a vertex-based count of the number of triangles associated with that vertex. For instance, vertex Mike (1) is connected to Kate (5), who is connected to Sarah (2), Sarah is connected to Mike (1), and so a triangle is formed. This can be useful for route finding where triangle free minimum spanning tree graphs need to be generated for route planning.

The code to execute a triangle count and print it is simple as shown next. The graph triangleCount method is executed for the graph vertices. The result is saved in the value tCount and printed:

```
val tCount = graph.triangleCount().vertices
println( tCount.collect().mkString("\n") )
```

The results of the application job show that vertices Flo (4) and Jim (6) have no triangles, while Mike (1) and Sarah (2) have the most as expected, as they have the most relationships:

```
(4,0)
(6,0)
(2,4)
(1,4)
(3,2)
(5,2)
```

Example 5 – connected components

When a large graph is created from data, it might contain unconnected sub graphs or sub graphs that are isolated from each other and might contain no bridging or connecting edges between them. These algorithms provide a measure of that connectivity. It might be important depending on your processing to know that all vertices are connected.

The Scala code for this example calls two graph methods, connectedComponents and stronglyConnectedComponents. The strong method required a maximum iteration count, which has been set to 1000. These counts are acting on the graph vertices:

```
val iterations = 1000
val connected = graph.connectedComponents().vertices
val connectedS = graph.stronglyConnectedComponents(iterations).vertices
```

The `vertex` counts are then joined with the original `vertex` records so that connection counts can be associated with the `vertex` information such as person name:

```
val connByPerson = vertices.join(connected).map {
    case (id, ( (person,age) , conn )) => (conn, id, person)
}
val connByPersonS = vertices.join(connectedS).map {
    case (id, ( (person,age) , conn )) => (conn, id, person)
}
```

The results are then output using a `case` statement and formatted for printing:

```
connByPerson.collect().foreach {
    case (conn, id, person) =>
        println ( f"Weak $conn $id $person" )
}
```

As expected, for the `connectedComponents` algorithm, the results show that, for each `vertex`, there is only one component. That means that all the vertices are members of a single graph as the graph diagram earlier in the chapter showed:

```
Weak 1 4 Jim
Weak 1 6 Flo
Weak 1 2 Sarah
Weak 1 1 Mike
Weak 1 3 John
Weak 1 5 Kate
```

The `stronglyConnectedComponents` method gives a measure of the connectivity in a graph, taking into account the direction of the relationships between them. The results for the `stronglyConnectedComponents` algorithm are output as follows:

```
connByPersonS.collect().foreach {
    case (conn, id, person) =>
        println ( f"Strong $conn $id $person" )
}
```

You might notice from the graph that the relationships `Sister` and `Friend` act from vertices `Flo` (6) and `Jim` (4) to `Mike` (1) as the `edge` and `vertex` data shows:

```
6,1,Sister
4,1,Friend

1,Mike,48
4,Jim,53
6,Flo,52
```

So the `strong` method output shows that, for most vertices, there is only one graph component signified by 1 in the second column. However, vertices 4 and 6 are not reachable due to the direction of their relationship, and so they have a vertex ID instead of a component ID:

```
Strong 4 4 Jim
Strong 6 6 Flo
Strong 1 2 Sarah
Strong 1 1 Mike
Strong 1 3 John
Strong 1 5 Kate
```

Summary

This chapter showed by example how Scala-based code can be used to call GraphX algorithms in Apache Spark. Scala has been used because it requires less code to develop the examples than Java, which saves time. Note that GraphX is not available for Python or R. A Scala-based shell can be used, and the code can be compiled into Spark applications.

The most common graph algorithms have been covered and you should have an idea now on how to solve any graph problem with GraphX. Especially since you've understood that a Graph in GraphX is still represented and backed by RDDs, so you are already familiar with using them. The configuration and code examples from this chapter will also be available for download with the book.

We hope that you found this chapter useful. The next chapter will delve into graph frames, which make use of DataFrames, Tungsten, and Catalyst for graph processing.

12
Apache Spark GraphFrames

GraphFrames is the new graph library of Apache Spark. It supports loss-less transformations of graph representations between GraphFrames and GraphX. While introducing another Apache Spark library equivalent to an existing one, we have to explain the motivation behind this decision. The motivation is the same as it was when introducing SparkML over MLlib. The idea was to have an equivalent to GraphX, which supports DataFrames, in order to make use of the optimizations that Catalyst and Tungsten bring.

Another goal was to progress further with unification by integrating graph algorithms and graph queries and optimizing their execution.

Although GraphX supports relational queries on graph structures, it doesn't support graph queries.

Therefore, GraphFrames was implemented with the goal of unifying graph algorithms, graph queries, and DataFrames (and therefore relational queries).

This chapter will cover the following topics:

- Architecture of GraphFrames
- Performance optimizations
- Practical examples in Scala

Architecture

Let's understand how GraphFrames works by taking a look at the architecture.

 The key thing in order to make use of DataFrames, Catalyst, and Tungsten is that the GraphFrames engine is based on relational queries.

This concept is illustrated in the following image:

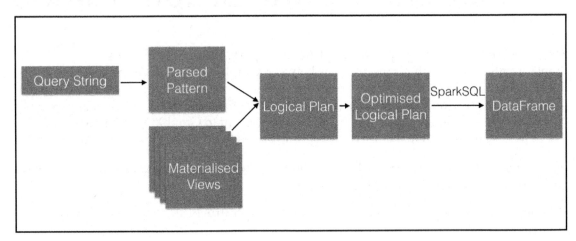

Graph-relational translation

So how can a graph query translate into a relational one?

Imagine that we have already found the vertex **A**, **B**, and **C**. Now we are searching for the edge from **C** to **D**. This query is illustrated in the following image:

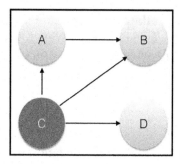

This is pretty straightforward as we can scan the vertex table and search for entries where the **Src** (**source**) field is **C**. Once we have found out that the **Dst** (**destination**) field points to **D** (let's assume that we are also interested in the properties of the node **D**), we finally join the vertex table in order to obtain these properties of **D**.

The following image illustrates such a practically complete query and the resulting join operations:

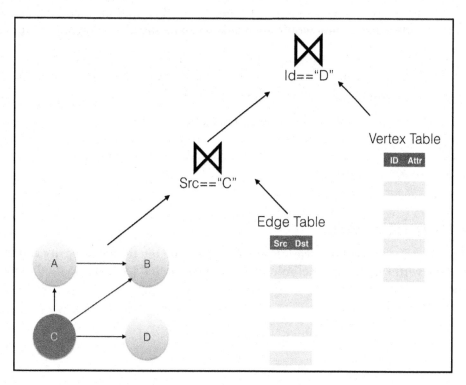

You might wonder at the fact that we are using a lot of joins in order to construct the query. This is true. However, there is a subsequent stage that is responsible for join elimination. So don't worry too much about this yet.

Materialized views

A common practice for query performance optimization in relational databases systems is materialized views.

A view is a subset of your data that (usually) cannot be updated directly but reflects the superset of the data it is based on. A materialized view is an extension to this concept by not only generating a view on a subset of data, but also storing the representation of that view to persistent storage. This especially makes sense if the construction of such a materialized view is computationally expensive. This is because, in subsequent queries making use of such a view, the amount of time that the creation of such a materialized view would have taken can be saved in each of those queries.

The same concept also applies for graph databases. Common subgraphs, which are used among multiple queries, can be defined as materialized views. Therefore, graph queries making use of these subgraphs can benefit using them.

In GraphX, only subgraphs with a triplet structure can be used but GraphFrames supports arbitrary subgraph structures. Materialized views in GraphFrames can be defined manually and all queries automatically make use of them.

Join elimination

As the vertex and edge table in GraphFrames satisfies the referential integrity constraint, the join of the vertex table can be eliminated if no field of that table is specified in the select statement.

So let's take a look at the following SQL statement:

```
SELECT src, dst from edges INNER JOIN vertices ON src = id
```

As the `attr` field of the vertices table is never read, this statements gets automatically rewritten:

```
SELECT src, dst from edges
```

GraphFrames added unique and foreign key hints to the optimizer of Catalyst. Therefore, Catalyst itself is now responsible for join elimination. Refer to `Chapter 3`, *The Catalyst Optimizer*, to read more about the **Catalyst Optimizer**.

Join reordering

Another way to improve query performance is join reordering.

Let's consider the following query structure with a binary relationship between edges **A** and **B** and incoming and outgoing relations (vertices) between **B, C, D**, and **E**:

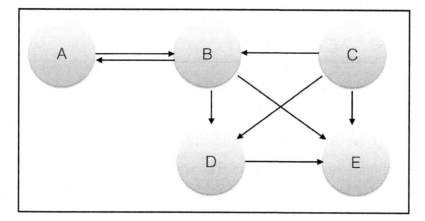

In a naive way, a query planner will create a query plan similar to this during the graph-relational translation where the resolution of each vertex between two edges basically leads to the creation of one join operation in the execution plan:

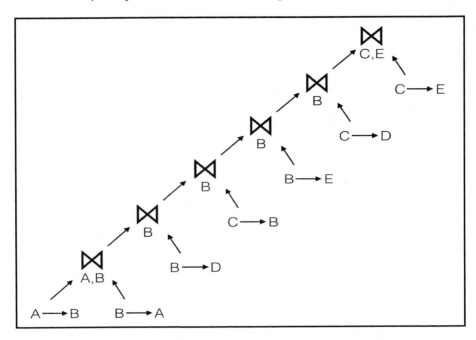

This is known as a left deep plan, which of course is not optimal as it can only be executed sequentially and also incorporates a lot of join operations that are computationally expensive. Finally, there is no common pattern or structure in such a left deep plan that would allow us to create materialized views to speed up things.

Now let's consider the following execution plan, which is semantically equivalent to the previous one but the joins have been reordered and the overall structure changed:

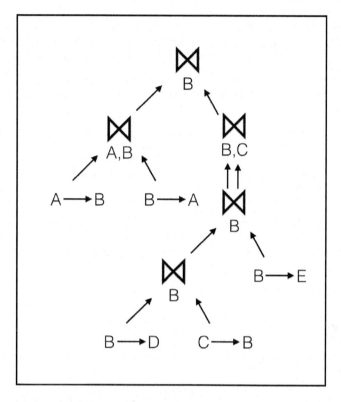

This is also known as a **bushy plan**, which builds up two intermediate results and joins them together. This leads to exactly the same results as the left deep plan, but it has a couple of advantages. They are listed as follows:

1. First, you might have noticed that there is one fewer join operation. Already good.
2. Second, as not all subsequent joins are waiting for the results of the previous join, this query can be run in parallel.
3. Then, often the intermediate results are smaller than in the left deep plan.
4. Finally, the complete right-hand side sub query can be defined as a materialized view.

Currently, there is research work in progress to create such materialized views based on query history automatically.

Graph structure query languages allow defining topological patterns, which are used to search for similar structures in the database. One very famous graph database is **Neo4J**. Its query language is called **cypher**. GraphFrames uses a subset of this query language, called **motifes** for now. More on Neo4J can be found here `https://neo4j.com/product/` and more on cypher can be found here `https://neo4j.com/developer/cypher/`.

Although GraphFrames is in its pretty early stages, comparisons to Neo4J show performance improvements by a factor of four, as stated by a Databricks software engineer during Spark Summit 2016.

Comparisons to GraphX show about the same performance. However, note that GraphX is pretty mature and a lot of work has been done for performance optimizations, and GraphFrames mostly takes only advantage of Catalyst and Tungsten through the DataFrames API.

Examples

Now let's look at a couple of examples in order to understand how to use the new GraphFrames API.

First of all, we need to create a GraphFrames object from data files. Before we do this, we need to install GraphFrames. Fortunately, this is very easy as the package is available on a Maven repository and we can just pass the dependency to the `spark-submit` and `spark-shell` commands:

```
spark-shell --packages graphframes:graphframes:0.5.0-spark2.1-s_2.11
```

Then, we need to import the required package:

```
import org.graphframes._
```

As our graph is based on two CSV files--one for the `vertices` and one for the `edges`--we need to create two DataFrames out of them:

```
val vertex = spark.read.option("header","true").csvgraph1_vertex.csv")
val edges = spark.read.option("header","true").csvgraph1_edges.csv")
```

Finally, we create a GraphFrames object out of these:

```
val graph = GraphFrame(vertex, edges)
```

Example 1 – counting

The graph has been loaded and we know the data volumes in the data files but what about the data content in terms of vertices and edges in the actual graph itself? It is very simple to extract this information using the vertices and edges count functions, as shown in the following code:

```
graph.vertices.count
graph.edges.count
```

As expected, we get 6 vertices and 12 edges.

Example 2 – filtering

What happens if we need to create a subgraph from the main graph and filter on the person's age or relationships? The following example code shows how this can be done.

First, we'll select only the vertices where age is greater than 40:

```
graph.vertices.filter("attr > 40").show
```

This returns a DataFrame, and using the show method, we obtain a print of the table:

```
[scala> graph.vertices.filter("attr > 40").show
+---+-----+----+
| id| name|attr|
+---+-----+----+
|  1| Mike|  48|
|  2|Sarah|  45|
|  4|  Jim|  53|
|  6|  Flo|  52|
+---+-----+----+
```

Now let's structure a query in order to find out the `vertices` taking part in a father or mother relationship.

As already mentioned, GraphFrames supports a subset of the cypher query language that Neo4J supports. Unfortunately, as of Apache Spark 2.2 and GraphFrames 0.5, this is not fully implemented to support this query in a nice way. Otherwise, the query would look as follows:

```
graph.find("(A)-[edge:Mother]->(B)").show
```

Therefore, let's implement the query in a slightly more verbose way:

```
GraphFrame(vertex, graph.edges.filter("attr=='Mother'")).show
```

Example 3 – page rank

The page rank algorithm provides a ranking value for each of the vertices in a graph; it makes the assumption that those vertices that are connected to the most edges, directly or indirectly, are the most important. Search engines use page rank to provide ordering for page display during a web search. So let's see how to implement this in GraphFrames.

1. First, we run the actual algorithm. It is important to notice that the algorithm returns no DataFrame. The algorithm returns a GraphFrames object again by merging the `pageRank` results into the `graph`:

   ```
   val results = graph.pageRank.resetProbability(0.15).tol(0.01).run()
   ```

2. So now take a look at this result:

   ```
   results.vertices.orderBy($"pagerank".desc).show
   ```

3. We are accessing the vertices of the graph. Note that the `pageRank` algorithm of GraphFrames created an additional attribute, `pagerank`, which we are now accessing through the DataFrame API.

4. In addition, we order the result by `pagerank`:

```
+---+-----+----+------------------+
| id| name|attr|          pagerank|
+---+-----+----+------------------+
|  1| Mike|  48|1.7447770383026542|
|  2|Sarah|  45|1.5460757395935596|
|  5| Kate|  22|1.0800834145716334|
|  3| John|  25|1.0800834145716334|
|  4|  Jim|  53|              0.15|
|  6|  Flo|  52|              0.15|
+---+-----+----+------------------+
```

Example 4 – triangle counting

The triangle count algorithm provides a vertex-based count of the number of triangles associated with that vertex. For instance, vertex `Mike` (1) is connected to `Kate` (5) who is connected to `Sarah` (2), `Sarah` is connected to `Mike` (1), and so a triangle is formed:

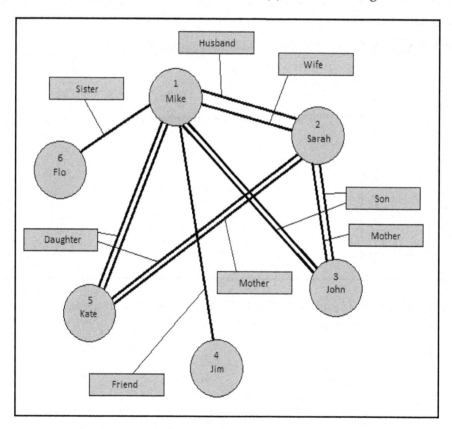

This can be useful for route finding where triangle-free minimum spanning tree graphs need to be generated for route planning.

The code to execute a triangle count and print it is simple, as shown in the following code. The GraphFrames `triangleCount` method is executed for the graph vertices. The result is saved in the value results, which is a DataFrame:

```
val results = graph.triangleCount.run()
```

Now let's plot the results:

```
results.select("id", "count").show()
```

The following image shows the result:

```
scala> results.select("id", "count").show()
+---+-----+
| id|count|
+---+-----+
|  3|    1|
|  5|    1|
|  6|    0|
|  1|    2|
|  4|    0|
|  2|    2|
+---+-----+
```

So let's have a look at this result. It basically lists the vertex IDs on the left-hand side and the number of triangles that this particular vertex is taking part in.

So let's again look at the structure of our sample graph:

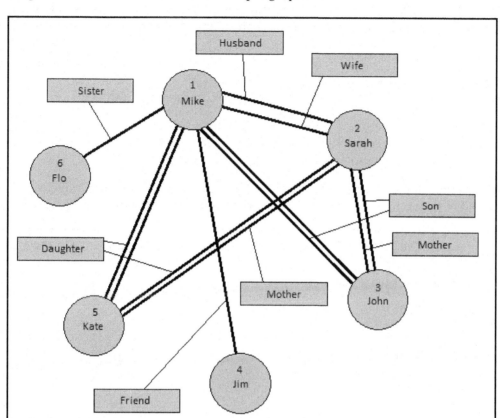

We can clearly see that the result is correct. `Mike` and `Sarah` are participating in two triangles, `John` and `Kate` only in one, and `Flo` and `Jim` on none. Done!

Example 5 – connected components

When a large graph is created from data, it might contain unconnected subgraphs--subgraphs that are isolated from each other and contain no bridging or connecting edges between them. These algorithms provide a measure of that connectivity; it might be important depending on your processing to know that all vertices are connected.

The code for this example calls two graph methods, `connectedComponents` and `stronglyConnectedComponents`. The strong method required a maximum iteration count, which has been set to 10. These counts are acting on the graph vertices.

So let's run the first code snippet:

```
val result = graph.connectedComponents.run()
result.select("id", "component").orderBy("component").show()
```

As expected for the `connectedComponents` algorithm, the results show that for each vertex, there is only one component. This can be verified as the algorithm result assigns each vertex to the same component ID.

This means that all the vertices are members of a single graph, as the graph diagram introduced in the Section on *Triangle Count* earlier in the chapter showed:

```
scala> result.select("id", "component").orderBy("component").show()
+---+------------+
| id|   component|
+---+------------+
|  1|154618822656|
|  2|154618822656|
|  3|154618822656|
|  4|154618822656|
|  5|154618822656|
|  6|154618822656|
+---+------------+
```

The `stronglyConnectedComponents` method gives a measure of the connectivity in a graph, taking into account the direction of the relationships between them. So let's run the corresponding code:

```
val result = graph.stronglyConnectedComponents.maxIter(10).run()
result.select("id", "component").orderBy("component").show()
```

You might notice from the graph that the relationships, `Sister` and `Friend`, act from vertices `Flo` (6) and `Jim` (4) to `Mike` (1) as the edge and vertex data, as shown in the following code:

```
6,1,Sister
4,1,Friend
...
1,Mike,48
4,Jim,53
6,Flo,52
```

So, the strong method output shows that for most vertices, there is only one graph. However, vertices 4 and 6 are not reachable due to the direction of their relationship and so they are assigned to another component, indicated by a different component ID:

```
scala> result.select("id", "component").orderBy("component").show()
17/06/18 07:21:05 WARN Executor: 1 block locks were not released by TID = 13624:
[rdd_1002_0]
+---+--------------+
| id|     component|
+---+--------------+
|  5|  154618822656|
|  2|  154618822656|
|  3|  154618822656|
|  1|  154618822656|
|  6|  644245094400|
|  4|1425929142272|
+---+--------------+
```

In order to make this example a bit clearer, let's add a disconnected vertex to the graph. This can be done by simply adding the following line to the `graph1_vertex.csv` file:

```
7,Stranger,52
```

Now, the vertex with ID 7 is not connected with the rest of the graph because we didn't add a connecting edge to the `graph1_edges.csv` file. Let's rerun the algorithm. Before we do this, we have to reread the files and recreate the GraphFrames object.

As expected, the `stronglyConnectedComponents` algorithm assigns vertex 7 to a different component ID:

```
scala> result.select("id", "component").orderBy("component").show()
17/06/18 07:24:25 WARN Executor: 1 block locks were not released by TID = 8717:
[rdd_545_0]
+---+------------+
| id|   component|
+---+------------+
|  7|  25769803776|
|  1| 154618822656|
|  2| 154618822656|
|  3| 154618822656|
|  5| 154618822656|
|  6| 644245094400|
|  4|1425929142272|
+---+------------+
```

During the last call, the `connectedComponents` algorithm assigned each vertex to the same component ID, but now we can see that vertex 7 gets its own component ID:

```
scala> result.select("id", "component").orderBy("component").show()
+---+------------+
| id|   component|
+---+------------+
|  7|  25769803776|
|  1|154618822656|
|  3|154618822656|
|  2|154618822656|
|  4|154618822656|
|  5|154618822656|
|  6|154618822656|
+---+------------+
```

Summary

This chapter started with an architectural overview on GraphFrames. We saw how GraphFrames can make use of the Catalyst and Tungsten optimizers by running on top of DataFrames.

Additional optimizations on top of these were explained. Finally, we showed, by example, how Scala-based code can be used to call GraphFrames algorithms in Apache Spark. Scala has been used because it requires less code to develop the examples, which saves time; a Scala-based shell can be used and the code can be compiled into Spark applications.

The configuration and code examples from this chapter are also available for download with the book. If you want to learn more on GraphFrames please refer to this link `https ://databricks.com/blog/2016/03/03/introducing-graphframes.html`.

Now let's have a look how Apache Spark can be used in the Cloud in conjunction with Jupyter in the next chapter. This is a very convenient user interface from which to do data science.

13
Apache Spark with Jupyter Notebooks on IBM DataScience Experience

When talking about the cloud, nearly everybody has a different view. Some think of virtual machines, which you can start and stop instantaneously, while some others think of file storage. But the cloud is more than that. In this chapter, we will talk about using Apache Spark in the cloud. But this is, of course, more than provisioning some virtual machines and installing an Apache Spark cluster on it.

We are talking about the so-called **Platform as a service clouds (PaaS)**, where everything is a service, ready to be consumed, and the operation of components is done by the cloud provider. Therefore, on PaaS clouds, Apache Spark is pre-installed. This is done in a way that workers can be added to and removed from the cluster on-the-fly. But not only is Apache Spark pre-installed, the required tooling around it is also available.

In this chapter, we'll introduce the following:

- Why notebooks are the new standard for data science
- A practical example in how to analyze bearing vibration data
- The trinity of data science programming languages (Scala, Python, R) in action
- Interactive, exploratory data analysis and visualization

In data science it is common practice now to use notebooks such as Juypter (covered in this chapter) and Zeppelin (covered in the next chapter on running Apache Spark on Kubernetes).

Another practice we are seeing more and more is that people tend to prefer Python and R over Scala and Java, especially for one-time scripts and visualization as opposed to long-term **Extract Transform Load** (ETL) processes where Scala and Java still are leaders.

Why notebooks are the new standard

Jupyter notebooks are rapidly becoming the default way to apply data science. They can be seen as Google Docs for analytics. Documentation, lines of code, and output from that code (text, data tables, charts, and plots) are all united.

In addition, such notebooks are easily shareable, even without a backend. Just export them as JSON documents.

Jupyter notebooks preserve all output cells even if the cell during execution has been connected on a large scale Apache Spark cluster processing hundreds of gigabytes of data.

In my experience, notebooks are used mostly in the following scenarios:

- Notebooks are an ideal tool for creating and sharing a knowledge base on best practices a core data science team executes. This way, their knowledge is documented in an executable way.
- Notebooks are used to document the variety of available data sources in an enterprise and to provide executable quick-start code.
- Creating master-templates - casting best practices and company coding conventions into derived notebooks in order to preserve quality of those.

- Dividing data science work between business analysts, data preparation, and senior data scientist within a single notebook, including knowledge transfer among those roles.

Learning by example

Let's have a look at an example in order to learn how to use this tool:

1. If you don't have a Bluemix account, register for one here: `ibm.biz/CloudFreemium`.
2. Once you have an account in place, go to `https://datascience.ibm.com`, and click on **Sign In**.
3. Click on **Sign-In with your IBM ID**, and follow the instructions.

Once you are ready to go, let's start with a small hello world project by creating a Jupyter notebook on Scala with Apache Spark 2.x.

As illustrated in the following screenshot, click on the **Create notebook** button:

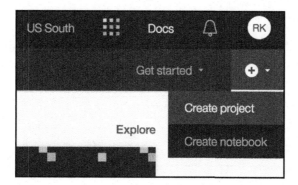

This opens the **Create notebook** dialog as illustrated here:

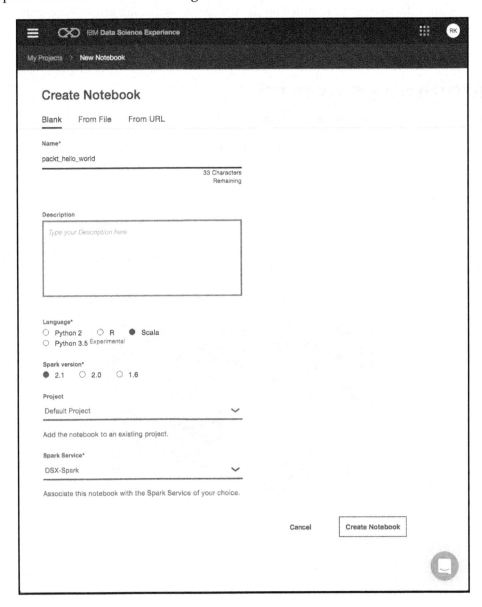

So let's have a look at what information we need to provide:

1. First of all, each notebook needs a name. We choose `packt_hello_world` as the name.
2. Then we select **Scala** as the programming language.
3. We want to run our code on an Apache Spark 2.x instance.
4. We choose **Default Project**. Putting notebooks into projects facilitates collaboration, resource assignments, and version management of third-party libraries.
5. Finally, we choose an Apache Spark instance running on the IBM Bluemix cloud, where our code has to be executed. This service is completely containerized; therefore, it can handle each of the supported Apache Spark versions and programming languages, which, at the time of writing this book, are Scala, Python 2.7, Python 3.5, and R on Apache Spark versions 1.6, 2.0, and 2.1.

So let's start with a motivating example and see how easy it is to interact with the `SparkSQL` object. This is the first time we will run Scala code within Apache Spark without using either the `spark-shell` command or the `spark-submit` command.

We'll also use Python, R and Scala interchangeably in different notebooks since each programming language has its own strengths--Jupyter notebooks make it easy to use such a hybrid approach because no further programming language-dependent skills, other than syntax such as IDEs or build tools, are required.

Let's consider the real-life scenario of a small industrial enterprise doing analytics in the cloud. As you've might have experienced, good data scientists are a rare species, and most of them don't come with a Scala background. Mostly, they work with MATLAB, R, and Python. The same holds for this enterprise. They have plenty of Java developers but only one data scientist. Therefore, it is a good idea to create different roles.

Finally, this data product development process based on Jupyter and Apache Spark as a service catalyzes communication and exchange between skill groups involved in data science projects. The software engineer becomes a better mathematician, and the mathematician becomes a better software engineer because everyone can have a look at (and modify) the assets created by the other since all are in one central place and not buried behind server logins and shell scripts. In addition, they are very readable since they contain not only code but also documentation and output from that code.

Let's start with the first example, where we perform the following steps:

1. The Java software engineer is responsible for implementing the ETL process. He pulls data from machines (in this example, we'll pull a dataset from the web), transforms it, and then loads data into a cloud object store. This is entirely done using a Scala notebook. Although the software engineer is not an expert in Scala, he has acquired enough knowledge for this task. The fact that he can use ANSI SQL for querying data really helps since most software engineers have basic SQL skills. Those notebooks can also be triggered and run automatically on a periodic basis in order to update data.

2. Once the data is prepared and available in the object store, the data scientist can create an interactive analytics notebook based on Python and the Pixiedust interactive data visualization library in order to get an idea of what the data looks like.
   Python is a very easy-to-learn programming language, so it can be seen as the intersection between software engineers and statisticians since you can pick it up really fast if you are coming from a Java and R/MATLAB background.

3. Use an R notebook and the famous `ggplot2` library for creating awesome, publishable plots.

ETL: Why is ETL always needed? Usually, the persons involved in the data sources responsible for export don't have the usability of their export in mind. They just want to make sure they have put enough information into the export and they want to keep the process slim on their side. That's the reason why data scientists always struggle with ETL. Either we have to cope with some lousy exported data or we have to directly access a **System of Records (SOR)** via, for example, a read-only materialized view.

The IEEE PHM 2012 data challenge bearing dataset

We are taking vibration sensor data from an accelerometer attached to a bearing in an experiment setup. This bearing is put on heavy load in order to make it fail fast.

The whole process has been extensively discussed in the following publication: Nectoux, R. Gouriveau, K. Medjaher, E. Ramasso, B. Morello, N. Zerhouni, C. Varnier. PRONOSTIA: *An Experimental Platform for Bearings Accelerated Life Test. IEEE International Conference on Prognostics and Health Management, Denver, CO, USA, 2012*

The basic experiment setup is as follows:

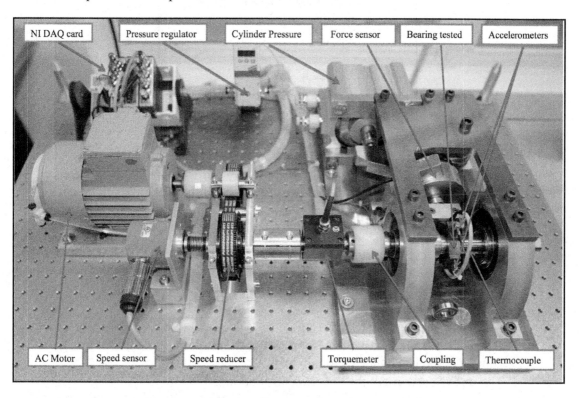

You don't have to understand each component on this setup, but the most important ones include the **Cylinder Pressure**, which generates force against the **Bearing tested** in order to make it fail fast, and the two **Accelerometers**, which record vibration data.

It is important to notice that those data points are recorded at a sampling frequency of 25.6 kHz for a period of 100 ms (2,560 data points per second), followed by a pause of 9,900 ms as illustrated in the following figure:

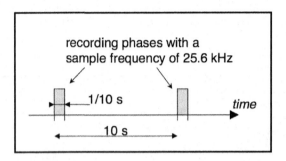

ETL with Scala

Let's have a look at the first Scala-based notebook where our ETL process is expressed. Fortunately, the IEEE website allows us to download a ZIP file containing all the data. We'll use a Scala-based notebook to perform the following steps:

1. Download the ZIP file to a local staging area within the Apache Spark driver. The download location is already included in the notebook file that you can download from the book's download page. But for more information on the data set please refer to http://www.femto-st.fr/en/Research-departments/AS2M/R esearch-groups/PHM/IEEE-PHM-2012-Data-challenge.php.
2. Unzip the file.
3. Create an Apache Spark DataFrame out of the nested folder structure to get a unique and queryable view of all data.
4. Use an SQL statement for data transformation.
5. Save the result into a single JSON file on the IBM Cloud OpenStack Swift-based ObjectStore.

So let's have a look at each individual step:

1. Downloading the ZIP file to the staging area:
   In the IBM Data Science Experience platform, the Apache Spark cluster lives in a Docker/Kubernetes-based environment (more on this in the next chapter). This also holds for the Apache Spark driver container. This means we can call ordinary shell commands within the driver container and also use this as the staging area:

```
                We download the zip file containing the data to the local stagin area

In [*]:   import sys.process._
          "wget http://www.femto-st.fr/f/d/Training_set.zip" !

          --2017-06-27 17:31:57--  http://www.femto-st.fr/f/d/Training_set.zip
          Resolving www.femto-st.fr (www.femto-st.fr)... 195.83.19.10
          Connecting to www.femto-st.fr (www.femto-st.fr)|195.83.19.10|:80... connected.
          HTTP request sent, awaiting response... 200 OK
          Length: 140424205 (134M) [application/zip]
          Saving to: 'Training_set.zip.1'

              0K .......... .......... .......... .......... ..........  0% 96.4K 23m42s
             50K .......... .......... .......... .......... ..........  0%  384K 14m49s
            100K .......... .......... .......... .......... ..........  0%  385K 11m51s
            150K .......... .......... .......... .......... ..........  0%  385K 10m22s
            200K .......... .......... .......... .......... ..........  0% 81.9M 8m18s
            250K .......... .......... .......... .......... ..........  0% 7.70M 6m58s
            300K .......... .......... .......... .......... ..........  0%  405K 6m46s
            350K .......... .......... .......... .......... ..........  0% 7.23M 5m57s
            400K .......... .......... .......... .......... ..........  0%  386K 5m57s
            450K .......... .......... .......... .......... ..........  0% 77.9M 5m21s
            500K .......... .......... .......... .......... ..........  0% 40.9M 4m52s
```

2. As you can see in the following screenshot, IBM provides plenty of free space in this staging area by mounting a GPFS cluster file system onto the driver container. In this case, we have more than 70 TB of space in this staging area. In case we need to load more than 70 TB, we need to split the data and incrementally load it. IBM Cloud OpenStack Swift-based ObjectStore provides unlimited storage capacity, and there is no need be concerned about scalability. The client is charged per GB on a monthly basis. More details on pricing can be found here `https://console-regional.ng.bluemix.net/?direct=classic&en v_id=ibm:yp:us-south#/pricing/cloudOEPaneId=pricing&paneId=pricingSh eet&orgGuid=3cf55ee0-a8c0-4430-b809-f19528dee352&spaceGuid=06d96c35- 9667-4c99-9d70-980ba6aaa6c3`:

```
In [3]:  "df -h" !

         Filesystem     Size  Used Avail Use% Mounted on
         /dev/sda3      930G   90G  840G  10% /
         devtmpfs       189G     0  189G   0% /dev
         tmpfs          189G     0  189G   0% /dev/shm
         tmpfs          189G  4.1G  185G   3% /run
         tmpfs          189G     0  189G   0% /sys/fs/cgroup
         /dev/sdb1      3.6T  9.1G  3.4T   1% /disk1
         /dev/sdf1      3.6T   89M  3.4T   1% /disk5
         /dev/sdj1      3.6T   89M  3.4T   1% /disk9
         /dev/sdd1      3.6T   89M  3.4T   1% /disk3
         /dev/sde1      3.6T   89M  3.4T   1% /disk4
         /dev/sdc1      3.6T   89M  3.4T   1% /disk2
         /dev/sdi1      3.6T   89M  3.4T   1% /disk8
         /dev/sdg1      3.6T   89M  3.4T   1% /disk6
         /dev/sdh1      3.6T   89M  3.4T   1% /disk7
         /dev/sda1      253M  163M   91M  65% /boot
         tmpfs           38G     0   38G   0% /run/user/0
         /dev/fs01      246T  173T   73T  71% /gpfs/global_fs01
```

3. Next let's unzip the data:

```
In [*]: "unzip  ./Training_set.zip" !

        Archive:  ./Training_set.zip
          creating: Learning_set/
          creating: Learning_set/Bearing1_1/
         inflating: Learning_set/Bearing1_1/acc_00001.csv
         inflating: Learning_set/Bearing1_1/acc_00002.csv
         inflating: Learning_set/Bearing1_1/acc_00003.csv
         inflating: Learning_set/Bearing1_1/acc_00004.csv
         inflating: Learning_set/Bearing1_1/acc_00005.csv
         inflating: Learning_set/Bearing1_1/acc_00006.csv
         inflating: Learning_set/Bearing1_1/acc_00007.csv
         inflating: Learning_set/Bearing1_1/acc_00008.csv
         inflating: Learning_set/Bearing1_1/acc_00009.csv
         inflating: Learning_set/Bearing1_1/acc_00010.csv
         inflating: Learning_set/Bearing1_1/acc_00011.csv
         inflating: Learning_set/Bearing1_1/acc_00012.csv
         inflating: Learning_set/Bearing1_1/acc_00013.csv
         inflating: Learning_set/Bearing1_1/acc_00014.csv
         inflating: Learning_set/Bearing1_1/acc_00015.csv
         inflating: Learning_set/Bearing1_1/acc_00016.csv
```

4. Now we have a huge number of individual CSV files, which we want to use to create a DataFrame. Note that we can filter individual files using a wildcard. So in this case, we are only interested in the accelerometer data, ignoring the temperature data for now:

```
In [7]: val bearing1_1_acc = spark.read.option("inferSchema","true").csv("./Learning_set/Bearing1_1/acc*")

In [8]: bearing1_1_acc.printSchema

root
 |-- _c0: integer (nullable = true)
 |-- _c1: integer (nullable = true)
 |-- _c2: integer (nullable = true)
 |-- _c3: decimal(5,-1) (nullable = true)
 |-- _c4: double (nullable = true)
 |-- _c5: double (nullable = true)


In [9]: bearing1_1_acc.show
+---+---+---+---------+------+------+
|_c0|_c1|_c2|      _c3|   _c4|   _c5|
+---+---+---+---------+------+------+
|  9| 38| 46|8.6566E+5|-1.626|-0.086|
|  9| 38| 46|8.6570E+5|-1.538|-0.299|
|  9| 38| 46|8.6574E+5|-0.969|-0.025|
|  9| 38| 46|8.6578E+5|-0.577| 0.008|
|  9| 38| 46|8.6582E+5| 0.143|-0.087|
|  9| 38| 46|8.6586E+5| 0.129|-0.611|
|  9| 38| 46|8.6590E+5| 0.636|-0.496|
|  9| 38| 46|8.6594E+5|-0.129| 0.588|
|  9| 38| 46|8.6598E+5|-0.323| 0.369|
|  9| 38| 46|8.6602E+5|-0.812| 0.019|
|  9| 38| 46|8.6605E+5|  -0.8| 0.642|
|  9| 38| 46|8.6609E+5|-0.845|-0.047|
|  9| 38| 46|8.6613E+5|-0.723| 0.117|
|  9| 38| 46|8.6617E+5|-0.527| 0.237|
|  9| 38| 46|8.6621E+5|-0.224| 0.334|
```

As we can see, we are double-checking whether the schema was inferred correctly, and we also have a look at the first rows of the dataset to get an idea of what's inside.

The column names represent the following:

- _c0: hour
- _c1: minute
- _c2: second
- _c3: millisecond
- _c4: horizontal acceleration
- _c5: vertical acceleration

5. It is obvious that some data transformation is necessary. The timestamp especially is in a very unusable format. The data scientist also told us to create an additional column containing an aggregation key called **cluster** composed of hours, minutes, and seconds.
   The following script does the job:

```
In [10]:  bearing1_1_acc.createOrReplaceTempView("bearing1_1_acc")
          val bearing1_1_acc_transformed = spark.sql("""
              SELECT concat(_c0,_c1,_c2) as cluster,
              (cast(timestamp(concat('1970-01-01 ',_c0,':',_c1,':',_c2,'.123')) as long) *1000000)+_c3 as ts,
              _c4 as hacc,
              _c5 as vacc
              from bearing1_1_acc
          """)
```

6. The final step is to store the resulting DataFrame as JSON into the IBM Cloud OpenStack Swift-based ObjectStore:

```
In [ ]:  bearing1_1_acc_transformed.write.json("swift://coursera." + name + "/bearing1_1_acc_transformed.json")
```

This concludes our ETL process. Once we are convinced that everything runs fine by manually running the notebook, we can automatically schedule it to run once every hour if we like:

Schedule Job

Name *

ETL Bearing

39 Characters Remaining

Description

Describe what this job is about.

Version

A version is saved to your notebook and scheduled.

Summary

"packt_hello_world" notebook from scheduled to run hourly starting on Wed, 28 June 2017, 01:52 AM until Wed, 28 June 2017, 11:59 PM.

Starts on *

28 June 2017

At time

01:52 AM

Repeats *

Hourly

Ends on

28 June 2017

Interactive, exploratory analysis using Python and Pixiedust

Now since our ETL process is in place, let's use a more lightweight programming environment based on Python for some exploratory data analysis in order to get an idea of what the data looks like. We'll use a visualizations/charting library called Pixiedust here.

The main advantage is that you can directly pass DataFrame objects to it, independent of their size, and Pixiedust will take care of the correct down sampling where necessary. It can create charts with only a single line of code whereas other libraries such as matplotlib need far more complex code to obtain similar charts. And the good news is: It is open source on the Apache V2 license but powered by IBM Watson Data Lab developers. More on Pixiedust can be found here: https://github.com/ibm-watson-data-lab/pixiedust.

We'll now implement this as a Python notebook executing the following steps:

1. Load the DataFrame from the ObjectStore.
2. Create an interactive chart using Pixiedust.

Let's go over every step in detail:

1. First, we load the DataFrame. Loading data as a DataFrame from the ObjectStore is straightforward. Here is how you go about it:

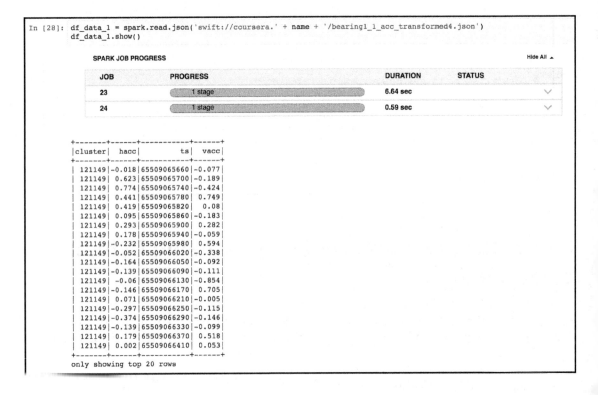

2. And so is using Pixiedust, which is just another two lines of Python code:

```
In [29]: import pixiedust

In [30]: display(df_data_1)
```

3. By default, you are presented with a table view containing the first rows of the dataset. It is important to notice that, independent of the size of the DataFrame, we can just visualize it, and Pixiedust takes care of using the Apache Spark DataFrame API to just pull the necessary data in order to prevent unnecessary operations:

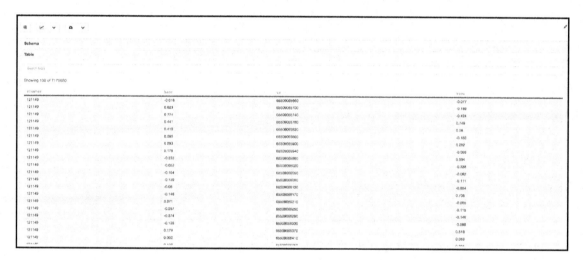

4. Now let's create a graph by clicking on the respective symbol:

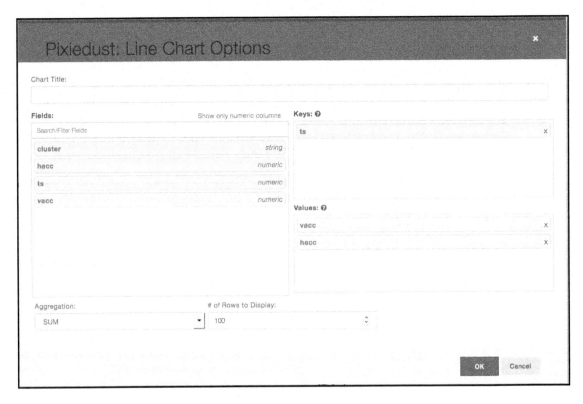

5. We have specified that the `ts` field containing the `timestamp`, which resides on the *x*-axis, and the `vacc` and `hacc` fields containing the vibration data are plotted against the `timestamp` on the *y*-axis.

The result looks like his:

```
In [30]: display(df_data_1)
```

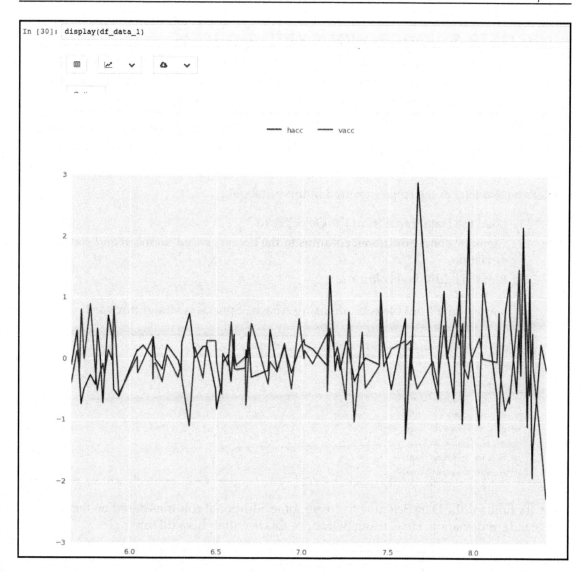

 Again, it is important to notice that we didn't do any sampling in order to visualize that data. And it doesn't matter whether the DataFrame contains one MB, one TB, or even one PB since Pixiedust uses the DataFrame API in order to obtain the required samples.

We can clearly see that the vibrations increase as time progresses and finally, at the end of the recordings, which is when the bearing breaks, they reach their maximum.

Real data science work with SparkR

Our Chief Data Scientist in the project is very skilled; unfortunately, he has no Apache Spark expertise since he is a mathematician mainly working with MATLAB and R. So in these cases, SparkR is a good choice to facilitate the transition to using Apache Spark. The following notebook is based on the R programming language. An Apache Spark expert created the initial DataFrame loading code, whereas the rest of the notebook was directly working on a local R DataFrame in contrast to an Apache Spark DataFrame — something the Data Scientist was familiar with.

So, let's have a look at the steps executed in this notebook:

1. Load the DataFrame from the ObjectStore.
2. Generate some additional columns in the dataset based on mean and standard deviation.
3. Plot the additional columns.

So again, loading data from ObjectStore using Apache SparkR is straightforward:

```
In [2]:  df.data.1 <- read.json(paste("swift://", "coursera", "." , name,"/", "bearing1_1_acc_transformed4.json", sep=""),
                  source = "org.apache.spark.sql.execution.datasources.csv.CSVFileFormat", header = "true")

         head(df.data.1)
```

cluster	hacc	ts	vacc
121149	-0.018	65509065660	-0.077
121149	0.623	65509065700	-0.189
121149	0.774	65509065740	-0.424
121149	0.441	65509065780	0.749
121149	0.419	65509065820	0.080
121149	0.095	65509065860	-0.183

Now it's time for the Data Scientist to create some additional columns based on the mean and standard deviation. He is using SQL since this is within his skill set:

```
In [13]:  df_grouped = sql("
            select cluster,
            mean(hacc) as mhacc,
            mean(vacc) as mvacc,
            STDDEV_POP(hacc) as sdhacc,
            STDDEV_POP(vacc) as sdvacc
            from data
            group by cluster
            order by cluster asc")

In [8]:   df_grouped_local = collect(df_grouped)
```

By calling `collect`, an R DataFrame called `df_grouped_local` is created, which can be used out-of-the-box by any R programmer without Apache Spark skills. This R DataFrame is used in order to plot those additional columns. Let's have a look at one:

```
In [12]:   attach(df_grouped_local)
           plot(cluster,sdhacc)
           detach(df_grouped_local)

           The following objects are masked from df_grouped_local (pos = 3):

               cluster, mhacc, mvacc, sdhacc, sdvacc
```

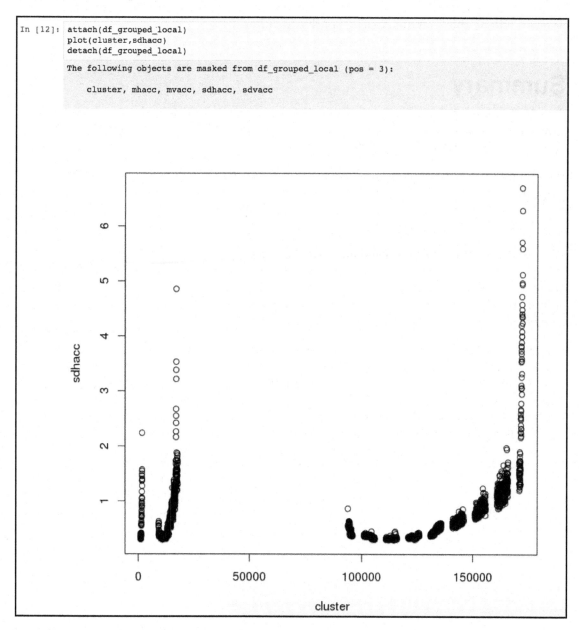

As can be seen from the preceding figure, the standard deviation of the horizontal vibrations dramatically increases as the life of the bearing approaches it's end. This is enough for our Data Scientist to do some magic in R, which we than can port back to Apache SparkML in order to scale. Of course in the long term we hope that our Data Scientist will be able to write Apache Spark code himself.

Summary

Apache Spark in the cloud is the perfect solution for data scientists and data engineers who want to concentrate on getting the actual work done without being concerned about the operation of an Apache Spark cluster.

We saw that Apache Spark in the cloud is much more than just installing Apache Spark on a couple of virtual machines. It comes as a whole package for the data scientist, completely based on open-source components, which makes it easy to migrate to other cloud providers or to local datacenters if necessary.

We also learned that, in a typical data science project, the variety of skills is huge, which is taken care of by supporting all common programming languages and open-source data analytics frameworks on top of Apache Spark and Jupyter notebooks, and by completely eliminating the necessity for operational skills required to maintain the Apache Spark cluster.

Sometimes just one level of increased access to the underlying infrastructure is necessary. Maybe some specific versions of patch levels of software are needed or very specific configuration settings need to be used. So normally this would be the cast for going back to IaaS and installing everything on our own. But this is not really necessary; fortunately there is a better solution that still provides a fair amount of automatizations and still pushing the hard parts of operations to the cloud provider.

This and more is explained in the next Chapter, *Apache Spark on Kubernetes*.

14
Apache Spark on Kubernetes

In this chapter, we'll talk about one of the most exciting movements in Apache Spark deployments: the deployments on the open source based Kubernetes cloud platform. In order to understand these concepts, this chapter explains the following:

- The difference between container and virtual machine based system abstraction
- Core concepts of the Docker platform
- Core concepts of Kubernetes
- Deployment of containerized Apache Spark on Kubernetes and Docker
- A practical example on Apache Spark deployment on Kubernetes

Bare metal, virtual machines, and containers

It turns out that until the late 1990s, most of IT applications were deployed to bare metal machines. This means that you used some sort of server hardware and installed an operating system on it, and on top of that, your applications were installed.

But virtual machines are quite old. In fact, by the early 1960s, IBM was capable of running virtual machines on their mainframes, but it took decades until virtual machines experienced huge market adoption. Most likely, the reason for this was that consumer grade hardware was not powerful enough to run virtual systems efficiently. However, as we all know, this has changed dramatically.

Nowadays, a modern server can run hundreds of virtual machines and thousands of containers, but let's have a look at one after the other. So how do virtual machines work? In the following section, we'll first contrast a bare metal deployment with a virtual machine one.

The following figure illustrates such a bare metal deployment:

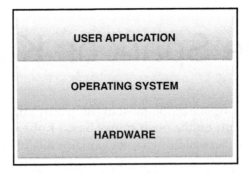

So as we can see on the bare metal hardware layer, an operating system is installed which accesses different hardware components through drivers and makes them available to the user application through a common API.

Let's contrast this to a virtual machine deployment:

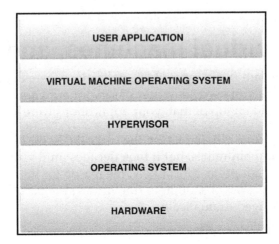

As we can see, there is an additional component present here, called **hypervisor**. This component basically runs as a user application on the bare metal operating system and emulates a complete hardware stack, so that it can host another operating system running user applications.

The operating system running on top (or within) of the hypervisor is called **guest** while the operating system running on top of the real bare metal hardware is called **host**. The idea is that the guest operating system is not aware that it is running inside a virtualized hardware, which has two main advantages:

- **Security**: The guest operating system and guest user application can't access resources on the host operating system without being controlled by the hypervisor.
- **Scalability and elasticity**: As the following figure illustrates, multiple guest systems can be run on a (powerful) host system allowing for scaling (imagine there are many host systems in the data center). Also, starting and stopping guest systems is relatively fast (in minutes), so a system can react to different load situations (especially in cloud deployments where virtually infinite resources are present across multiple host systems).

USER APPLICATION	USER APPLICATION	USER APPLICATION	USER APPLICATION	USER APPLICATION
VIRTUAL MACHINE OS	VIRTUAL MACHINE OS	VIRTUAL MACHINE OS	VIRTUAL MACHINE OS	VIRTUAL MACHINE OS
HYPERVISOR				
OPERATING SYSTEM				
HARDWARE				

As you can see, there is a huge overhead. In the previous figure, there are six operating systems running to serve five user applications. Five are labeled as **VIRTUAL MACHINE OS** inside the virtual machine and one is still necessary running on top of the real hardware, labeled as **OPERATING SYSTEM**.

There is a special case where no host operating system is required, and therefore the so-called hypervisor runs directly on the bare metal hardware.

Not all virtual machine environments support running a hypervisor directly on bare metal, but the deployment would look like the following, where the guest operating system functionality basically is provided by the hypervisor itself:

USER APPLICATION	USER APPLICATION	USER APPLICATION	USER APPLICATION	USER APPLICATION
VIRTUAL MACHINE OS	VIRTUAL MACHINE OS	VIRTUAL MACHINE OS	VIRTUAL MACHINE OS	VIRTUAL MACHINE OS
HYPERVISOR				
HARDWARE				

Containerization

Operating system processes are the central units of work that an operating system runs. So each user application, which basically is nothing other than a set of machine code on permanent storage, is transformed into a running process by reading it from disk, mapping it to the main memory, and starting to execute the contained set of instructions on the processor.

An application can contain one or more processes, and on Linux, each application thread is executed as a separate process sharing the same memory area. Otherwise, a process can't access memory that the other processes are using; this is an important concept for security and stability. But still, all processes can see and use the same set of resources that the operating system provides.

With hypervisors directly running on the bare metal hardware, at least we got rid of the host operating system and saved some resources. But is there a better way? Can't we get rid of the guest operating systems as well? Let's have a look at containerization:

As you might have noticed, we got rid of the guest operating systems and replaced them with containers. So what's the advantage here?

A container does not run on top of a virtualized hardware stack. In fact, all user applications are run directly on the host operating system. The only difference is that the individual operating system processes (the runtime components making up a user application) are fenced against each other and also against the host operating system. In fact, a user application has the feeling that it is alone on the host operating system since it doesn't see what's going on, on the host operating system, and therefore also doesn't see the contents of other containers.

So how is this achieved? This concept was born on the Linux kernel and is the de facto standard for container-based virtualization. There are two major Linux kernel extensions, which make this possible: cgroups and namespaces.

Namespaces

With isolation as the goal, Linux needed some way to separate resource views of different operating system processes from each other. The answer was namespaces. There are currently six namespaces implemented:

- `mnt`: controls access to the filesystems
- `pid`: controls access to different processes

- `net`: controls access to networking resources
- `ipc`: controls inter-process communication
- `uts`: returns a different hostname per namespace
- `user`: enables separate user management per process

In order to use namespaces, only one single system call has been implemented: `setns()`.

The following figure shows the namespace mapping of a random process with ID `2000`:

```
[root@ubuntu:~# ls -al /proc/2000/ns/
total 0
dr-x--x--x 2 root           root           0 Jun 30 23:22 .
dr-xr-xr-x 9 romeokienzler romeokienzler 0 Jun 20 01:25 ..
lrwxrwxrwx 1 root           root           0 Jun 30 23:22 cgroup -> cgroup:[4026531835]
lrwxrwxrwx 1 root           root           0 Jun 30 23:22 ipc -> ipc:[4026531839]
lrwxrwxrwx 1 root           root           0 Jun 30 23:22 mnt -> mnt:[4026531840]
lrwxrwxrwx 1 root           root           0 Jun 30 23:22 net -> net:[4026531957]
lrwxrwxrwx 1 root           root           0 Jun 30 23:22 pid -> pid:[4026531836]
lrwxrwxrwx 1 root           root           0 Jun 30 23:22 user -> user:[4026531837]
lrwxrwxrwx 1 root           root           0 Jun 30 23:22 uts -> uts:[4026531838]
```

It can be seen that the root name spaces are mapped to encapsulated and controlled namespaces with a specific ID. Since every process (or group of processes) is assigned to a sub-namespace of all the six groups mentioned earlier, access to filesystems, other processes, network resources, and user IDs can be restricted. This is an important feature for security.

So the only thing missing is a mechanism to prevent a single process from eating up all the CPU power of the host machine. This is done using control groups.

Control groups

Control groups are the last piece of the puzzle to create containers in a Linux environment. The cgroups subsystem provides means of processing resource management to the Linux kernel.

This subsystem is used to control resources such as:

- Main memory quota
- CPU slices
- Filesystem quota
- Network priority

In addition to that, cgroups provide an additional transient filesystem type. This means that, all data written to that filesystem is destroyed after reboot of the host system. This filesystem is ideal for being assigned to a container. This is because, as we'll learn later, access to real (persistent) filesystems is not possible within a container. Access to persistent filesystems must be specified through mounts during the start of the containers.

Linux containers

So now let's fuse together namespaces, cgroups, and some common version baseline in the Linux kernel, and you'll get **LXC**, which stands for **Linux containers**.

LXC has been part of the vanilla Linux kernel since February 20, 2014, and therefore can be used out-of-the-box on every Linux server.

Understanding the core concepts of Docker

So now it's time to further unfold the topic by introducing Docker. Docker basically makes use of LXC but adds support for building, shipping, and running operation system images. So there exists a layered image format, which makes it possible to pack the filesystem components necessary for running a specific application into a Docker images file.

Although not necessary for this chapter because it is already provided by the following `minikube` package we are using, Docker can be easily installed on different operating systems. Since Docker uses functionality only present in the Linux kernel, it can be run natively only on Linux (and only there you will see the performance benefits over using virtual machines). But you still can use it on macOS and Windows, where a separate hypervisor is running Docker on Linux in the background. So on Ubuntu Linux, we'll just provide the command here since it is so simple: `sudo apt install docker.io`.
Please have a look at the following link in order to install Docker on all other flavors of Linux and on other operating systems: `https://www.dock er.com/community-edition`

The advantage is that this format is layered, so downstream changes to the image result in the addition of a layer. Therefore, a Docker image can be easily synchronized and kept up to date over a network and the internet, since only the changed layers have to be transferred. In order to create Docker images, Docker is shipped with a little build tool which supports building Docker images from so-called **Dockerfiles**.

The following listing shows such a Dockerfile for creating a single container Apache Spark cluster using the **standalone** cluster manager:

```
#This image is based on the ubuntu root image version 16:04
FROM ubuntu:16.04
#Update and install required packages
RUN apt-get update
RUN apt-get install -y curl wget python openssh-server sudo
#Install the JVM
RUN mkdir -p /usr/java/default
RUN curl -Ls
'http://download.oracle.com/otn-pub/java/jdk/8u102-b14/jdk-8u102-linux-x64.
tar.gz' |tar --strip-components=1 -xz -C /usr/java/default/
#Install and configure ApacheSpark
RUN wget http://d3kbcqa49mib13.cloudfront.net/spark-2.0.0-bin-hadoop2.7.tgz
RUN tar xvfz spark-2.0.0-bin-hadoop2.7.tgz
RUN chown -R 1000:1000 /spark-2.0.0-bin-hadoop2.7
RUN echo "SPARK_LOCAL_IP=127.0.0.1" > /spark-2.0.0-bin-
hadoop2.7/conf/spark-env.sh
RUN groupadd -g 1000 packt
RUN useradd -g 1000 -u 1000 --shell /bin/bash packt
RUN usermod -a -G sudo packt
RUN mkdir /home/packt
RUN chown packt:packt /home/packt
RUN echo "StrictHostKeyChecking no" >> /etc/ssh/ssh_config
RUN echo "packt ALL=(ALL) NOPASSWD: ALL" >> /etc/sudoers
USER packt
RUN ssh-keygen -f /home/packt/.ssh/id_rsa -t rsa -N ''
RUN cp /home/packt/.ssh/id_rsa.pub /home/packt/.ssh/authorized_keys
ENV JAVA_HOME=/usr/java/default/
ENV SPARK_HOME=/spark-2.0.0-bin-hadoop2.7/
RUN echo "export JAVA_HOME=/usr/java/default/" >> /home/packt/.bashrc
RUN echo "export SPARK_HOME=/spark-2.0.0-bin-hadoop2.7/" >>
/home/packt/.bashrc
RUN echo ". ~/.bashrc" >> /home/packt/.bash_profile
#Allow external connections to the cluster
EXPOSE 8080
EXPOSE 0001
```

So let's have a look at the most important commands in order to understand the contents of the Dockerfile. Before we do that, it is important to notice that everyone with an active internet connection is able to create a Docker image from a Dockerfile. Therefore, besides savings on transfer times, it brings along an important security aspect. You know exactly what's inside the images and don't have to trust the provider of the image blindly anymore. So here are the most important directives used in this Dockerfile:

- FROM: This is the start of each Dockerfile and tells Docker, based on which (official or unofficial) root image, this image should be based on. We are based on Ubuntu 16.04 here, which is the latest **Long Time Support (LTS)** version of Ubuntu. It contains a minimal subset of components and basically provides us with an empty Ubuntu Linux installation. Of course, you can base your image also on other images you have created before.
- RUN: Everything after the RUN directive is directly executed as a shell command during the image creation, so the important steps done here are:
    1. Installing components using the apt command.
    2. Downloading, extracting, and installing a JVM and Apache Spark.
    3. Creating users and groups.
    4. Configuring ssh.
- USER: During the image creation, we are running as user **root**. In case we want to run as an underprivileged user, we can change it using the USER directive.
- ENV: This directive allows us to set operating system wide environment variables during runtime of the image.
- EXPOSE: This directive tells Docker during runtime of the image which IP ports should be made available from outside. It acts as some sort of firewall where per default all ports from outside are closed. These values can be reconfigured during the start of the image and are not fixed to the image itself.

If you now run the following command, a Docker image is created from the Docker file:

```
docker build -t me/apachespark:2.0 .
```

. specifies that the Docker daemon should pick the Dockerfile from the current location and build the image.

You can now start this Docker container with the following command:

```
docker run --name spark -it me/apachespark:2.0
```

But as we know, an Apache Spark cluster is built using multiple machines and not just one. In addition, it makes no sense to divide a single node into multiple containers using Apache Spark since we want to achieve exactly the opposite--Apache Spark makes multiple nodes behave like a single, big one. This is the one and only reason for using a data parallel framework, such as Apache Spark, to create virtual bigger compute resources out of small ones. So why does this all make sense? Let's have a look at Kubernetes first.

Understanding Kubernetes

Kubernetes (K8s) is an orchestrator of containers. It supports various container technologies, but here we'll concentrate on Docker.

 More on Kubernetes can be found here: `https://kubernetes.io/docs/co ncepts/overview/what-is-kubernetes/#kubernetes-is`.

So let's have a look at the Kubernetes architecture:

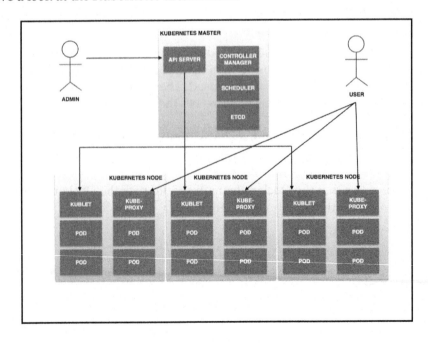

As in nearly every cluster infrastructure, there exists a master node managing the whole of the cluster. So let's have a brief look at the responsibilities of each of its components:

- **API server**: The API server provides a means of communication between the Kubernetes cluster and external system administrators. It provides a REST API used by the `kubectl` command line tool. This API can also be used by other consumers, making it possible to plug-in Kubernetes in existing infrastructures and automated processes.
- **Controller manager**: The controller manager is responsible for managing the core controller processes within a Kubernetes cluster.
- **Scheduler**: The scheduler is responsible for matching the supply of resources provided by the aggregated set of Kubernetes nodes to the demand of resources of the currently undeployed pods (pods are the basic scheduling units of Kubernetes; more on this later).
  In addition, the scheduler also needs to keep track of the user-defined policies and constraints, such as node affinity or data locality, in order to take the correct decisions as to where to place the container.

> Data locality is only considered by Kubernetes during deployment and shouldn't be confused with data locality provided by the **Hadoop Distributed File System (HDFS)**. More on data locality in HDFS can be found here: `http://hadoopinrealworld.com/data-locality-in-hadoop/`.

- **Etcd**: Etcd is a reliable key-value store, storing the overall state of the cluster and all deployed applications at any given point in time.

But without any workers, a cluster manager is useless, so let's have a look at the components running on the Kubernetes nodes:

- **POD**: PODs are the basic scheduling units of Kubernetes. A POD consists of at least one or more containers, which are co-located on the same node, so that they can share resources. Such resources include IP addresses (in fact, one physical IP is assigned to each POD so no port conflicts arise between them) and local disk resources which are assigned to all containers of the POD.

- **Kublet**: The kublet is the Kubernetes manager for each Kubernetes node. It is responsible for starting and stopping containers as directed by the controller. It is also responsible for maintaining a PODs state (for example, the number of active containers) and monitoring. Through regular heartbeats, the master is informed about the states of all PODs managed by the kublet.
- **Kube-proxy**: The kube-proxy serves as a load balancer among the incoming requests and PODs.

There exists an abundance of additional components supporting very complex deployment scenarios, but for the sake of simplicity, we'll skip those here.

Using Kubernetes for provisioning containerized Spark applications

So what's in it for Apache Spark here? Let's assume we have a set of powerful nodes in our local data center. What is the advantage of using Kubernetes for deployment over just installing Apache Spark on bare metal? Let's take the question the other way round. Let's have a look at the disadvantages of using Kubernetes in this scenario. Actually, there is no disadvantage at all.

 The link `http://domino.research.ibm.com/library/cyberdig.nsf/pap ers/0929052195DD819C85257D2300681E7B/$File/rc25482.pdf`is a 2014 paper of IBM Research, stating that performance within a Docker container is nearly identical to bare metal.

So this means that the only disadvantage is the effort you invest in installing and maintaining Kubernetes. But what you gain are the following:

- Easy installation and updates of Apache Spark and other additional software packages (such as Apache Flink, Jupyter, or Zeppelin)
- Easy switching between different versions
- Parallel deployment of multiple clusters for different users or user groups
- Fair resource assignment to users and user groups
- Straightforward hybrid cloud integration, since the very same setup can be run on any cloud provider supporting Kubernetes as a service

So how do we get started? The following section provides a step-by-step example of how to set up a single node installation of Kubernetes on your machine and how to deploy an Apache Spark cluster, including Zeppelin, on it; so stay tuned!

Example--Apache Spark on Kubernetes

This example is taken directly from the Kubernetes GitHub page, which can be found at `htt ps://github.com/Kubernetes/Kubernetes/tree/master/examples/spark`. We've done some modification to that example, since we are using a very specific Kubernetes deployment called **Minikube**. But we still want it to be based on the original example, since when you are using this link, you are guaranteed to always obtain an updated version compatible with the latest Kubernetes version in place. So these are the required steps, which are explained in detail in the next sections:

1. Install Minikube local Kubernetes to your machine.
2. Deploy the Apache Spark master node.
3. Deploy the Apache Spark worker nodes.
4. Deploy the Apache Kubernetes notebook application and test the whole cluster (optional).

The following section describes the prerequisites to run the example on your own.

Prerequisites

In order to get started quickly, it is highly recommended to either use one of the existing cloud services for Kubernetes (for example, from IBM you get a free 30 days trial at `https ://console.bluemix.net/docs/containers/container_index.html`) or use Minikube, which creates a single node Kubernetes cluster on your machine.

The `minikube` package needs a hypervisor. Although many are supported, the most straightforward way is to use VirtualBox. Instructions for installation can be found at `https://www.virtualbox.org/wiki/Down loads`. VirtualBox is free of charge.

Then, `minikube` and the `kubectl` command line tool have to be installed, as explained at `https://Kubernetes.io/docs/tasks/tools/install-mi nikube/`.

Finally, the following command will start your Kubernetes cluster, and we are ready to go:

```
minikube start
```

Deploying the Apache Spark master

Now let's start with deploying the Apache Spark master service. This is straightforward. We just need to run the following command:

```
kubectl create -f
https://raw.githubusercontent.com/Kubernetes/Kubernetes/master/examples/spa
rk/spark-master-controller.yaml
```

This command results in the following:

```
romeos-mbp:~ romeokienzler$ kubectl create -f https://raw.githubusercontent.com/kubernetes/kubernetes/master/examples/spark/spark-master-service.yaml
service "spark-master" created
```

So this command basically deployed a POD containing the Apache Spark master Docker image. The exact image location is specified in the `spark-master-controller.yaml` configuration file.

So let's have a look at the actual status of this POD:

```
[romeos-mbp:~ romeokienzler$  kubectl get pods
NAME                             READY   STATUS            RESTARTS   AGE
spark-master-controller-ljvq1    0/1     ContainerCreating 0          6s
```

As we can see, the POD is still under construction, since the actual status is `ContainerCreating`. Let's wait a bit and re-issue the command:

```
[romeos-mbp:~ romeokienzler$  kubectl get pods
NAME                             READY   STATUS    RESTARTS   AGE
spark-master-controller-ljvq1    1/1     Running   0          17m
```

Now we are lucky. The POD's status is `Running`. It took quite a while, but don't forget that this is a test environment running inside a virtual machine.

In order to be 100 percent sure that the deployment succeeded, let's have a look at the logs:

```
romeos-mbp:~ romeokienzler$ kubectl logs spark-master-controller-ljvQ1
17/07/02 05:47:14 INFO Master: Registered signal handlers for [TERM, HUP, INT]
17/07/02 05:47:15 INFO SecurityManager: Changing view acls to: root
17/07/02 05:47:15 INFO SecurityManager: Changing modify acls to: root
17/07/02 05:47:15 INFO SecurityManager: SecurityManager: authentication disabled; ui acls disabled; users with view permissions: Set(root); users with modify permissions: Set(root)
17/07/02 05:47:15 INFO Slf4jLogger: Slf4jLogger started
17/07/02 05:47:15 INFO Remoting: Starting remoting
17/07/02 05:47:16 INFO Remoting: Remoting started; listening on addresses :[akka.tcp://sparkMaster@spark-master:7077]
17/07/02 05:47:16 INFO Utils: Successfully started service 'sparkMaster' on port 7077.
17/07/02 05:47:16 INFO Master: Starting Spark master at spark://spark-master:7077
17/07/02 05:47:16 INFO Master: Running Spark version 1.5.2
17/07/02 05:47:26 INFO Utils: Successfully started service 'MasterUI' on port 8080.
17/07/02 05:47:26 INFO MasterWebUI: Started MasterWebUI at http://172.17.0.2:8080
17/07/02 05:47:26 INFO Utils: Successfully started service on port 6066.
17/07/02 05:47:26 INFO StandaloneRestServer: Started REST server for submitting applications on port 6066
17/07/02 05:47:26 INFO Master: I have been elected leader! New state: ALIVE
```

So this looks very nice. But as of now, there is no way that our application running inside the POD is reached via an IP connection from outside Kubernetes since no ports are mapped on the Docker container where the application runs in. Therefore, we have to create a so-called service:

```
romeos-mbp:~ romeokienzler$ kubectl create -f https://raw.githubusercontent.com/kubernetes/kubernetes/master/examples/spark/spark-ui-proxy-controller.yaml
replicationcontroller "spark-ui-proxy-controller" created
```

By creating a service, we basically allow ports from outside the containers to be mapped to ports inside the containers. Let's examine the `spark-master-service.yaml` file:

```
kind: Service
apiVersion: v1
metadata:
  name: spark-master
spec:
  ports:
    - port: 7077
      targetPort: 7077
      name: spark
    - port: 8080
      targetPort: 8080
      name: http
  selector:
    component: spark-master
```

The key `port` specified the outside port (we'll explain later what **outside** exactly means in Kubernetes) and the key `targetPort` is the port inside the Docker containers of the POD where we want to map to from outside.

Now it's time to talk about what **outside** means. Generally, Kubernetes runs in cloud infrastructures and expects that a load balancer is already there for it to use. The load balancer is dynamically and transparently updated when creating a **service** in Kubernetes, so that the load balancer forwards the specified ports to the correct PODs. We are using the Minikube test system but our scenario is in a production scale Kubernetes real-world installation.

The following command would inform us about the actual endpoint of our application:

```
[romeos-mbp:~ romeokienzler$ kubectl get svc spark-ui-proxy -o wide
NAME              CLUSTER-IP    EXTERNAL-IP    PORT(S)        AGE    SELECTOR
spark-ui-proxy    10.0.0.146    <pending>      80:30621/TCP   16s    component=spark-ui-proxy
```

But as we are running Minikube, our single node test environment for Kubernetes, there is no load balancer present, which we can update with our new port mappings. Therefore, we need to use the following command in order to access our application endpoint within the POD. This command is not a Kubernetes but a `minikube` command:

```
[romeos-mbp:~ romeokienzler$ minikube service spark-ui-proxy --url
http://192.168.99.100:30621
```

This command basically simulates the load balancer and allows us to access the endpoint within the POD; in this case, it is the UI of the Apache Spark master:

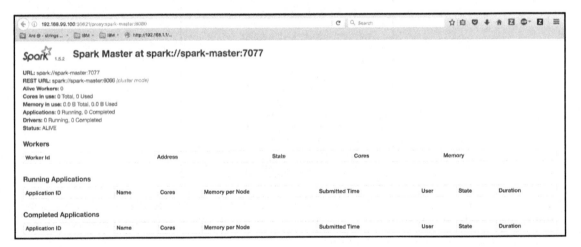

Deploying the Apache Spark workers

This looks very nice, but note that there are no workers present. An Apache Spark master without workers is useless. Therefore, let's create the PODs for two workers:

```
romeos-mbp:~ romeokienzler$ kubectl create -f https://raw.githubusercontent.com/kubernetes/kubernetes/master/examples/spark/spark-worker-controller.yaml
replicationcontroller "spark-worker-controller" created
```

Again, let's check the status of the additional POD:

```
[romeos-mbp:~ romeokienzler$ kubectl get pod
NAME                               READY     STATUS     RESTARTS   AGE
spark-master-controller-ljvq1      1/1       Running    0          23h
spark-ui-proxy-controller-k3nqs    1/1       Running    23         22h
spark-worker-controller-cz8rx      1/1       Running    0          4s
spark-worker-controller-l121v      1/1       Running    0          4s
```

As we can see, the two additional workers are already running successfully. Since this happened very fast, let's examine the log file of the master once again in order to see if they've been registered correctly:

```
romeos-mbp:~ romeokienzler$ kubectl logs spark-master-controller-ljvq1
17/07/02 05:47:14 INFO Master: Registered signal handlers for [TERM, HUP, INT]
17/07/02 05:47:15 INFO SecurityManager: Changing view acls to: root
17/07/02 05:47:15 INFO SecurityManager: Changing modify acls to: root
17/07/02 05:47:15 INFO SecurityManager: SecurityManager: authentication disabled; ui acls disabled; users with view permissions: Set(root); users with modify permissions: Set(root)
17/07/02 05:47:15 INFO Slf4jLogger: Slf4jLogger started
17/07/02 05:47:16 INFO Remoting: Starting remoting
17/07/02 05:47:16 INFO Remoting: Remoting started; listening on addresses :[akka.tcp://sparkMaster@spark-master:7077]
17/07/02 05:47:16 INFO Utils: Successfully started service 'sparkMaster' on port 7077.
17/07/02 05:47:16 INFO Master: Starting Spark master at spark://spark-master:7077
17/07/02 05:47:16 INFO Master: Running Spark version 1.5.2
17/07/02 05:47:26 INFO Utils: Successfully started service 'MasterUI' on port 8080.
17/07/02 05:47:26 INFO MasterWebUI: Started MasterWebUI at http://172.17.0.2:8080
17/07/02 05:47:26 INFO Utils: Successfully started service on port 6066.
17/07/02 05:47:26 INFO StandaloneRestServer: Started REST server for submitting applications on port 6066
17/07/02 05:47:26 INFO Master: I have been elected leader! New state: ALIVE
17/07/03 04:42:53 INFO Master: Registering worker 172.17.0.6:35693 with 2 cores, 1024.0 MB RAM
17/07/03 04:42:53 INFO Master: Registering worker 172.17.0.7:36563 with 2 cores, 1024.0 MB RAM
```

This was a complete success. We've added two Apache Spark workers in a matter of seconds! Isn't that great?

As you've just seen, adding (and also removing) Apache Spark workers to a master is very fast on Kubernetes. There exist cloud services which provide Kubernetes as a service. This means you can use Kubernetes and the required resources backed by Docker containers running on real hardware as an offering in clouds and you are charged on individually deployed Docker containers (and maybe their main memory and CPU consumption) on an hourly basis. We would suggest that you start off with a minimal Apache Spark configuration just like the one we are currently creating here, and in case you run into heavy analytics and resource demands, you can dynamically grow and shrink your Apache Spark cluster on demand. This is called **elasticity** and is one of the main reasons many companies have recently started to run Apache Spark on Kubernetes as a service in the cloud. One cloud provider is IBM and there is a free 30-day trial on the Kubernetes cloud service. An excellent tutorial on this can be found here: `http://www.developer.com/cloud/using-kub ernetes-k8s-on-ibm-bluemix.html`.

To complete the picture, let's check the UI of the master again:

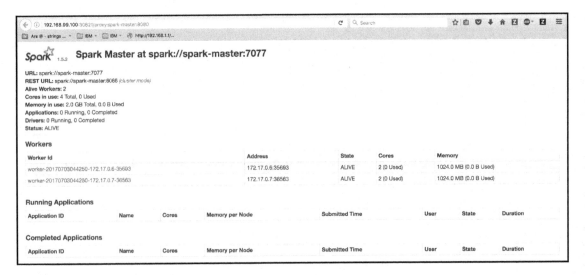

And here we are. We have installed an Apache Spark cluster with one master and two workers on Kubernetes with just a couple of commands.

We can already use this cluster, but let's follow along this example a bit more, since a very interesting component will be installed, that is Zeppelin.

Deploying the Zeppelin notebooks

Apache Zeppelin is the answer of the Apache Foundation to Jupyter notebooks. Jupyter notebooks have been introduced in the earlier chapter on Apache Spark in the cloud where we've introduced the IBM Data Science Experience offering which is based on Jupyter notebooks.

So why do we need another notebook implementation? The first thing you might notice if you use Jupyter is that the UI seems to be quite outdated. And this is sad, but true.

Zeppelin is based on modern technologies such as AngularJS and Bootstrap. One very nice feature is that you can create customized forms within Zeppelin and the variables are directly passed to the embedded R, Scala, or Python code running in the notebook. In addition, Zeppelin has a built-in charting function, whereas in Jupyter you have to use external libraries. Finally, Zeppelin allows you to mix multiple programming languages, whereas in Jupyter you are bound to a single programming language per notebook. Jupyter has a much larger community but Zeppelin seems to be slowly catching up. So it is at least worth having a look at it.

Zeppelin could run completely outside Kubernetes and access Apache Spark remotely, but since installing things in Kubernetes is so straightforward, let's use Kubernetes to deploy a Zeppelin POD:

```
romeos-mbp:~ romeokienzler$ kubectl create -f https://raw.githubusercontent.com/kubernetes/kubernetes/master/examples/spark/zeppelin-controller.yaml
replicationcontroller "zeppelin-controller" created
```

Again, we want to make sure that the POD is up and running, so we regularly check:

```
[romeos-mbp:~ romeokienzler$ kubectl get pod
NAME                              READY   STATUS             RESTARTS   AGE
spark-master-controller-ljvq1     1/1     Running            0          23h
spark-ui-proxy-controller-k3nqs   1/1     Running            23         22h
spark-worker-controller-cz8rx     1/1     Running            0          3m
spark-worker-controller-l121v     1/1     Running            0          3m
zeppelin-controller-csmvr         0/1     ContainerCreating  0          3s
```

We wait until the POD is running:

```
[romeos-mbp:~ romeokienzler$ kubectl get pod
NAME                               READY   STATUS    RESTARTS   AGE
spark-master-controller-ljvq1      1/1     Running   0          23h
spark-ui-proxy-controller-k3nqs    1/1     Running   23         23h
spark-worker-controller-cz8rx      1/1     Running   0          33m
spark-worker-controller-l121v      1/1     Running   0          33m
zeppelin-controller-csmvr          1/1     Running   0          29m
```

Since default ports within PODs are not accessible, we need to create a service as well:

```
romeos-mbp:~ romeokienzler$ kubectl create -f https://raw.githubusercontent.com/kubernetes/kubernetes/master/examples/spark/zeppelin-service.yaml
service "zeppelin" created
```

And again, since Minikube lacks a load balancer, we have to use a `minikube` command in order to get the ports defined in the service mapped to somewhere accessible:

```
[romeos-mbp:~ romeokienzler$ minikube service zeppelin --url
http://192.168.99.100:30510
```

So let's open this URL location and check what's happening:

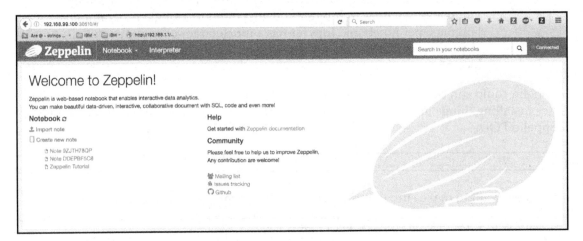

Here we are! With just three Kubernetes commands, we've been able to create and access a Zeppelin notebook server environment that is already perfectly configured with our existing Apache Spark cluster. If you click on **Create new note**, you can basically start to write an Apache Spark notebook in R, Scala, or Python, but this is beyond the scope of this book. But since we've come so far, let's at least create a simple notebook and run a basic Apache Spark job in order to test if the whole installation is correct:

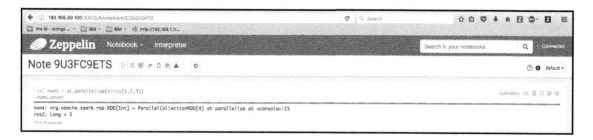

So, that is it! Don't forget `minicube stop` for a graceful shutdown of your Kubernetes cluster, and we are done.

Summary

We saw that containerization is the new way to go and that managing an abundance of containers requires orchestrations. We learned that Kubernetes is such an orchestrator and we saw how it can be used to create a simple Apache Spark cluster within minutes. We used a local test installation for playing around with Kubernetes, but the example shown can be used out-of-the-box on any Kubernetes installation.

We also saw that using Kubernetes as a service in the cloud can be very beneficial when used in conjunction with Apache Spark, since in the cloud the underlying Docker containers are charged on an hourly basis, therefore making it possible to elastically grow and shrink the Apache Spark cluster on the fly, as needed.

Finally, using Kubernetes in the cloud and in the local data center as well allows a broader usage scenario in a so-called hybrid cloud approach. In such an approach, depending on constraints such as data protection laws and resource requirements, an Apache Spark cluster can be provisioned within minutes. Therefore, Apache Spark can be used to execute a specific task and once the results are written back to persistent storage the cluster can be destroyed in order to free the cloud and local data center resources as soon as they are not used anymore.

Index

CPSIA information can be obtained
at www.ICGtesting.com
Printed in the USA
LVOW04s2046301117
558160LV00004B/350/P